LEGAL FOUNDATIONS OF EDUCATION

Educational Foundations

edited by Bruce Maxwell and Lauren Bialystock

Education, as an academic field taught at universities around the world, emerged from a range of older foundational disciplines. The *Educational Foundations* series comprises six volumes, each covering one of the foundational disciplines of philosophy, history, sociology, policy studies, economics, and law. This is the first reference work to provide an authoritative and up-to-date account of all six disciplines, showing how each field's ideas, methods, theories, and approaches can contribute to research and practice in education today. The six volumes cover the same set of key topics within education, which also form the chapter titles:

- Mapping the Field
- Purposes of Education
- Curriculum
- Schools and Education Systems
- Learning and Human Development
- Teaching and Teacher Education
- Assessment and Evaluation

This structure allows readers to study the volumes in isolation, by discipline, or laterally, by topic, and facilitates a comparative, thematic reading of chapters across the volumes. Throughout the series, attention is paid to how the disciplines comprising the educational foundations speak to social justice concerns such as gender and racial equality.

Volume 1: Philosophical Foundations of Education
edited by Winston C. Thompson

Volume 2: Historical Foundations of Education
edited by Theodore Michael Christou

Volume 3: Sociological Foundations of Education
edited by Claire Maxwell, Miri Yemini, and Laura Engel

Volume 4: Policy Foundations of Education
edited by Andrew Wilkins

Volume 5: Economic Foundations of Education
edited by Álvaro Choi

Volume 6: Legal Foundations of Education
edited by J.C. Blokhuis

LEGAL FOUNDATIONS OF EDUCATION

edited by
J.C. Blokhuis

BLOOMSBURY ACADEMIC
LONDON • NEW YORK • OXFORD • NEW DELHI • SYDNEY

BLOOMSBURY ACADEMIC
Bloomsbury Publishing Plc
50 Bedford Square, London, WC1B 3DP, UK
1385 Broadway, New York, NY 10018, USA
29 Earlsfort Terrace, Dublin 2, Ireland

BLOOMSBURY, BLOOMSBURY ACADEMIC and the Diana logo are
trademarks of Bloomsbury Publishing Plc

First published in Great Britain 2023

Cover design: Charlotte James
Cover image © CSA Images/ Getty Images

A catalogue record for this book is available from the British Library.

A catalog record for this book is available from the Library of Congress.

ISBN: HB: 978-1-3501-7126-8
ePDF: 978-1-3501-7127-5
eBook: 978-1-3501-7128-2
Set: 978-1-3501-7152-7

Typeset by Integra Software Services Pvt. Ltd.
Printed and bound in Great Britain

To find out more about our authors and books visit www.bloomsbury.com
and sign up for our newsletters.

CONTENTS

GENERAL EDITORS' PREFACE

BRUCE MAXWELL
UNIVERSITY OF MONTREAL
LAUREN BIALYSTOK
UNIVERSITY OF TORONTO

Readers of a certain age will undoubtedly remember Choose Your Own Adventure children's books. In a normal novel, the author leads the reader through a series of fixed events and experiences lived by some other person. Choose Your Own Adventure books were different because they made the reader the protagonist. Every few pages, options were proposed about what to do next so that the story unfolded in different ways depending on the reader's choices. The net effect, enhanced by the uncustomary use of the second person throughout, is that readers themselves determine the reading experience. We offer this six-volume book series on educational foundations in much the same spirit. It does not have to be read sequentially, but rather can be delved into according to one's personal, academic, or professional interests and informational needs. These are books made for exploration.

THE AIM AND STRUCTURE OF THE SERIES

If a reference work in educational foundations like this one is to be comprehensive, it must necessarily be extremely long. If conciseness is the aim, comprehensiveness is out of the question. The foundations, after all, comprise a set of disciplinary approaches to education whose boundaries are porous and contested, and which take up a vast array of topics. The relevant literatures span centuries and their influence is global. Yet at the same time, the study of educational foundations is nearly always, and rightly so, adapted to local contexts and current educational unknown—what topics and issues are examined under this heading, and even the very academic disciplines it is thought to include, can thus vary considerably from place to place and shift as the decades recede behind us. From an editorial standpoint, faced with this surfeit of material, the choice between offering selected tidbits from the great canvass of the education foundations or taking a deep dive into one particular conception of the educational foundations may seem inevitable. The result of the first choice is superficiality. The result of the second is neglect.

In the design of this series, we have attempted to avoid these compromises. We have tried to offer a substantial but also comparative view of educational foundations that highlights the distinct contributions of six selected foundations disciplines. The six volumes are devoted, respectively, to the disciplines of philosophy (Volume 1), history (Volume 2), sociology (Volume 3), politics (Volume 4), economics (Volume 5), and law (Volume 6), but the structure of the volumes is consistent in that the same set of chapter headings appears in each of the volumes and in the same order. The goal of this parallel structure is to encourage the chapter authors, all internationally recognized experts in their fields, to explore the same key topics in education from the vantage point of their respective disciplines. Using a style accessible to a wide audience of education students, teacher educators, and others interested in educational issues, their writ was to produce informative and rigorous statements on how their home academic discipline approaches the topic they were assigned and how their field has contributed to the advancement of knowledge in these areas.

In the first chapter of each volume in this series, "Mapping the Field," the volume editors survey the characteristic sources, methods, and concerns of their field as it has engaged with education. In the ensuing chapters, the contributing authors address the six themes that we selected to encompass a range of broad topics that have been of perennial interest to educational thinkers across cultures at least since the advent of mass, compulsory schooling. The first three chapters in each volume are concerned with the wider conceptual and institutional contexts of schooling. The chapters titled "Purposes of Education" (Chapter 2) address the general aims of teaching and learning as they occur within schools and education systems. The chapters on "Curriculum" (Chapter 3) and "Schools and Education Systems" (Chapter 4) deal with what children and young people are taught in school and why, and the institutional frameworks through which the curriculum is transmitted and particular aims are pursued. The final three chapters in the volumes turn to matters closer to pedagogy and instruction. The chapters on "Learning and Human Development" (Chapter 5) consider how children and young people acquire what is taught in school and how education shapes them as persons. The chapters on "Teaching and Teacher Education" (Chapter 6) examine how adults help children and young people acquire what is taught in school and how to prepare adults to occupy the educator role. The final chapter in each volume deals with "Assessment and Evaluation" (Chapter 7), or how we judge students' progress in acquiring what is taught in school as well as the outcomes of educational systems.

The advantage of the overarching structure of the series is that it facilitates a vertical and horizontal reading, which makes the set of books conducive to exploration. Readers interested in one disciplinary perspective only could study that volume in depth. And, since each volume covers the same set of topics and the common themes appear as the titles of the chapters, readers interested in a particular topic can read across the volumes to find out what different academic disciplines have to say about it.

THE EDUCATIONAL FOUNDATIONS IN CONTEXT

The publication of this book series comes at a curious moment in the history of the field of educational foundations. The choices that led to the design of this series were very much the product of this historical context.

Educational foundations as a core subject in teacher education has never been so uncertain (Neuman 2009; Shutz and Butin 2013). The widespread belief among teacher educators that future teachers need to be versed to some extent in the educational foundations is a vestige of a once-dominant liberal arts model of teacher education. Taking hold during the first half of the twentieth century under the influence of John Dewey and likeminded progressivists (see Butin 2005b), the idea that the humanities should be central to teacher education came increasingly under attack after the Second World War, and has lost ground steadily through to the present. Under pressure from government and trustee institutions, faculties of education in North America and Europe have been gravitating for some time toward a professional training model for teachers and away from the liberal arts model that made humanistic studies so central to teacher education (Colgan and Maxwell 2019). With these changes came the slow but ineluctable erosion of educational foundations content in teacher education. While instruction in the foundations of education was once typically separated into discrete areas of study, under the influence of a professional training model and neoliberal pressures, professional preparation in the foundations has been consolidated and diluted. Two generations ago, education students could expect tens of hours of instruction dedicated exclusively to educational philosophy and theory, the history of educational systems and ideas, and the sociological analysis of educational methods and institutions. Today, the curricular diet of the average education student contains but a few hours of educational foundations material, in which the constitutive disciplines may be blurred together. Although the phrase "foundations of education" promises to transmit the collected wisdom of multiple traditions, most courses in educational foundations are taught by a single instructor with relevant expertise and qualifications in at most one discipline in the humanities or social sciences.

Furthermore, the great variety of topics addressed under the heading of "educational foundations" is testimony to a state of deep uncertainty among teacher educators and foundations scholars themselves about what the educational foundations are all about (see Butin 2005a; Ryan 2006; Neumann 2006; Kerr, Mandzuk, and Raptis 2011; Hartlep et al. 2015). Some adopt a discipline-based view, limiting educational foundations to three areas of scholarly inquiry: philosophy of education, history of education, and sociology of education, usually in that order (e.g., Semel 2010). Others add to the list of disciplinary lenses that constitute the educational foundations anthropology, policy studies, law, and economics (e.g., Pope and Stemhagen 2008). Still others expand educational foundations to include such diverse forms of scholarship as cultural studies, gender studies, religious studies, indigenous ontologies, critical theory, and comparative and international education (see Committee on Academic Standards and Accreditation 2013; Hartlep et al. 2015). In the United Kingdom, much more so than in North America, psychology is often considered a foundations discipline. Indeed, the lists of topics and fields that have been proposed to define "the foundations of education" give the impression it is a catch-all term for anything to do with education that is theoretical, critically reflective, or abstract, as opposed to content that relates to the practical matters of effective instruction, evaluation, and classroom management. The scales fall from one's eyes, however, when one peruses the tables of contents of textbooks explicitly positioned as works on the educational foundations, social foundations of education, or education studies. Such books routinely contain chapters on assessment, classroom management, and reflective teaching practice (e.g., Curtis et al. 2013; Edmunds et al. 2015). In the end, perhaps the practical and the theoretical in teaching are not that distinct.

It is common knowledge that the foundations of education—which we take to be essentially coextensive with "social foundations of education" and "education studies"—lie at the epicenter of an ideological earthquake that has been shaking teacher education and educational research since about the turn of the twenty-first century. Given the depth of the identity crisis facing the educational foundations, it is a small wonder that a consensus has emerged around educational foundations as a vehicle for advancing the cause of social justice concerns in education and denouncing data-driven educational decision-making. If those invested in educational foundations are looking for a way to demonstrate its relevance to teacher education, who can deny that the problem of educational inequality is bad and getting worse and that unbridled managerialism in education can create more problems than it solves? Teachers need to know this.

As the debates rage on about what the educational foundations are and what role they should play in teacher preparation, over the last thirty years, interest in educational issues has quietly grown, not only within academic disciplines typically associated with educational foundations—philosophy, history, sociology—but also in other disciplines that fall outside the educational foundations' customary sphere. The latter include political science, economics, and law. This newfound interest in educational research has led to a proliferation of research associations, academic journals, and scholarly conferences dedicated to the study of education from a particular disciplinary perspective. At their best, these sites operate as a meeting ground where fruitful exchange occurs between researchers based in education departments and faculties (who tend to be better versed in the realities of classroom instruction, mass schooling, and teacher formation) and researchers who are more inclined to tackle educational issues from within the boundaries of specific academic disciplines. Academic expertise in educational issues is no longer the exclusive purview of scholars affiliated with education departments in universities.

This book series seeks to leverage this exciting new scholarly interest in educational matters, both for the benefit of those engaged in educational theory, research, and practice, and for the benefit of the field of educational foundations itself. We believe that educational justice can be served by asking what we can learn from specific academic disciplines in the social sciences and humanities and how they frame, study, and understand the universal and recurrent questions in education, as well as how they can help us to think about evolving realities within and outside schools.

SELECTING THE SIX FOUNDATIONS DISCIPLINES

Setting out the general objectives for the book series was, relatively speaking, the easy part. Settling on which disciplinary perspectives would (and would not) be represented in the series involved some tough choices. As we saw above, there is no authoritative list of the fields that make up educational foundations. Our gambit in this series is that certain disciplines deserve to be read independently as part of the mosaic that makes up educational studies. Our selection of the six disciplines that were elected for inclusion in this series—philosophy, history, sociology, policy studies, economics, and law—reflects some degree of overlapping consensus among those who debate the contents of educational foundations, but does not purport to be definitive or immutable. We chose these six fields, not as a function of how frequently they are recognized as foundational, but because they met our criteria for the kinds of disciplines that would work in this series.

First, we wanted to include only fields with a long-standing and recognized history in academia, ones characterized by fairly well-defined objects of study as well as methods of inquiry proper to them. The application of this criterion led us to exclude, most notably, a volume on the cultural foundations of education. Cultural studies is a relative newcomer on the academic scene and its distinctive area of concern and methodological and analytic approaches are still very fluid. Nevertheless, many of the concerns of cultural studies are captured within more established disciplines, especially critical sociology, for which the sociological foundations volume gives a forum. Second, we wanted to ensure that each volume had a relatively distinct identity in terms of content and to avoid undue overlap with any other volume in the series. The application of this criterion led us to exclude, most notably, a volume on the anthropological foundations of education, as we felt that repetition with a sociology volume would have been inevitable. Third, we wanted to make sure that any discipline selected for the series would have something substantive to say about the wide range of recurrent issues in education articulated in the series' chapter headings. The application of this criterion led us to rule out a volume on the psychological foundations of education. While psychologists undoubtedly have much to say on such topics as learning and human development and assessment, topics such as the purposes of education and the curriculum generally fall outside psychology's individual-oriented scope.

While the six disciplines retained for this series all met our criteria, there are noteworthy differences between them as well. Some, history and philosophy in particular, have been recognized as areas of formal inquiry for millennia. Indeed, philosophy, previously known as the "queen of the sciences," may have hitherto subsumed many of the methods and areas of inquiry that branched into their own disciplines during modernity, and which are still splintering today. Moreover, educational questions were always present in philosophical thought, going back in the Western tradition at least as far as Plato's *Republic*. In the contemporary academy, educational questions are less often addressed in philosophy departments, but philosophical questions seem to permeate the study of education. Along with philosophy, the trio of classical foundational disciplines most commonly taught today includes history and sociology. Understood in opposition to the technical or practical dimensions of teaching, these disciplines are now widely regarded as constituting the core of the "educational foundations" and often operate as a beachhead for the social sciences and humanities in faculties of education.

In contrast to the classical foundations, economics, policy studies, and law have developed as branches of educational study only recently, but now provide perspectives on all aspects of formal schooling. These fields have rapidly gained substantial influence and may be, in the eyes of educational policymakers and administrators at any rate, the most important areas of educational study. Educational economics has shaped the twenty-first-century view of education as an investment good that is crucial to microeconomics as well as to global markets and national growth. This focus follows naturally from global shifts in economic policy toward neoliberalism and privatization, which have resulted in stronger connections between education and labor markets. However, contrary to popular belief, perhaps, educational economists are also concerned with the effects of inequality, both as inputs into educational systems and as outcomes of educational marketization. Policy studies uses empirical and theoretical methods to examine political forces in education, and especially the processes by which governments make educational choices. Drawing from other critical social sciences, policy studies is especially well suited to understanding relations of power and authority in education. The discipline of law traditionally studies how legal systems determine and interpret legal norms, but educational law has become a focus of legal scholarship only comparatively recently. Developing in tandem with the judicialization of American education, educational law focuses on the analysis of case law from around the world on such issues as parents' rights in education, the need for schools to respect students' basic rights, and the role the courts have played in advancing the cause of educational justice and equality.

As much as philosophy, history, sociology, policy studies, economics, and law offer distinct perspectives and resources for understanding educational phenomena, these disciplines all broadly apply the methods of the humanities and social sciences to questions of curriculum, learning, teaching, and schooling. We do not conceive of a discipline as a monolithic tradition of study; educational scholars borrow liberally from one another and move toward similar goals, all while advancing their respective traditions. The layout of this series is intended to showcase similarities across disciplines that tend to work on parallel problems in relative isolation from one another. These volumes feature recurrent methods of analysis—for instance, critiques of power and interpretations of social processes—as well as appeals to shared intellectual ancestors—such as John Dewey, Michel Foucault, or Émile Durkheim. Taken together, the six disciplines that anchor this book series provide panoramic perspectives on a battery of educational issues. By presenting them as a symmetrical set, we hope to advance understanding of the meaning and importance of educational foundations, separately and collectively.

ADVANCING EDUCATIONAL JUSTICE WITH THE SOCIAL SCIENCES AND HUMANITIES

While the academic origins of much educational research have been pushed out of teacher education, the critical spirit of the humanities and social sciences is alive and well in many faculties of education. As mentioned earlier, when teacher education tips into the non-technical, it is often oriented toward a social justice agenda that highlights how education systems reproduce and can exacerbate patterns of oppression and inequality. These concerns have gained traction in the context of global racial reckonings, the climate crisis, and the COVID-19 pandemic, which intensified all manner of disparities and challenges in education.

We take seriously the demands of educational justice in both research and practice, but social justice education is not a discipline in its own right, nor can it be said to be an academic foundation that has shaped the study of education through modernity. We believe it is through an appreciation of the educational foundations that social justice concerns can best be understood and leveraged to create change. Concerns about equity and the injustice of background conditions suffuse these volumes, highlighting the ongoing relevance of educational foundations for interpreting the world and challenging educational practices. Schools and universities, like other institutions, are presently in the throes of diversity, equity, and inclusion (DEI) discourse and corresponding mandates to rid themselves of racist legacies and biases. Severed from historical understanding or reasoned explanation, these institutional positions have at times been criticized for paying lip service to social justice while reinforcing neoliberal structures. By engaging deeply with the academic work that calls these structures into question, these volumes offer a means of contextualizing and interpreting the need for DEI in all aspects of formal education.

Given the political context and professional pressures we have described, this series is intended to be both backward-looking and forward-looking. The contributors—a diverse group hailing from five continents—are leading scholars who have their finger on the pulse of their fields and directions for future research. By articulating the contributions of academic disciplines to educational studies and the state of research in those fields, these volumes can inform rigorous scholarship, educational policy, and professional practice. However much of the series you read, and in whatever order, we hope that these books will leave you enlightened and with a renewed appreciation for the richness that the social sciences and humanities have to offer the study of education.

REFERENCES

Butin, Dan W. (2005a), "Guest Editor's Introduction: How Social Foundations of Education Matters to Teacher Preparation: A Policy Brief," *Educational Studies*, 38 (3): 214–29.

Butin, Dan W. (2005b), *Teaching Social Foundations of Education*, New York: Routledge.
Colgan, Andrew D. and Bruce Maxwell, eds. (2019), *The Importance of Philosophy in Teacher Education: Mapping the Decline and its Consequences*, Abingdon, UK: Routledge.
Committee on Academic Standards and Accreditation: Sandra Winn Tutweiler (Chair), Kathleen deMarrais, David Gabbard, Andrea Hyde, Pamela Konkol, Huey-li Li, Yolanda Medina, Joseph Rayle, and Amy Swain (2013), "Standards for Academic and Professional Instruction in Foundations of Education, Educational Studies, and Educational Policy Studies, third edition, 2012, draft presented to the educational community by the American Educational Studies Association's Committee on Academic Standards and Accreditation," *Educational Studies*, 49 (2): 107–18.
Curtis, Will, Stephen Ward, John Sharp, and Les Hankin, eds. (2013), *Education Studies: An Issue Based Approach*, London: Learning Matters.
Edmunds, Alan, Jodi Nickel, Kenneth Rea Badley, and Gail Edmunds (2015), *Educational Foundations in Canada*, Don Mills, ONT: Oxford University Press.
Hartlep, Nicholas D., Bradley J. Porfilio, Stacy Otto, and Kathleen O'Brien (2015), "What We Stand *For*, Not *Against*: Presenting our Teacher Education Colleagues with the Case for Social Foundations in PK–12 Teacher Preparation Programs," *Educational Foundations*, 28: 135–50.
Kerr, Donald, David Mandzuk, and Helen Raptis (2011), "The Role of the Social Foundations of Education in Programs of Teacher Preparation in Canada," *Canadian Journal of Education*, 34 (4): 118–34.
Neumann, Richard (2009), "Highly Qualified Teachers and the Social Foundations of Education," *Phi Delta Kappan*, 91 (3): 81–5.
Plato (1974), *The Republic*, trans. G.M.A. Grube, Indianapolis, IN: Hackett.
Pope, Nakia S. and Kurt Stemhagen (2008), "Social Foundations Educators of the World Unite! An Action Plan for Disciplinary Advocacy," *Educational Studies*, 44 (3): 247–55.
Ryan, Ann Marie (2006), "The Role of Social Foundations in Preparing Teachers for Culturally Relevant Practice," *Multicultural Education*, 13 (3): 10–13.
Schutz, Aaron, and Dan W. Butin (2013), "Beyond Dependency: Strategies for Saving Foundations," *Critical Questions in Education*, 4 (2): 60–71.
Semel, Susan F., ed. (2010), *Foundations of Education: The Essential Texts*, New York: Routledge.

Introduction

J.C. BLOKHUIS

Generally speaking, the legal foundations of education include the statutory frameworks within which schools and education systems operate in jurisdictions throughout the world. These frameworks are comprised of the laws and policies through which particular states (a) establish and maintain public school systems; (b) require parents and guardians to enroll the children in their care in approved educational programs; (c) mandate that particular subjects be taught in particular ways by persons with particular credentials; (d) regulate teacher certification standards and teacher employment; and (e) ensure school safety, effectiveness, and efficiency. While these and other related matters fall squarely within the metes and bounds of the Legal Foundations of Education, they also fall within those of the Policy Foundations of Education and to a lesser extent those of the Philosophical Foundations of Education.

While the title of this volume suggests an overview of the laws and rules regulating public schools and education systems throughout the world, its scope is narrower. As indicated in Chapter 1—Mapping the Field—the task at hand is to introduce a *specific* field to an international audience of nonspecialists. Accordingly, this volume focuses on education law, memorably defined by M.A. McGhehey (1961: 1) as, "that area of the law which is concerned with legal relationships and legal problems growing out of the operation of the [American] public school system."

In the United States, the federal Constitution protects individual freedoms by limiting the scope of government action. Because American public school officials are state agents, the Constitution regulates their interactions with school employees, parents, and students. All state education laws, public school and district policies, and administrative practices must be consistent with the Constitution. Under Section 1983 of the federal Civil Rights Act, individuals may sue government agencies and individual state actors for alleged violations of First Amendment guarantees of freedom of speech and religion, Fourth Amendment protection from unreasonable searches, Fourteenth Amendment due process and equal protection requirements, and a host of civil rights protected under federal statutes. Section 1983 lawsuits against states, school districts, and public school officials have generated a vast number of judicial decisions. Collectively, these decisions constitute the case law with which practitioners, scholars, and students of education law work.

Scholars and practitioners of education law can be readily distinguished from others working within the legal foundations of education and other foundational domains by their focus on (a) the constitutional rights of students, teachers and other personnel in American public schools; and (b) constitutional limits on the authority of public school officials in the United States. Accordingly, this volume features illustrative work by leading scholars and practitioners in the field of education law, as follows:

In Chapter 1, "Mapping the Field," J.C. Blokhuis traces the development of education law to legal and social developments in United States following the watershed US Supreme Court decision in *Brown v. Board of Education*, 347 U.S. 483 (1954). During the ensuing civil rights era, the ascription of limited constitutional rights to minors in public schools; the emergence of rights-supportive lawyers, law firms, and interest groups; and the expansion of government agency liability under Section 1983 of the Civil Rights Act generated an explosion of lawsuits against states, school districts, and public school officials. The resulting body of case law is both the lifeblood of education law and its *sine qua non*. Professor Blokhuis attributes the judicialization of American education and the rise of the Education Law Association to an American jurisprudential context profoundly reshaped by *Brown*.

In Chapter 2, "Purposes of Education," Maryam Ahranjani and J.C. Blokhuis consider the aims and purposes of public education according to liberal philosophers of education, which typically include the preparation of children for democratic citizenship; the facilitation of their prospective autonomy; preparation for economic participation and mobility; and for the exercise of the quintessentially American right to "life, liberty, and the pursuit of happiness." They then review significant cases in which the US Supreme Court characterized of the aims and purposes of education in broad terms (favoring more expansive constitutional rights and freedoms for students) from 1940 to 1970, noting how this shifted to increasingly narrow characterizations (favoring more expansive authority for school officials to maintain order and control) from 1975 to the present.

In Chapter 3, "Curriculum," J.C. Blokhuis and David Hòa Khoa Nguyễn review US Supreme Court decisions establishing constitutional limits on prayer, Bible reading, religious observances, and the use of religious books and music in American public schools, focusing on three clauses within the First Amendment—the Free Speech Clause, the Free Exercise Clause, and the Establishment Clause. They then consider "released time" policies allowing students in public schools in a number of US states to earn credits for private religious instruction received offsite during the school day. They then review persistent religious objections to aspects of the science curriculum and explore how state legislatures, local school districts, and individual teachers have turned to the courts in a century-long battle over the teaching of evolution in American public schools.

In Chapter 4, "Schools and Education Systems," Jonathan Feldman and J.C. Blokhuis review the history of constitutional and federal civil rights litigation in the wake of *Brown v. Board of Education*, 347 U.S. 483 (1954), the watershed case in which US Supreme Court overruled the "separate but equal" doctrine and found segregated public schools unconstitutional. This victory launched the civil rights movement, putting public schools and education systems at the vanguard of a rights revolution that continues to this day. While the US Constitution and federal civil rights statutes regulate the operation of public schools nationwide, de facto school segregation in many American cities remains a serious problem.

In Chapter 5, "Learning and Human Development," Katherine Covell and R. Brian Howe consider the influence of the United Nations Convention on the Rights of the Child on children's learning and development, particularly in states that have ratified and implemented its provisions. All UN member states *except* the United States have ratified this extraordinary treaty, largely because ratification would require a two-thirds majority vote in a polarized US Senate. Using the framework of children's rights *to* education, *in* education, and *through* education, Professors Covell and Howe analyze the meaning of these rights and review problems in their implementation worldwide. They then describe initiatives in education on children's rights and studies of their effects on children's learning and development. They conclude with a brief look at how states have incorporated children's rights education in public schools in compliance with the CRC, obstacles to compliance, and prospects for change.

In Chapter 6, "Teaching and Teacher Education," Suzanne E. Eckes and Charles J. Russo review the legal landscape for the education, certification, and employment of teachers in the United States. They then examine First Amendment issues associated with the regulation of the speech and the conduct of teachers, both inside and outside of the classroom. Can American public school teachers be dismissed for voicing opinions on matters of public concern? Can they lose their certification if school officials disapprove of their preferred teaching methods or materials? Can public school teachers be dismissed for what they say or do while off duty or online? Professors Eckes and Russo review recent decisions from federal and state courts and from media reports on these questions and others in the American constitutional context.

In Chapter 7, "Assessment and Evaluation," Patrick J. McGuinn explores how the federal government has increased its influence in American public education over the past sixty years. It has done this through financial incentives for states and school districts, including statutory frameworks for the assessment and evaluation of students, teachers, and schools. While the original version of the Elementary and Secondary Education Act of 1965 contained little about assessment and evaluation, subsequent reauthorizations have expanded federal legal mandates on student and teacher performance and school quality.

The volume editor, series editors, and everyone on the Bloomsbury team would like to thank the contributors to this volume for their willingness to share their expertise with a global audience. We would also like to thank the Education Law Association, the leading professional organization for scholars and practitioners in the field (including many of the contributors to this volume), for its ongoing assistance with and support for this project.

REFERENCE

McGhehey, M.A. (1961), *Research and Reporting Activities in Legal Problems of Education*, Washington, DC: US Department of Health, Education, and Welfare.

CHAPTER ONE

Mapping the Field

Education Law in a Jurisprudential Context Profoundly Reshaped by Brown

J.C. BLOKHUIS

The emergence of education law as a field of practice and scholarly inquiry was facilitated by legal and social developments in the United States following the watershed decision by the US Supreme Court in *Brown v. Board of Education*, 347 U.S. 483 (1954). In this landmark civil rights case, the highest American court found that racially segregated public school systems violated the Equal Protection Clause of the Fourteenth Amendment, which prohibits any state from denying to any person within its jurisdiction equal treatment under the law. For a unanimous Court, Chief Justice Earl Warren overturned the "separate but equal" doctrine enunciated in *Plessy v. Ferguson*, 163 U.S. 537 (1896), describing segregated schools as "inherently unequal."

The *Brown* decision galvanized the nascent civil rights movement in the United States. One year later, activist Rosa Parks would spark the first of many boycotts, sit-ins, and demonstrations by refusing to give up her seat on a Montgomery, Alabama bus. The boycotts and sit-ins and protests of the ensuing decade led to the passage of federal legislation protecting Americans from racial discrimination in public life, including the Civil Rights Act of 1964, the Voting Rights Act of 1965, and the Fair Housing Act of 1968 (Pruitt 2021). While the American civil rights movement formally began in 1954 and ended in 1968, the *Brown* decision was a major step in the quest for equity, diversity, and inclusion in American schools and society that continues to this day.

It also marked a turning point in American jurisprudence. Until the political question doctrine was repudiated by the US Supreme Court in *Baker v. Carr*,

369 U.S. 186 (1962), political matters on which the Constitution offered no clear guidance were considered nonjusticiable. The federal courts left political questions to democratically elected legislators to decide. The *Brown* decision did not, in and of itself, desegregate American public schools. It merely served as a judicial cudgel of sorts, forcing an otherwise reluctant Congress into action. Law may be a blunt instrument in the ongoing pursuit of justice in American society, but the *Brown* decision would not have been necessary if desegregation had been achievable by political means (Blokhuis and Curren 2021: 16).

Ran Hirschl (2013) describes the process by which judges are increasingly relied upon to resolve intractable political and administrative disputes as *judicialization*. "National high courts worldwide have been frequently asked to resolve a range of issues from the scope of expression and religious liberties and privacy to property, trade and commerce, education, immigration, labor, and environmental protection," he writes. Education law developed in tandem with the judicialization of American education in the wake of *Brown*, a phenomenon associated with the judicial review of administrative decisions by public school officials in lawsuits filed in the American federal courts, usually by or on behalf of students or school personnel alleging constitutional rights violations (Blokhuis and Curren 2021: 1). Legal and social developments in the United States during the civil rights movement included the ascription of limited constitutional rights to minors in public schools and other custodial contexts; the emergence of rights-supportive lawyers, law firms, interest groups, and professional associations; and the expansion of government agency liability and concomitant proliferation of lawsuits under Section 1983 of the Civil Rights Act. In short, the *Brown* decision prompted the judicialization of American education, the founding of the Education Law Association, and the emergence of education law as a quintessentially American field of practice and scholarly inquiry.

EDUCATION LAW WITHIN AND BEYOND THE UNITED STATES

As a field of practice and scholarly enquiry, education law is both US-centered and US-centric. Leading American textbooks in the field include *Education Law, 6th edition*, the latest in a series launched in 1992 by Tyll van Geel and Michael Imber, who passed the torch to Jonathan Feldman and J.C. Blokhuis (Blokhuis et al. 2021) more than a decade ago. Of the 1,862 decisions listed in the Table of Cases, none is from a foreign court or jurisdiction. The same holds true for *Legal Rights of School Leaders, Teachers, and Students, 8th edition*, by Martha M. McCarthy, Suzanne E. Eckes, and Janet R. Decker (2019); for *American Public School Law, 9th edition*, by Kern Alexander and M. David Alexander (2019); for *The Law of Public Education, 10th edition*, by Charles J. Russo (2018b); and for *Education Law, 2nd edition*, a newer series by John

Dayton (2019). In *Educational Policy and the Law*, 4th edition, by Mark G. Yudof, David L. Kirp, Betsy Levin, and Rachel F. Moran (2002), there were 1,236 items in the Table of Contents, including one non-US case.

By comparison, the leading Canadian textbook in the field is *Education Law, 5th edition*, by Anthony F. Brown, Marvin A. Zuker, Nicola Simmons, and Robert G. Keel (2019). Of the nearly six hundred decisions in its Table of Cases, roughly a third are decisions from the realm of family law, including child welfare and protection, divorce, and juvenile justice systems through which the state regulates the custodial authority of adults in the interests of children. This may reflect a broader conceptualization of the term "education" in Canadian jurisprudence, a term often coupled at common law with the term "maintenance" to function as a synonym, more or less, with "childrearing" or "upbringing." About 1 percent of the decisions listed in the Table of Cases in the leading Canadian education law textbook are from the United Kingdom, and roughly 10 percent are American, including many of the watershed US Supreme Court decisions explored in the chapters of this volume.

Those who practice education law *outside* the United States may look to American jurisprudence for inspiration and context, but their counterparts *within* the United States tend not to reciprocate that interest. Indeed, the international influence of American constitutional jurisprudence in general appears to have been on the wane for decades. "One of our great exports used to be constitutional law," Anne-Marie Slaughter bemoaned to Adam Liptak of the *New York Times* in 2008. According to his report, from 1990 through 2002, the US Supreme Court of Canada cited US Supreme Court decisions about a dozen times a year. From 2002 to 2008, the citation rate fell by half (Liptak 2008). The same thing was occurring in Australia, where American decisions were cited 208 times in 1995 and only seventy-two times in 2005 (Liptak 2008).

To the extent that education law is practiced or studied *beyond* the United States, it is to a considerable degree an exercise in comparative education law, a field of study in its own right. Charles J. Russo, editor of the *Encyclopedia of Education Law* (2008), has also produced a four-volume series in comparative education law exploring legal issues in education in selected countries in the British Commonwealth (2017a), East Asia (2017b), Europe (2018a), and Africa and the Americas (2019). The practice and study of law is very much a comparative endeavor, not least because the bedrock common law principle in American jurisprudence requiring like cases be treated alike demands it (Winston 1974; Strauss 2002; Marmor 2005). Education law *within* the United States is very much a comparative endeavor because the American system of state and local control complicates education law. Rules, policies, and standards can vary from state to state, from district to district, and from building to building. In states allowing charter schools—publicly funded schools that operate independently of the school districts and even the facilities in which they operate—the rules, policies, and standards can vary from one part of a building to the next (Blokhuis et al. 2021: 2).

According to the National Center for Education Statistics (NCES), 88 percent of kindergarten through grade 12 (K–12) students in the United States were enrolled in public schools, 7 percent were enrolled in parochial schools, 2 percent in other private schools, while 3 percent were reported by their parents as being homeschooled in 2016 (Wang, Rathbun, and Misu 2019: 7). Because they are not state agents, private school officials are not subject to the federal Constitution and cannot be sued under Section 1983 of the Civil Rights Act. Nor are parents educating their children at home. This fundamental difference between public and private schools and schools systems in American jurisprudence adds an important dimension to the comparative nature of education law for scholars and practitioners alike.

The American federal court system adds another comparative dimension. There are ninety-five federal trial courts (called US district courts) in the United States and thirteen federal intermediate appellate courts (called US courts of appeals or circuit courts). The First Circuit includes Maine, Massachusetts, New Hampshire, Puerto Rico, and Rhode Island; the Second Circuit includes Connecticut, New York, and Vermont; the Third Circuit includes New Jersey, Pennsylvania, and the US Virgin Islands; the Fourth Circuit includes Maryland, North Carolina, South Carolina, Virginia, and West Virginia; the Fifth Circuit includes Louisiana, Mississippi, and Texas; the Sixth Circuit includes Kentucky, Ohio, Michigan, and Tennessee; the Seventh Circuit includes Illinois, Indiana, and Wisconsin; the Eight Circuit includes Arkansas, Iowa, Minnesota, Missouri, Nebraska, and the Dakotas; the Ninth Circuit includes Alaska, Arizona, California, Guam, Hawaii, Idaho, Montana, Nevada, the Northern Mariana Islands, Oregon, and Washington; the Tenth Circuit includes Colorado, Kansas, New Mexico, Oklahoma, Utah, and Wyoming; the Eleventh Circuit includes Alabama, Florida, and Georgia; while the DC Circuit covers the District of Columbia. The American federal court system plays an important role in shaping education law because it deals almost exclusively with cases involving the federal Constitution, federal statutes, and federal regulations. When inconsistencies arise in rulings issued by the circuit courts on a particular legal question, debates among scholars and practitioners fill the pages of law reviews and scholarly journals with a focus on education law. Leading academic journals in the field include the *Journal of Law and Education*, founded in 1972 and hosted by the University of South Carolina School of Law and the *BYU Education and Law Journal*, founded in 1992 by the School of Education at Brigham Young University. Unless and until the Supreme Court resolves inconsistencies in circuit court decisions, the specific contours of the constitutional rights of students or teachers in American public schools may vary between the states within the various circuit court jurisdictions noted above.

The Supreme Court of the United States serves as the highest authority on the meaning of federal statutes and the US Constitution. As such, it tends to hear appeals in cases on which there have been inconsistent rulings between and among the federal circuit courts and in cases with important jurisprudential consequences. Although the Supreme Court receives more than 7,000 appeal requests each year, it generally agrees to hear only about 2 percent of them (Blokhuis et al. 2021: 8). Of these decisions, no more than one or two each year entail major developments for scholars and practitioners of education law.

To illustrate how the study and practice of education law is a comparative endeavor, let us consider some key judicial opinions from within and beyond the United States.

EXHIBIT A: THE FREE SPEECH RIGHTS OF STUDENTS IN AMERICAN PUBLIC SCHOOLS

The First Amendment reads, "*Congress shall make no law* respecting an establishment of religion, or prohibiting the free exercise thereof; or *abridging the freedom of speech*, or of the press; or the right of the people peaceably to assemble, and to petition the Government for a redress of grievances." The portions italicized above are commonly referred to as the Free Speech Clause.

A watershed Supreme Court decision on the free speech rights of students in public schools was issued at the end of the civil rights movement. In *Tinker v. Des Moines Independent Community School District*, 393 U.S. 503 (1969), a group of middle school students who were suspended for wearing black armbands to protest American involvement in Vietnam claimed school officials violated their free speech rights. The Supreme Court agreed, holding that political speech by students in public schools is protected by the First Amendment, provided it does not materially or substantially disrupt the educational work of the school or interfere with the rights of others. "First Amendment rights, applied in light of the special characteristics of the school environment, are available to teachers and students," wrote Justice Abe Fortas for the Court. "It can hardly be argued that either students or teachers shed their constitutional rights to freedom of speech or expression at the schoolhouse gate" (see Driver 2018).

Until recently, the various circuit courts had applied the "material and substantial disruption" standard enunciated in *Tinker* inconsistently in cases involving student speech originating off-campus (typically on the internet or a social media platform). In *Wisniewski v. Board of Education*, 494 F.3d 34 (2d Cir. 2007), *cert. denied*, 552 U.S. 1296 (2008), a student was suspended for creating an icon for his instant message account depicting one of his teachers being shot in the head, along with the caption, "Kill Mr. VanderMolen." The Second Circuit (Connecticut, New York, and Vermont) upheld the decision by school officials to suspend him, finding that the icon "pose[d] a reasonably foreseeable risk that [it] would come to the attention of school authorities and … materially and substantially disrupt the work and discipline of the school." For similar reasons, in *Doninger v. Niehoff*, 527 F.3d 41 (2d Cir. 2008), *cert. denied*, 565 U.S. 976 (2011), the Second Circuit allowed school officials to disqualify a student from running for office after he referred to them as "douchebags" in a blog post (McCarthy 2021: 440; see Blokhuis et al. 2021: 156).

Conversely, the Third Circuit (Delaware, New Jersey, Pennsylvania, and the US Virgin Islands) found in favor of students in both *J.S. v. Blue Mountain School District*, 650 F.3d 915 (3d Cir. 2011), *cert. denied*, 565 U.S. 1156 (2012) and *Layshock v. Hermitage School District*, 650 F.3d 205 (3d Cir. 2011), *cert. denied*, 565 U.S. 1156 (2012). Both cases involved students who created vulgar MySpace profiles on their school principals. In the former case, the student was suspended for ten days; in the latter case, the student was placed in an alternate education program and barred from participating in graduation ceremonies. In both cases, the Third Circuit regarded the profiles as parodies unlikely to be taken seriously. The Third Circuit also expressed doubt about the applicability of *Tinker* to off-campus student speech in general (McCarthy 2021: 440; see Blokhuis et al. 2021: 161).

In *Kowalski v. Berkeley County Schools*, 652 F.3d 565 (2011), *cert. denied*, 565 U.S. 1173 (2012), a student was suspended for violating her school's anti-harassment policy after she created a "hate website" describing a classmate as a "slut" [*sic*] with a venereal disease. Basing its ruling on a "nexus" between the website and the school, the Fourth Circuit (Maryland, North Carolina, South Carolina, Virginia, and West Virginia) applied the disruption standard from *Tinker* and concluded the student could be punished without violating the First Amendment. The Fifth Circuit (Louisiana, Mississippi, and Texas) reached a similar conclusion in *Bell v. Itawamba County School District*, 799 F.3d 379 (5th Cir. 2015), a case involving a student who posted a homemade rap video online, with lyrics alleging sexual misconduct against two coaches and threats to shoot them in the face. Applying the material and substantial disruption test from *Tinker*, the Court found in favor of school officials who suspended the student. The Ninth Circuit (Alaska, Arizona, California, Guam, Hawaii, Idaho, Montana, Nevada, Northern Mariana Islands, Oregon, and Washington) likewise applied the disruption test from *Tinker* in *Wynar v. Douglas County School District*, 728 F.3d 1062 (9th Cir. 2013), a case involving a student who was expelled after making online threats to engage in a shooting spree at his school (McCarthy 2021: 440; see Blokhuis et al. 2021: 246–7).

In 2021, the Supreme Court granted leave to appeal the Third Circuit's decision in *Mahanoy Area School District v. B.L.*, 594 U.S. ___ (2021), a case involving a cheerleader who had been denied a promotion to her school's varsity team. While at a shopping center one weekend, she and a friend posted pictures of themselves on Snapchat, middle fingers raised, with vulgar captions making liberal use of the word associated with the gesture. B.L. was later dropped from the cheerleading team for violating a school rule requiring that cheerleaders avoid using foul language and inappropriate gestures online. On June 23, 2021, the Supreme Court issued its ruling in the case, finding the school district had violated the First Amendment when it punished B.L. for her social media posts. Writing for an 8–1 majority, Justice Stephen G. Breyer resolved the inconsistent approach of the Third Circuit to the regulation of off-campus student speech: "Unlike the 3rd Circuit, we do not believe the special characteristics that give schools additional license to regulate student speech always disappear when a school regulates speech that takes place off campus" (Walsh 2021).

Free speech claims have come rather a long way from the *Tinker* case in 1969 (involving students who wore black armbands in class to protest an unpopular military operation in Vietnam) to the *Mahanoy* case in 2021 (involving a cheerleader who used vulgar language and gestures on social media). What these and all the other cases discussed above have in common are claims that school officials violated the First Amendment filed by or on behalf of students under Section 1983 of the Civil Rights Act (42 U.S.C. § 1983).

EXHIBIT B: STUDENT PRIVACY RIGHTS IN AMERICAN AND CANADIAN PUBLIC SCHOOLS

The Fourth Amendment to the US Constitution guarantees that individuals are "to be secure in their persons, houses, papers, and effects, against unreasonable searches and seizures." In *Katz v. United States*, 389 U.S. 347 (1967), an important Civil Rights era decision, the Supreme Court held that the Fourth Amendment protects the *privacy* interests of individuals, alongside their persons and their property. In criminal contexts, the Fourth Amendment requires that police officers obtain a warrant based on probable cause before undertaking a search. Search warrants must be supported by an oath or affirmation, and must describe in detail the places to be searched, the items to be seized, and the individuals to be arrested. There are exceptions, however. Search warrants are not required in exigent circumstances, when evidence is in plain view, or when a search is conducted with valid consent. For scholars and practitioners of education law, perhaps the most important exception to Fourth Amendment search warrant requirements applies to public school officials investigating student misconduct.

The US Supreme Court enunciated this exception in *New Jersey v. T.L.O.*, 469 U.S. 325 (1985), a watershed case involving a fourteen-year-old student who denied smoking cigarettes in a school bathroom when questioned by a teacher. Upon searching the student's purse in an attempt to find cigarettes, an assistant vice-principal subsequently found cigarettes and rolling papers. He continued searching the purse and found marijuana, drug paraphernalia, cash, and a list of names of students owing money for marijuana purchases. The student later confessed to police that she had indeed been selling marijuana and was charged with delinquency. The student claimed the search of her purse by the assistant vice-principal violated her Fourth Amendment rights. While acknowledging that students have privacy interests which must be balanced against the duty to maintain a safe and orderly learning environment, the Court held that public school officials do not need probable cause or a warrant to search a student if the search is justified at its inception and its scope is reasonable in the circumstances.

In the years since the *T.L.O.* decision, widespread public concerns about school safety have led many school officials throughout the United States to adopt relatively nonintrusive search procedures applicable to all students, without the need for individualized suspicion. The use of metal detectors at school entrances is a "search" for Fourth Amendment purposes, but American courts have found the practice reasonable, given the minimal infringement of privacy and the overriding public interest in keeping weapons out of schools. Indeed, in the interests of maintaining a secure and orderly learning environment, many public schools now feature surveillance cameras in common areas and drug testing programs for students involved in extracurricular activities. In other contexts, agents of the state could not require such things of adults, much less punish them for noncompliance, as this would violate their constitutional rights. But again, the Fourth Amendment rights of American public school students are not coextensive with those of adults in other contexts.

Shortly before its decision in *T.L.O.*, the Supreme Court found that the use of sniffer dogs to search luggage at airports is not a "search" for Fourth Amendment purposes in *United States v. Place*, 462 U.S. 696 (1983). It also affirmed that the Fourth Amendment protects people, not *places*, in *Segura v. United States*, 468 U.S. 796 (1984). Thus in American public schools, where students have a reduced expectation of privacy when using common areas, including desks, lockers, and parking lots, sniffer dogs may be used to search virtually everything *except* their persons.

In *Burlison v. Springfield Public Schools*, 708 F.3d 1034 (8th Cir. 2013), two police officers arrived at the school with sniffer dogs to search a science classroom. Students were instructed to leave their backpacks and personal items and wait outside in the hallway for five minutes. One student who believed his backpack had been opened alleged his Fourth Amendment rights had been violated and filed suit under Section 1983. The Eighth Circuit (Arkansas, Iowa, Minnesota, Missouri, Nebraska, North Dakota, and South Dakota) disagreed:

> Assuming that C.M.'s belongings were seized in this case when the school police officer directed that they be left in the classroom for approximately five minutes while the drug dog survey occurred, we conclude that the seizure was part of a reasonable procedure to maintain the safety and security of students at the school. Since C.M. is a high school student, he has a "lesser expectation of privacy" than the general public...
>
> The district and its officials have shown an immediate need for a drug dog procedure because there is substantial evidence showing there was a drug problem in district buildings. The Supreme Court has repeatedly emphasized the strong government interest in preventing drug use by students ... We conclude that the brief separation of C.M. and his belongings was reasonable and did not deprive him of a constitutionally protected right.

Similarly, the Supreme Court of Canada has ruled that public school principals may search students as part of their duty to maintain order and discipline, provided there are reasonable grounds to conduct a search and the matter is disciplinary and not criminal in nature (Brown et al. 2019: 290). The leading Canadian case is *R. v. M. (M.R.)*, [1998] 3 S.C.R. 393, a counterpart in many respects to *T.L.O.* The Canadian case involved a thirteen-year-old alleged to be dealing drugs at a school dance. When the student arrived at the dance, the vice-principal escorted him to his office and called the police. An officer watched as the vice-principal found a cellophane bag of marijuana in the student's sock. Charges against the student were later dismissed on the ground that the vice-principal was acting as an agent of the police and had violated the student's rights under Section 8 of the Charter of Rights and Freedoms. Section 8 provides that "Everyone has the right to be secure against unreasonable search or seizure," and excludes anything seized in violation of this right from being entered into evidence at trial. Canadian courts have defined a "search" for Section 8 purposes as any action by an agent of the state that interferes with an individual's reasonable expectation of privacy.

At the Court of Appeal, Justice Bruce E. Pugsley applied the same two-step test deployed by the US Supreme Court in *T.L.O.*, finding no violation of Section 8 because the search undertaken by the vice-principal was justifiable at its inception and was reasonable in its scope. On appeal, the Supreme Court of Canada agreed, holding that the constitutional standards applicable to searches by public school officials depend on whether they are acting as agents of the police (Brown et al. 2019: 293). Searches by school officials undertaken in the course of maintaining a safe learning environment must be reasonable, authorized by statute, and carried out in a reasonable manner. Because the vice-principal was not acting as a police officer in this case, the search was not unreasonable in the circumstances.

However, in *R. v. M. (A.)*, [2006] 79 O.R. (3d) 481 (C.A.), the Ontario Court of Appeal reached a different conclusion than that of the Eighth Circuit in *Burlison*, despite similar underlying facts. In the Canadian case, three police officers conducted a sniffer dog search of a high school without the prior knowledge of the principal, who asked students to remain in their classrooms for the duration of the impromptu search. A student who was later charged for possession for the purpose of trafficking after the sniffer dog found marijuana and "magic mushrooms" in his backpack claimed the search violated his constitutional rights under Section 8 of the Charter (Brown et al. 2019: 295–6). The Ontario Court of Appeal agreed with the student, describing the search as "a warrantless, random search with the entire school body held in detention. It was not authorized by either the criminal law or the Education Act and subsidiary school policies." On further appeal, a majority on the Supreme Court of Canada ruled in favor of the student:

> This was a random speculative search. What was done here may have been seen by the police as an efficient use of resources, and by the principal of the school as an efficient way to advance a zero-tolerance policy. But these objectives were achieved at the expense of the privacy interest (and constitutional rights) of every student in the school . . . A hunch is not enough to warrant a search of citizens or their belongings by police dogs.

EXHIBIT C: PARENTAL RIGHTS IN AMERICAN AND CANADIAN JURISPRUDENCE

In *Wisconsin v. Yoder*, 406 U.S. 205 (1972), the US Supreme Court granted an exemption from compulsory schooling laws to a group of Amish parents. Jonas Yoder and Wallace Miller were members of an Old Order Amish community; Adin Yutzy was a Conservative Amish Mennonite. All three refused to send their children to public schools after the eighth grade. They were convicted of truancy under Wisconsin's compulsory school attendance law (see Peters 2003: 1). Chief Justice Warren Burger, writing for six members of the US Supreme Court, began his opinion for the Court by affirming the duties of the state: "There is no doubt as to the power of a State, having a high responsibility for education of its citizens, to impose reasonable regulations for the control and duration of basic education." Ultimately, however, he found the free exercise rights of Amish parents outweighed the state interest in providing public education to children beyond the eighth grade. In his view, the compulsory schooling laws of Wisconsin forced Yoder, Miller, and Yutzy to violate their sincerely held religious beliefs while imperiling the survival of their faith communities. If children born to Amish parents were to attend public school beyond the eighth grade, "they must either abandon belief and be assimilated into society at large, or be forced to migrate to some other and more tolerant region."

While Justice Byron White concurred with the Chief Justice, he offered a vigorous affirmation of the state interest in the upbringing of children, quoting Chief Justice Warren two decades earlier in *Brown* (1954):

> Today, education is perhaps the most important function of state and local governments. Compulsory school attendance laws and the great expenditures for education both demonstrate our recognition of the importance of education to our democratic society. It is required in the performance of our most basic public responsibilities, even service in the armed forces. It is the very foundation of good citizenship. Today it is a principal instrument in awakening the child to cultural values, in preparing him for later professional training, and in helping him to adjust normally to his environment.

The *Yoder* decision was based in part on *Pierce v. Society of Sisters*, 268 U.S. 510 (1925), a due process challenge by a Catholic school and a private military academy to a proposed law in Oregon that would have required all parents in the state to enroll their children in public schools. This law, if enacted, would have put private schools out of business. "We think it entirely plain that the Act of 1922 unreasonably interferes with the liberty of parents and guardians to direct the upbringing and education of children under their control," wrote Justice James Clark McReynolds. "The fundamental theory of liberty upon which all governments in this Union repose excludes any general power of the State to standardize its children by forcing them to accept instruction from public teachers only." Three years earlier, Justice McReynolds had made similar pronouncements on the scope of parental liberties under the Fourteenth Amendment in *Meyer v. Nebraska*, 262 U.S. 390 (1923). In that case, a Nebraska statute requiring that children be taught in English only was found to restrict the substantive due process rights of parents and teachers. "Without a doubt, [the Fourteenth Amendment] includes not merely freedom from bodily restraint, but also the right of the individual to marry, establish a home and bring up children and generally to enjoy those privileges long recognized at common law as essential to the orderly pursuit of happiness by free men [*sic*]," he wrote. Both cases were decided under the due process provisions of the Fourteenth Amendment rather than free exercise provisions of the First Amendment because it was unclear at the time whether state governments were bound by the First Amendment. In *Gitlow v. New York*, 268 U.S. 652 (1925), decided just one week after *Pierce*, the Supreme Court determined that the Fourteenth Amendment made the First Amendment applicable to state governments (Blokhuis et al. 2021: 21).

In *R. v. Jones*, [1986] 2 S.C.R. 284, the Supreme Court of Canada considered whether compulsory schooling laws in Alberta infringed upon parental rights and freedoms under Sections 2(a) and 7 of the Canadian Charter of Rights and Freedoms, which are similar in some respects to the First and Fourteenth Amendments to the US Constitution. The First Amendment reads, "Congress shall make no law respecting an establishment of religion, or prohibiting the free exercise thereof; or abridging the freedom of speech, or of the press; or the right of the people peaceably to assemble, and to petition the Government for a redress of grievances." By way of comparison, Section 2(b) of the Canadian Charter of Rights and Freedoms reads, "Everyone has the following fundamental freedoms: (a) freedom of conscience and religion." The Due Process Clause of the Fourteenth Amendment to the US Constitution reads, "nor shall any State deprive any person of life, liberty, or property, without due process of law." By way of comparison, Section 7 of the Canadian Charter of Rights and Freedoms reads, "Everyone has the right to life, liberty and security of the person and the right not to be deprived thereof except in accordance with the principles of fundamental justice."

Thomas Larry Jones was a fundamentalist pastor who provided lessons to his three children (and twenty others) in the basement of his church. He refused to send his children to a public school, in accordance with provincial legislation. The same legislation permitted parents to apply to the local school superintendent to determine whether their children were receiving efficient instruction at home or at an approved private school. The legislation also permitted Jones to register his church basement academy as a private school. Jones, however, believed he did not need public permission to do what God required and claimed that the act of applying for an exemption from compulsory schooling laws would constitute an acknowledgment that the state, not God, had the final authority over the education of his children.

The trial court concluded that Jones's religious freedoms under Section 2(a) had not been infringed by the compulsory schooling laws of Alberta. However, Jones's Section 7 claim that the legislation deprived him of his parental "liberty" to bring up his children as he pleased was sustained. The decision was subsequently reversed by the Court of Appeal, which entered convictions against Jones for truancy. Eight justices of the Supreme Court of Canada heard Jones's appeal, issuing three concurring opinions and one dissenting opinion, borrowing heavily from the US Supreme Court in *Brown* (1954) and *Yoder* (1972).

Justice Gérard La Forest agreed with the trial court that there had been no infringement of Jones's Section 2(a) religious freedoms. The compulsory schooling laws of Alberta did not give the province absolute control over the education of children. No parent was forced to send any child to a public school in Alberta. Invoking the language of the US Supreme Court in *Brown* (1954), Justice La Forest continued, "Education is today a matter of prime concern to government everywhere. Activities in this area account for a very significant part of every provincial budget." He then added, "No proof is required to show the importance of education in our society or its significance to government. The legitimate, indeed compelling, interest of the state in the education of the young is known and understood by all informed citizens." In his view, "it would be reasonable to permit the appellant to ignore the province's laws on a matter as important as the education of the young."

Justice Bertha Wilson agreed. "In my view, the *School Act* does not offend religious freedom; it accommodates it." While she did not point out the rather obvious irony that a man loath to acknowledge the state as the final authority in the education of his children should turn to the highest court in the land to vindicate his claim that God was the "final authority" in the education of his children, she nonetheless concluded Jones had failed to show that taking advantage of the exemption procedures within provincial legislation would have any substantive effect on his belief that God had the final say.

While Justice La Forest declined to include "a right of parents to educate their children as they see fit" within the ambit of Section 7 of the Charter, Justice Wilson was willing to do so, drawing on US constitutional jurisprudence:

> In the United States the constitutionally protected status of family relations has been recognized [citing *Meyer*, *Pierce*, and *Yoder*] ... Further, the court has specifically protected the right of the parent to educate the child. However, the appellant's proposition that he has a right to educate his children "as he sees fit" goes too far. Having regard to the structure of the Constitution and the values it explicitly identifies as worthy of protection, I believe that the liberty interest protected is the parent's right to educate his children in accordance with his conscientious beliefs and I think this is in fact the right the appellant is asserting in this case.

Notably, Section 7 of the Charter does not include protection for property rights. "This omission is no accidental oversight," notes Peter H. Russell (1994: 168). By his account, progressives in the Canadian Parliament insisted on the deletion of references to property rights in exchange for their support for the 1982 Charter. This fundamental difference between the Fourteenth Amendment in the United States and Section 7 of the Charter in Canada helps to explain why Canadian education has not experienced the same degree of judicialization as American education, and more broadly why education law remains a predominantly American field of practice and scholarly inquiry.

"MODERN EDUCATION LITIGATION PAYS—SOMETIMES LITERALLY"

"Youth advocates in the late 1960s and early 1970s embraced a political-legal strategy that had been successfully developed by the Civil Rights Movement … utiliz[ing] court challenges to advance the social interests of children," notes Richard Arum (2003: 6). Perhaps the most important statutory vehicle for such challenges, and thus for the judicialization of American education, is Section 1983 of the Civil Rights Act (42 U.S.C. § 1983). This federal legislation provides as follows:

> Every person who, under color of any statute, ordinance, regulation, custom or usage of any State or Territory or the District of Columbia, subjects or causes to be subjected, any citizen of the United States or other person within the jurisdiction thereof to the deprivation of any rights, privileges, or immunities secured by the Constitution and laws, shall be liable to the party injured in any action at law, suit in equity, or other proper proceeding for redress.

In *Wood v. Strickland*, 420 U.S. 308 (1975), the US Supreme Court held that public school officials could be liable under Section 1983 for knowingly violating the constitutional rights of students, including their due process rights (Friendly 1975: 1274–5). Three years later, in *Monell v. Department of Social Services*, 436 U.S. 658 (1978), a challenge to the compulsory maternity leave policies of both the Department of Social Services and the Board of Education of the City of New York, the Supreme Court held that local government agencies could be liable under Section 1983 (see Blokhuis and Curren 2021: 12–13).

Monell and *Wood* vaulted Section 1983 from relative obscurity to a leading role in the judicialization of American education. Damages awarded under Section 1983 are based on actual losses sustained by plaintiffs, not the importance of the violated right. Although punitive damages against school districts are not permitted in Section 1983 suits, plaintiffs can nonetheless receive large awards. "Thus attorneys working in such areas as religion, free speech, desegregation, and school discipline, who previously donated their services or relied on charitable contributions, could reasonably expect an independent source of funding," note West and Dunn (2009: 6), adding, "modern education litigation pays—sometimes literally."

PROPERTY RIGHTS, DUE PROCESS, AND JUDICIALIZATION AFTER *BROWN*

In *Bolling v. Sharpe*, 347 U.S. 497 (1954), the US Supreme Court unanimously interpreted the term "liberty" in the Due Process Clause of the Fourteenth Amendment even more broadly than Justice McReynolds had done in *Meyer* (1923), noting that it "extends to the full range of conduct which the individual is free to pursue, and it cannot be restricted except for a proper governmental objective." The very same day, in *Brown* (1954), the Court unanimously overruled the "separate but equal" doctrine, finding race-based segregation in public schools contrary to the Equal Protection Clause of the Fourteenth Amendment.

The subsequent explosion in litigation involving public schools and school districts (Zirkel 1997: 341) in the late 1960s and early 1970s exemplifies judicialization through civil rights jurisprudence. Like the *Brown* case itself, litigation in this period "did not emerge spontaneously from grassroots student and parental efforts, but required a supportive legal infrastructure" (Arum 2003: 18), including the Office of Economic Opportunity (OEO) and its Legal Services offices (established in 1965), offices of the Legal Service Corporation (established in 1974), and other public interest law firms using court challenges to advance the constitutional rights and interests of racialized children in the United States.

In *Goldberg v. Kelly*, 397 U.S. 254 (1970), the US Supreme Court found that because welfare benefits are a statutory entitlement, recipients have a corresponding property interest protected by the Fourteenth Amendment. Accordingly, the Due Process Clause requires notice and opportunity to confront and cross-examine adverse witnesses, to present oral arguments, and to obtain counsel before benefits may be withdrawn, even for a brief interval. Twenty years after *Brown*, civil rights groups had come to view the suspension of racialized students from public schools as a "rearguard attempt of school officials to perpetuate dual school systems, a problem calling for the exercise of judicial remedial powers just as surely as the breakup of *de jure* segregation mandated by *Brown*" (Wilkinson 1975: 31). Thus, in *Goss v. Lopez*, 419 U.S. 565 (1975), a Section 1983 case involving nine racialized students suspended for ten days for damaging a school cafeteria, the Supreme Court recognized that children have a property interest in receiving the public education guaranteed them under state statutes, and that a ten-day suspension without a hearing would violate their rights under the Fourteenth Amendment.

Like *Brown*, the *Goss* case made its way to the Supreme Court through the efforts of the Center for Law and Education at Cambridge, Massachusetts; the Office of Economic Opportunity's Legal Services office in Cleveland, Ohio; and numerous organizations submitting *amicus curiae* briefs, including the American Civil Liberties Union (ACLU) and the National Association for the Advancement of Colored People (NAACP) (Arum 2003: 19). "If in *Brown* the racial question was very much on the surface, in *Goss* it lay not very far below," notes J. Harvie Wilkinson III (1975: 30).

As Martin R. West and Joshua M. Dunn (2009: 5–6) note, "the creation of the Legal Services Program within the Office of Economic Opportunity marked a shift in federal policy away from subsidizing legal advice for the poor and [instead] filing test cases intended to alter policy nationwide." Litigation initiated and supported by Legal Services and various civil rights groups in this period challenged school funding inequities on equal protection grounds. American predominance in the field of education law accordingly owes much to this program, which provided legal resources to desegregate public schools in the wake of *Brown* (1954); to challenge racial injustice in the punishment of students in *Goss* (1975); and to address—unsuccessfully—disparities in public school funding (see Blokhuis and Curren 2021: 1; Arum 2003: 8; Blum and Burkholder 2021). In *San Antonio Independent School District v. Rodriguez*, 411 U.S. 1 (1973), the Supreme Court rejected claims that public education was a fundamental right, holding that relative—as opposed to absolute—deprivations of educational rights arising from local property tax-based funding systems did not violate the Fourteenth Amendment.

According to Arum (2003: 8), legal challenges to local public school disciplinary practices occurred in large part because of federal funding and support for legal activism during the Civil Rights era. He singles out the Legal Services Program established by the Office of Economic Opportunity (OEO), established in 1965 "with a mandate that was interpreted to include promoting law reform as part of the War on Poverty under President Johnson." By his account, more than half of its federal funding supported new legal service organizations that stressed law reform: "In 1967, the OEO Legal Services Program received $27 million in federal funding and employed nearly 1200 lawyers; by 1972, the program received $71.5 million and employed over 2000 lawyers" (9; see Blokhuis and Curren 2021: 11). There was a corresponding increase in state and federal litigation involving schools in this period, from 2,452 cases in the 1950s, to 3,413 cases in the 1960s, to 6,788 in the 1970s (Zirkel 1997).

THE ASCRIPTION OF RIGHTS TO MINORS IN CUSTODIAL CONTEXTS IN THE CIVIL RIGHTS ERA

In *Kent v. United States*, 383 U.S. 541 (1966), a sixteen-year-old was taken into custody and questioned for twenty-four hours before confessing to criminal charges. The Juvenile Court of the District of Columbia waived its jurisdiction without a hearing or investigation, allowing Kent to be tried as an adult. The

US Supreme Court overturned Kent's conviction, holding that the Juvenile Court had violated his due process rights under the Fourteenth Amendment in waiving its jurisdiction. The following year, in *In re Gault*, 387 U.S. 1 (1967), a fifteen year old was taken into custody after a neighbor alleged he had made a lewd phone call. The Juvenile Court declared him a delinquent and sent him to an industrial school until he turned twenty-one. The Supreme Court reviewed the due process rights of adults under the Fifth Amendment, including the right to receive notice of charges, the right to counsel, the right to confront one's accuser, the right against self-incrimination, and the right to cross-examine witnesses and found that for juveniles, "departures from established principles of due process have frequently resulted not in enlightened procedure, but in arbitrariness." Two years later, in *Tinker* (1969), discussed earlier, three students were suspended for wearing black armbands in school to protest American military action in Vietnam. The Supreme Court ascribed limited First Amendment protections to public school students engaging in nondisruptive political speech. Six years later, as noted earlier, the Supreme Court held that due process requires notice and a hearing for students suspended from public schools in *Goss* (1975) (see Blokhuis and Curren 2021: 9).

The ascription of due process and other constitutional rights to minors in custodial contexts during the Civil Rights era created a need for lawyers to work in the previously nonexistent field of children's rights (Guggenheim 2005: ix), initially to represent children in juvenile court proceedings subsequently in Section 1983 lawsuits after *Goss*. Thousands of law school graduates took up the call, creating what Ran Hirschl (2006: 725) has described as the "support structure for legal mobilization—a nexus of rights-advocacy organizations, rights-supportive lawyers and law schools, governmental rights-enforcement agencies, and legal aid schemes," which facilitated the judicialization of American education (see Blokhuis and Curren 2021: 10).

Among legal services organizations emerging in the *Brown* era, the National Organization on Legal Problems in Education (NOLPE) looms large. It is no coincidence that NOLPE was organized as the Supreme Court was preparing its landmark decision in *Brown* (1954). According to ELA historian Martha M. McCarthy (1984: 37), "The organization's founders correctly anticipated that the *Brown* ruling would mark a new era of judicial intervention in the educational domain and that litigation and legislation would become increasingly significant in determining school policies and practices."

Prior to *Brown* and the founding of NOLPE, there was not much by way of case law or legal information in the inchoate field of education law. Floyd G. Delon (2008: xxix) identifies two textbooks of note from the 1920s and three from the 1930s, including *Essentials of School Law*, by Harry R. Trusler (1927); and *Handbook of Indiana School Law*, by Frank R. Stephenson (1929); *Legal*

Authority of the American Public School as Developed by a Study of Liabilities to Damages, by J.F. Weltzin (1931); *Education as a Function of the State*, by Lee O. Garber (1934); and *The Courts and Public School Property*, by Harold H. Punke (1936). Also worthy of note from the period was the *Yearbook of School Law* published annually by M.M. Chambers from 1933 to 1942, when the nation's preoccupation with the war brought such publications to a halt.

NOLPE was founded Frank Heinich, an Omaha attorney, and Madaline Kinter Remmlein, an employee of National Education Association (NEA), which has since become the largest labor union in the United States. After Remmlein's request to establish a department on school law issues at the NEA was denied, Edward C. Bolmeier, the president of Duke University, and Lee O. Garber proposed a school law organization independent of the union. This became a topic for discussion at the American Education Research Association convention in February 1954. Four months later, at a school law conference at Duke University, NOLPE was born (McCarthy 1984: 37; see also Karanxha 2009, 2010).

On January 3, 1955, Remmlein was named president; Garber was named secretary-treasurer; and Bolmeier was named to the executive committee as the representative for schools of education.

Reviewing the inaugural edition of Remmlein's magistral *School Law* (1950) for the *Elementary School Journal*, Bolmeier (1951) observed, "Despite the increasing legal ramifications of school administration, no general book on school law has been published during the past decade." Remmlein's pathbreaking series would continue for thirty years, with thirteen editions between 1950 and 1979. In addition, she published *An Evaluation of Existing Forms of School Laws, with Recommendations for their Improvement* (with Martha L. Ware), with multiple editions between 1959 and 1963; *The Law of Local Public School Administration*, with numerous editions between 1953 and 1981; and *Legal Provisions for Summer Schools* (1964).

Working alongside Newton Edwards, Garber launched a number of long-running series in education law, including *The Law Governing Pupils* (1962d); *The Law Governing Teaching Personnel* (1962a); *The Courts and the Public Schools: The Legal Basis of School Organization and Administration* (1971); *The Law Governing School Board Members and School Board Meetings* (1963a); *The Law Relating to the Creation, Alteration, and Dissolution of School Districts* (1962c); *Law and the School Business Manager* (1957); *The Public School in our Governmental Structure* (1962b); and *Tort and Contractual Liability of School Districts and School Boards* (1963b).

In 1994, NOLPE changed its name to the Education Law Association (ELA) and moved its headquarters from Topeka, Kansas (home of the plaintiffs in *Brown*) to the University of Dayton, Ohio in 1997. In 2013, the ELA moved to

Cleveland, Ohio (home of the Office of Economic Opportunity Legal Services branch in *Goss*). It is now a virtual organization that continues to publish the *School Law Reporter* and an array of periodicals and reference items. The ELA has a membership of about 1,200, including practicing attorneys; education law professors; faculty members from graduate schools of education; school board members; public and private school K–12 and higher educational administrators; teachers; staff members of state and federal education agencies and professional associations; law librarians; hearing officers; policymakers; advocates; graduate students and law students (ELA 2021).

In addition to the *Education Law Reporter*, sponsored by the Education Law Association and published by West for its members and library subscribers, the ELA has published an Ed Law Update since April, 2021, succeeding its *School Law Reporter* as a repository for case commentaries on notable decisions in the field. The ELA continues to publish a *Yearbook of Education Law* (Russo 2021) along with a host of monographs by leading authorities in the field including *Search and Seizure in the Public Schools*, by Lawrence F. Rossow and Jacqueline A. Stefkovich (2014); *Social Media, Public Schools, and the Law*, by R. Stewart Mayers (2015); *A Guide to Special Education Law*, by Elizabeth A. Shaver and Janet R. Decker (2017); *Education Finance Law*, by R. Craig Wood, David C. Thompson, John Dayton, and Christine Kiracofe (2015); and *Legal Issues of Faith-based and Other Nonpublic Schools*, edited by Charles J. Russo and Steve Permuth (2018).

REFERENCES

Alexander, Kern and M. David Alexander (2019), *American Public School Law*, 9th edn., St. Paul, MN: West Academic.

Arum, Richard (2003), *Judging School Discipline: The Crisis of Moral Authority*, Cambridge, MA: Harvard University Press.

Blokhuis, J.C. and Randall Curren (2021), "The Judicialization of American Education," in Kathy Hytten (ed.), *Oxford Research Encyclopedia of Education*, New York: Oxford University Press. https://doi.org/10.1093/acrefore/9780190264093.013.1602.

Blokhuis, J.C., Jonathan Feldman, Michael Imber, and Tyll van Geel (2021), *Education Law*, 6th edn., New York: Routledge.

Blum, Lawrence and Zoe Burkholder (2021), *Integrations: The Struggle for Racial Equality and Civic Renewal in Public Education*, Chicago: University of Chicago Press.

Bolmeier, Edward C. (1951), "School Law, by Madeline Kinter Remmlein," *Elementary School Journal*, 52 (1): 53–5.

Brown, Anthony F., Marvin A. Zuker, Nicola Simmons, and Robert Keel (2019), *Education Law*, 5th edn., Toronto: Thomson Reuters.

Chambers, M.M. (1933), *The First Yearbook of School Law*, Oakland: University of California Press.

Dayton, John (2019), *Education Law: Principles, Policies, and Practice*, 2nd edn., Athens, GA: Wisdom Builders.

Delon, Floyd G. (2008), "Foreword," in Charles J. Russo (ed.), *Encyclopedia of Education Law*, Vol. 1, xxviii–xxx, Thousand Oaks, CA: Sage.

Driver, Justin (2018), *The Schoolhouse Gate: Public Education, the Supreme Court, and the Battle for the American Mind*, New York: Pantheon.

Education Law Association (2021), "The History of ELA," Educationlaw.org. Available online: https://educationlaw.org/about-ela/mission (accessed November 2, 2021).

Edwards, Newton and Lee O. Garber (1971), *The Courts and the Public Schools: The Legal Basis of School Organization and Administration*, Chicago: University of Chicago Press.

Friendly, Henry J. (1975), "Some Kind of Hearing," *University of Pennsylvania Law Review*, 123 (6): 1267–317.

Garber, Lee O. (1934), *Education as a Function of the State*, Minneapolis, MN: Educational Testing Bureau.

Garber, Lee O. (1957), *Law and the School Business Manager*, Danville, IL: Interstate Printers and Publishers.

Garber, Lee O. and Newton Edwards (1962a), *The Law Governing Teaching Personnel*, Danville, IL: Interstate Printers and Publishers.

Garber, Lee O. and Newton Edwards (1962b), *The Law Governing Pupils*, Danville, IL: Interstate Printers and Publishers.

Garber, Lee O. and Newton Edwards (1962c), *The Law Relating to the Creation, Alteration, and Dissolution of School Districts*, Danville, IL: Interstate Printers and Publishers.

Garber, Lee O. and Newton Edwards (1962d), *The Public School in Our Governmental Structure*, Danville, IL: Interstate Printers and Publishers.

Garber, Lee O. and Newton Edwards (1963a), *The Law Governing School Board Members and School Board Meetings*, Danville, IL: Interstate Printers and Publishers.

Garber, Lee O. and Newton Edwards (1963b), *Tort and Contractual Liability of School Districts and School Boards*, Danville, IL: Interstate Printers and Publishers.

Guggenheim, Martin (2005), *What's Wrong with Children's Rights?* Cambridge, MA: Harvard University Press.

Hirschl, Ran (2006), "The New Constitutionalism and the Judicialization of Pure Politics Worldwide," *Fordham Law Review*, 75 (2): 721–54.

Hirschl, Ran (2013), "The Judicialization of Politics," in Robert E. Goodin (ed.), *The Oxford Handbook of Political Science*. https://doi.org/10.1093/oxfordhb/9780199604456.013.0013.

Karanxha, Zorka (2009), "Education Law Association," in Charles J. Russo (ed.), *Encyclopedia of Law and Higher Education*, 147–50, New York: Sage.

Karanxha, Zorka (2010), "Education Law Association," *Educational Leadership and Policy Studies Faculty Publications*, 44. Available online: https://scholarcommons.usf.edu/els_facpub/44 (accessed July 31, 2021).

Liptak, Adam (2008), "U.S. Court Is Now Guiding Fewer Nations," *New York Times*, September 17. Available online: https://www.nytimes.com/2008/09/18/us/18legal.html (accessed October 19, 2021).

Marmor, Andrei (2005), "Should Like Cases Be Treated Alike?" *Legal Theory*, 11 (1): 27–38.

Mayers, R. Stewart (2015), *Social Media, Public Schools, and the Law*, Cleveland, OH: Education Law Association.
McCarthy, Martha M. (1984), "The National Organization on Legal Problems of Education: Serving the Profession," *Educational Considerations*, 11 (1): 37–8.
McCarthy, Martha M. (2021), "The Fate of Student Off-Campus Expression: *Mahanoy Area School District v. B.L.*," *Education Law Reporter*, 387: 439–47.
McCarthy, Martha M., Suzanne E. Eckes, and Janet R. Decker (2019), *Legal Rights of School Leaders, Teachers, and Students*, 8th edn., Boston: Pearson.
McGhehey, Marion A. (1961), *Research and Reporting Activities in Legal Problems of Education*, Washington, DC: US Department of Health, Education, and Welfare.
Peters, Shawn Francis (2003), *The Yoder Case: Religious Freedom, Education, and Parental Rights*, Lawrence: University Press of Kansas.
Pruitt, Sarah (2021), "*Brown v. Board of Education*: The First Step in the Desegregation of America's Schools," *History.com*, March 16. Available online: https://www.history.com/news/brown-v-board-of-education-the-first-step-in-the-desegregation-of-americas-schools (accessed October 19, 2021).
Punke, Harold H. (1936), *The Courts and Public School Property*, Chicago: University of Chicago Press.
Remmlein, Madaline Kinter (1950), *School Law*, New York: McGraw-Hill.
Remmlein, Madaline Kinter (1953), *The Law of Local Public School Administration*, New York: McGraw-Hill.
Remmlein, Madaline Kinter (1964), *Legal Provisions for Summer Schools*, Washington, DC: National Education Association.
Remmlein, Madaline Kinter and Martha L. Ware (1959), *An Evaluation of Existing Forms of School Laws, with Recommendations for Their Improvement*, Cincinnati, OH: W.H. Anderson.
Rossow, Lawrence F. and Jacqueline Anne Stefkovich (2014), *Search and Seizure in the Public Schools*, Cleveland, OH: Education Law Association.
Russell, Peter H. (1994). "Canadian Constraints on Judicialization from Without," *International Political Science Review*, 15 (2): 165–75.
Russo, Charles J., ed. (2008), *Encyclopedia of Education Law*, Vols. 1 and 2, Thousand Oaks, CA: Sage.
Russo, Charles J., ed. (2017a), *Handbook of Comparative Education Law: British Commonwealth Nations*, Vol. 1, Lanham, MD: Rowman & Littlefield.
Russo, Charles J., ed. (2017b), *Handbook of Comparative Education Law: Selected Asian Nations*, Vol. 2, Lanham, MD: Rowman & Littlefield.
Russo, Charles J., ed. (2018a), *Handbook of Comparative Education Law: Selected European Nations*, Vol. 3, Lanham, MD: Rowman & Littlefield.
Russo, Charles J. (2018b), *The Law of Public Education*, 10th edn., Goleta, CA: Foundation Press.
Russo, Charles J., ed. (2019), *Handbook of Comparative Education Law: Selected Nations from Africa and the Americas*, Vol. 4, Lanham, MD: Rowman & Littlefield.
Russo, Charles J., ed. (2021), *Yearbook of Education Law*, Cleveland, OH: Education Law Association.
Russo, Charles J. and Steve Permuth, eds. (2018), *Legal Issues of Faith-based and Other Nonpublic Schools*, Cleveland, OH: Education Law Association.
Shaver, Elizabeth A. and Janet R. Decker (2017), *A Guide to Special Education Law*, Cleveland, OH: Education Law Association.

Stephenson, Frank Robert (1929), *Handbook of Indiana School Law*, Fowler, IN: Benton Review Shop.

Strauss, David A. (2002), "Must Like Cases Be Treated Alike?" University of Chicago Public Law & Legal Theory Working Paper No. 24. Available online: https://chicagounbound.uchicago.edu/cgi/viewcontent.cgi?referer=&httpsredir=1&article=1197&context=public_law_and_legal_theory (accessed December 4, 2021).

Trusler, Harry Raymond (1927), *Essentials of School Law*, Milwaukee, WI: Bruce Publishing.

Walsh, Mark (2021), "U.S. Supreme Court Rules for Cheerleader Who Posted Vulgar Snapchat Message," *Education Week*, June 23. Available online: https://www.edweek.org/policy-politics/u-s-supreme-court-rules-for-student-on-regulation-of-off-campus-speech/2021/06 (accessed October 31, 2021).

Wang, Ke, Amy Rathbun, and Lauren Musu (2019), *School Choice in the United States: 2019*, NCES 2019–106, US Department of Education, Washington, DC: National Center for Education Statistics. Available online: https://nces.ed.gov/pubs2019/2019106.pdf (accessed December 4, 2021).

Weltzin, J. Frederick (1930), *The Legal Authority of the American Public School as Developed by a Study of Liabilities to Damages*, Grand Forks: University of North Dakota Press.

West, Martin R. and Joshua M. Dunn (2009), "The Supreme Court as School Board Revisited," in Joshua M. Dunn and Martin R. West (eds.), *From Schoolhouse to Courthouse: The Judiciary's Role in American Education*, 3–16, Washington, DC: Fordham Institute.

Wilkinson, J. Harvie, III (1975), "*Goss v. Lopez*: The Supreme Court as School Superintendent," *Supreme Court Review 1975*: 25–76.

Winston, Kenneth I. (1974), "On Treating Like Cases Alike," *California Law Review*, 62 (1): 1–39.

Wood, R. Craig, David C. Thompson, John Dayton, and Christine Kiracofe (2015), *Education Finance Law*, Cleveland, OH: Education Law Association.

Yudof, Mark G., David L. Kirp, Betsy Levin, and Rachel F. Moran (2002), *Educational Policy and the Law*, 4th edn., Belmont, CA: Wadsworth/Thomson Learning.

Zirkel, Perry A. (1997), "The 'explosion' in Educational Litigation: An Update," *Education Law Reporter*, 114: 341–51.

CHAPTER TWO

Purposes of Education

"The Very Foundation of Good Citizenship"

MARYAM AHRANJANI AND J.C. BLOKHUIS

According to liberal philosophers of education, a basic purpose of public education is to prepare children for democratic citizenship. Individual and collective flourishing is both the highest aim of the state and thus the highest aim of public schools and education systems (Brighouse 2005; see also Callan 1997; Gutmann 1999; Curren 2000, 2006). Public education should also promote the prospective autonomy of children, exposing them to diverse ways of living and conceptions of the good so that they can make good choices, governing themselves and their affairs in accordance with reason and reasonable laws. And it should facilitate equality of opportunity and social mobility by preparing children to participate in the economy in accordance with their particular abilities and preferences, which may differ from those of their parents or caregivers. An education that fulfills these purposes—autonomy facilitation, economic participation, and democratic engagement—enhances the likelihood that every child will lead a flourishing life (Brighouse 2005).

In the United States, public education is supposed to secure the "unalienable" rights of the American people, framed in the Declaration of Independence as "life, liberty and the pursuit of happiness." A republican government is legitimate insofar as it safeguards these rights. In this two-part chapter, we examine the purposes of education in the United States as they are reflected in the constitutional framework for its public school systems. In the first part, we review significant Supreme Court decisions in which the Court found no express or implied rights to education in the *federal* Constitution (while recognizing and affirming the aims and purposes of education in the United States). We note how the Court's characterization of the aims and purposes of education in increasingly broad terms (favoring students) from 1940 to 1970 gave way to increasingly narrow characterizations (favoring school officials) from 1975 to the present. In the second part, we consider the implications of the fact that all fifty *state* constitutions in the United States provide a framework for the provision of public schools and corresponding rights for all children (while in some cases describing the aims and purposes of public education in broad and sometimes lofty terms).

THE EVOLUTION OF "COMMON" OR PUBLIC SCHOOLS

The growth of the American Republic over the course of its first century relied on a delicate balance between federal oversight and local control. Jurisdictional disputes are familiar to citizens of federal republics such as Germany and Switzerland, and of course within the European Union. In the nascent United States, Congress wanted each territory aspiring to statehood to create its own constitution, but it also wanted the people in each state admitted to the Union to identify, in the words of the Pledge of Allegiance in 1892, as members of "one nation, indivisible, with liberty and justice for all." Created in the nineteenth century through land grants from Congress, common school systems were intended to further the federal interest in creating citizens with a shared commitment to republican ideals and institutions (Tyack, James, and Benavot 1987: 14–15). Congress wrote detailed requirements about public schools into its enabling acts for new states and donated 77,630,000 acres for common schools, with numerous strings attached (22). Expansion westward brought more elaborate systems of organizing public education (21), particularly after the Civil War (1861–5). Congress established the federal Department of Education (ED) in 1867 (22). Then as now, the ED creates regulations and Congress offers subsidies, while public school systems remain decentralized, funded, and managed at the state and local level (22).

In reflecting on how the systems developed, what was included in the curriculum, and how schools were managed, scholars have observed some common purposes. Amy Gutmann (1999: 287) points out that civic education was necessary to reproduce society and sustain a liberal democratic political order. Public schools promoted development of moral—as defined by the majority—character (Tyack, James, and Benavot 1987: 169; Gutmann 1999: 41). John Dewey (1966: 54) famously observed that education is training for the responsibilities and privileges of adult life, which in his view, includes democratic participation. Bruce Fuller and Arun Rasiah (2005: 81) note that common schooling helps immigrants to adapt and assimilate. By compelling all parents to send their children to school, each American state sought to ensure that children within its territorial jurisdiction had access to instruction and opportunities for social and economic mobility and for civic participation beyond what their parents alone might be willing or able to provide. Parents were incidentally freer to manage the competing demands of domestic life and paid employment (Curren and Blokhuis 2011: 1). Two important realities shaped and continue to shape the evolution of public education: population growth and increasing diversity in terms of national origin, race, ethnicity, religion, sexual orientation, gender, and other aspects of identity.

"THE VERY FOUNDATION OF GOOD CITIZENSHIP"

There is no explicit language in the US Constitution addressing education. Further, the US Supreme Court—the highest court in the land and thus the final arbiter of the federal Constitution—has declined to find an implied right to education. This means there are no *federal* Constitutional rights to education for any of the nearly 57 million school-age children in the United States. However, the Supreme Court *has* addressed education in the course of affirming of other constitutional rights.

Since 1899, the Supreme Court has heard no fewer than ninety-six cases—an average of about one case per year—on civil rights claims and public education. The issues considered by the Court include, inter alia, student free speech and free exercise rights; freedom from unreasonable searches and seizures; rights to equal treatment regardless of race, gender, or national origin; and due process rights in the context of school discipline. While the Supreme Court has maintained that there is no federal Constitutional right to education, it has repeatedly acknowledged aims and purposes of public education that are consistent with those identified by liberal philosophers of education as conducive to leading a flourishing life, including the facilitation of the skills associated with critical thinking or autonomy, economic participation, and democratic engagement. In six watershed cases involving federal Constitutional rights in the context of public schools, the Supreme Court expounded at length on the purposes of education in the United States: *West Virginia v. Barnette* (1943), *Brown v. Board of Education* (1954), *Tinker v. Des Moines* (1969), *Wisconsin v. Yoder* (1972), *San Antonio v. Rodriguez* (1973), and *Plyler v. Doe* (1982). We will consider each of these cases in turn.

West Virginia v. Barnette, 319 U.S. 624 (1943)

Three years before its watershed opinion in *West Virginia v. Barnette*, the Supreme Court held that a school could expel a student for refusing to recite the Pledge of Allegiance without violating the First Amendment in *Minersville School District v. Gobitis*, 310 U.S. 586 (1940). Under the First Amendment of the US Constitution, "Congress shall make no law respecting an establishment of religion, or prohibiting the free exercise thereof." The first part is the Establishment Clause, which prohibits the federal and state governments from using public funds to promote or sponsor any specific faith or religion, from advancing or inhibiting religion in general, or privileging one faith over another. The second part is the Free Exercise Clause, which prohibits governments from interfering with individual religious beliefs.

In the wake of the *Gobitis* decision, the West Virginia legislature amended its education statutes to require that all schools in the state, including private and parochial schools, foster a "spirit of Americanism" by requiring teachers and students to salute the flag. Any student who refused would be expelled for insubordination. Worse, schools were to treat expelled children as truants, making their parents liable for fines of up to $50. This is precisely what happened to Marie and Gathie Barnette, elementary school students who were expelled for refusing to salute the flag or recite the Pledge of Allegiance in accordance with their parents' wishes and subsequently expelled.

In *West Virginia v. Barnette*, the Supreme Court overruled *Minersville*, finding the state violated free speech rights in compelling students to salute the flag. The application of the Bill of Rights—the first ten amendments to the US Constitution—to *state* governments had begun in *Gitlow v. New York*, 268 U.S. 652 (1925), a landmark case in which the Supreme Court held that the Fourteenth Amendment to the United States Constitution required that state governments respect the freedom of speech and freedom of the press provisions of the First Amendment. Writing for the majority in the *Barnette* case (in a decision issued on Flag Day, a holiday commemorating the adoption of the US flag on June 14, 1777), Justice Jackson aligned the purposes of public education with respect to the principles enshrined in the Bill of Rights:

> The Fourteenth Amendment, as now applied to the States, protects the citizen against the State itself and all of its creatures – Boards of Education not excepted. These have, of course, important, delicate, and highly discretionary functions, but none that they may not perform within the limits of the Bill of Rights. That they are educating the young for citizenship is reason for scrupulous protection of Constitutional freedoms of the individual, if we are not to strangle the free mind at its source and teach youth to discount important principles of our government as mere platitudes . . . .
>
> If there is any fixed star in our constitutional constellation, it is that no official, high or petty, can prescribe what shall be orthodox in politics, nationalism, religion, or other matters of opinion or force citizens to confess

> by word or act their faith therein. If there are any circumstances which permit an exception, they do not now occur to us. We think the action of the local authorities in compelling the flag salute and pledge transcends constitutional limitations on their power and invades the sphere of intellect and spirit which it is the purpose of the First Amendment to our Constitution to reserve from all official control.

Brown v. Board of Education, 347 U.S. 483 (1954)

Brown is arguably the most famous decision in American education law and constitutional jurisprudence. It was a landmark decision in which the Supreme Court overruled the "separate but equal" doctrine it had established in *Plessy v. Ferguson*, 163 U.S. 537 (1896). Finding separate schools for African American children to be "inherently unequal" to schools for white children, the Court concluded that the African American plaintiffs in the consolidated case had been "deprived of the equal protection of the laws guaranteed by the Fourteenth Amendment." In reaching its momentous (and unanimous) decision in *Brown*, the Court described in considerable detail the purposes of education in the United States:

> Today, education is perhaps the most important function of state and local governments. Compulsory school attendance laws and the great expenditures for education both demonstrate our recognition of the importance of education to our democratic society. It is required in the performance of our most basic public responsibilities, even service in the armed forces. It is the very foundation of good citizenship. Today it is a principal instrument in awakening the child to cultural values, in preparing him [*sic*] for later professional training, and in helping him [*sic*] to adjust normally to his [*sic*] environment. In these days, it is doubtful that any child may reasonably be expected to succeed in life if he [*sic*] is denied the opportunity of an education. Such an opportunity, where the state has undertaken to provide it, is a right which must be made available to all on equal terms.

As Justin Driver (2018: 249) explains, "Americans have long imbued education with special meaning, and [it was] … this exaltation of the schooling environment that made *Brown* the Supreme Court's most indispensable decision of the twentieth century." In a single paragraph, the Court affirmed the purposes of education in terms of facilitating autonomy, economic participation, active citizenship in a democratic society, and individual flourishing as the highest function of state governments. While the decision did not, in and of itself, desegregate American public schools, it galvanized the civil rights leaders who led the civil rights movement of the 1950s and 1960s. Only a year after the *Brown* decision, activist Rosa Parks was arrested for refusing to give up her seat to a white person on a segregated bus in Montgomery, Alabama. Her actions triggered the first of countless boycotts, sit-ins, and demonstrations across the American South. These prompted the passage of federal legislation such as the Civil Rights Act of 1964, the Voting Rights Act of 1965, and the Fair Housing Act of 1968.

Tinker v. Des Moines Independent School District, 393 U.S. 503 (1969)

Until the civil rights movement was well under way in the United States, children were regarded as having custodial interests, not liberty interests. They were subject to the care and control of their parents, who had legal authority at common law to make decisions on their behalf. Students in public and private schools were expected to obey their teachers in much the same way they were expected to obey their parents, because teachers in both private and public schools stood *in loco parentis* (Blokhuis et al. 2021: 118). Apart from the Supreme Court ruling in *West Virginia v. Barnette* prohibiting school officials from requiring that students salute the flag, there were no constitutional limits on the authority of public school officials to discipline students.

In the 1960s, the situation changed dramatically as the Supreme Court issued three decisions extending constitutional protection to minors in custodial contexts. In *Kent v. United States*, 383 U.S. 541 (1966), the Court concluded that a minor charged with an offense received "neither the protections accorded to adults nor the solicitous care and regenerative treatment postulated for children" under the *parens patriae* doctrine, which requires the "state as parent" to regulate the custodial authority of adults in the interests of children. The following year, the Court applied the due process protections of the Fourteenth Amendment to juvenile court proceedings in *In re Gault*, 387 U.S. 1 (1967). The third decision occurred two years later, in the midst of widespread protests over the Vietnam War, the Court ascribed limited First Amendment rights to students in public schools (Blokhuis et al. 2021: 118).

In *Tinker v. Des Moines*, a group of students were suspended for wearing black armbands to protest American military involvement in Vietnam. Supported by the American Civil Liberties Union, the students and their parents argued that the school policy under which they had been disciplined violated their constitutional rights. Ultimately, the Supreme Court agreed, finding that students do not "shed their constitutional rights to freedom of speech or expression at the schoolhouse gate." Here, too, the Supreme Court expounded on the purposes of education in American jurisprudence:

> In our system, state-operated schools may not be enclaves of totalitarianism. School officials do not possess absolute authority over their students. Students

> in school as well as out of school are "persons" under our Constitution. They are possessed of fundamental rights which the State must respect, just as they themselves must respect their obligations to the State. In our system, students may not be regarded as closed-circuit recipients of only that which the State chooses to communicate. They may not be confined to the expression of those sentiments that are officially approved. In the absence of a specific showing of constitutionally valid reasons to regulate their speech, students are entitled to freedom of expression of their views.

The lofty language in *Tinker* built on Justice Brennan's famous words in *Keyishian v. Board of Regents*, 385 U.S. 589 (1967):

> The vigilant protection of constitutional freedoms is nowhere more vital than in the community of American schools … The classroom is peculiarly the "marketplace of ideas." The Nation's future depends upon leaders trained through wide exposure to that robust exchange of ideas which discovers truth out of a multitude of tongues, [rather] than through any kind of authoritative selection.
>
> The principle of these cases is not confined to the supervised and ordained discussion which takes place in the classroom. The principal use to which the schools are dedicated is to accommodate students during prescribed hours for the purpose of certain types of activities. Among those activities is personal intercommunication among the students. This is not only an inevitable part of the process of attending school; it is also an important part of the educational process.

Wisconsin v. Yoder, 406 U.S. 205 (1972)

Compulsory schooling laws in the United States have often engendered conflict between the educational aims of state governments and the preferences of individual parents. In *Wisconsin v. Yoder*, a group of Old Order Amish parents who had been charged with truancy and fined $5 for educating their children at home claimed that the compulsory schooling laws of Wisconsin violated their free exercise rights under the First Amendment and their due process rights under the Fourteenth Amendment (Blokhuis et al. 2021: 22). Prioritizing the interests of the parents over those of their children and the State of Wisconsin, the Supreme Court granted an unprecedented constitutional exemption from compulsory schooling laws to Amish parents. Nonetheless, the Court strongly affirmed both the legitimacy of compulsory schooling laws and the purposes of public education in American jurisprudence. For a majority on the Court, Chief Justice Burger wrote:

> Formal high school education beyond the eighth grade is contrary to Amish beliefs not only because it places Amish children in an environment hostile to Amish beliefs, with increasing emphasis on competition in class work and sports and with pressure to conform to the styles, manners, and ways of the peer group, but also because it takes them away from their community, physically and emotionally, during the crucial and formative adolescent period of life. During this period, the children must acquire Amish attitudes favoring manual work and self-reliance and the specific skills needed to perform the adult role of an Amish farmer or housewife. They must learn to enjoy physical labor. Once a child has learned basic reading, writing, and elementary mathematics, these traits, skills, and attitudes admittedly fall within the category of those best learned through example and "doing," rather than in a classroom. And, at this time in life, the Amish child must also grow in his faith and his relationship to the Amish community if he is to be prepared to accept the heavy obligations imposed by adult baptism…
>
> There is no doubt as to the power of a State, having a high responsibility for education of its citizens, to impose reasonable regulations for the control and duration of basic education. … Providing public schools ranks at the very apex of the function of a State…
>
> The essence of all that has been said and written on the subject is that only those interests of the highest order and those not otherwise served can overbalance legitimate claims to the free exercise of religion. We can accept it as settled, therefore, that, however strong the state's interest in universal compulsory education, it is by no means absolute to the exclusion or subordination of all other interests…
>
> The State advances two primary arguments in support of its system of compulsory education. It notes, as Thomas Jefferson pointed out early in our history, that some degree of education is necessary to prepare citizens to participate effectively and intelligently in our open political system if we are to preserve freedom and independence. Further, education prepares individuals to be self-reliant and self-sufficient participants in society. We accept these propositions.

In a concurring opinion, Justice White memorably elaborated on the purposes of education, broadly construed, in American jurisprudence, writing:

> In the present case, the State is not concerned with the maintenance of an educational system as an end in itself, it is rather attempting to nurture and develop the human potential of its children, whether Amish or non-Amish: to expand their knowledge, broaden their sensibilities, kindle their imagination, foster a spirit of free inquiry, and increase their human understanding and tolerance. It is possible that most Amish children will wish to continue living the rural life of their parents, in which case their

> training at home will adequately equip them for their future role. Others, however, may wish to become nuclear physicists, ballet dancers, computer programmers, or historians, and for these occupations, formal training will be necessary. There is evidence in the record that many children desert the Amish faith when they come of age. A State has a legitimate interest not only in seeking to develop the latent talents of its children but also in seeking to prepare them for the life style that they may later choose, or at least to provide them with an option other than the life they have led in the past.

In the wake of the *Yoder* decision, Joel Feinberg (2007: 113) decried the Court's violation of what he termed, "the child's right to an open future," noting that children have a right to have their future options kept open until they are fully formed, self-determining adults capable of making decisions for themselves. Effectively, the Supreme Court ascribed both an Amish identity and an Amish destiny to children born to Amish parents in Wisconsin, narrowing their future options to whatever their parents might prefer. "American courts have long held that the state has a 'sovereign power of guardianship' over minors and other legally incompetent persons which confers upon it the right, or perhaps even the duty, to look after the interests of those who are incapable of protecting themselves," he noted, affirming the State of Wisconsin's position that it had a duty, as *parens patriae*, to apply its compulsory schooling laws to all parents in the interests of *all* children in its jurisdiction (Feinberg 2007: 114).

In his view, had the Court refused to grant the exemption sought by the Amish parents in the case this would put them in the same position as all other parents in the state, they would be in the same kind of position vis-a-vis their children as all other parents who must "take their chances with outside influences" when sending their children to school (115). By the same token, had the Court refused to grant the exemption sought by the Amish parents in the case, Amish children would be put on the same position as all other children in the state as "nuclear physicists, ballet dancers, computer programmers, or historians," or whatever life course they might chose for themselves in the future. Justice Douglas, in dissent, most explicitly affirmed that the educational rights of parents were nonexclusive in this important sense: "I agree with the Court that the religious scruples of the Amish are opposed to the education of their children beyond the grade schools," he wrote, "yet I disagree with the Court's conclusion that the matter is within the dispensation of parents alone."

San Antonio Independent School District v. Rodriguez, 411 U.S. 1 (1973)

In *Brown*, the Court found that segregated schools and the "separate but equal" doctrine violated the Equal Protection Clause of the Fourteenth Amendment. Two decades later, in *San Antonio v. Rodriguez*, the Supreme Court considered whether state systems of school finance resulting in interdistrict inequalities were unconstitutional. Property-poor districts could not match the money raised by property-rich districts, and state and federal subsidies could not compensate for differences in local property bases. Realizing that their chances of winning would be greatly enhanced if the Court employed strict scrutiny, the appellants argued that wealth-based discrimination, like race-based discrimination in *Brown*, should trigger the use of the strict scrutiny test (Blokhuis et al. 2021: 373). The Court found there was no right to education under the Constitution and refused to apply strict scrutiny, the highest standard of judicial review, which is normally applied cases involving alleged deprivations of fundamental rights. Instead, it applied the default standard of rational basis scrutiny and found that the property tax-based school financing system had a rational basis consistent with the Fourteenth Amendment. In reaching this conclusion, the Court did not dispute the plaintiffs' claims that "the right to speak is meaningless unless the speaker is capable of articulating his thoughts intelligently and persuasively" and that the right to vote "cannot be divorced from the educational foundation of the voter." Instead, the Court deferred to state legislatures to find institutional mechanisms for the achievement of educational aims associated with autonomy and civic participation.

Plyler v. Doe, 457 U.S. 202 (1982)

It is important to note that the individual rights and freedoms guaranteed under the US Constitution are not limited to US citizens. In 1975, Texas began withholding funds from local school districts in which the children of undocumented migrants were enrolled. In response, one school district began charging tuition to recover lost revenue. In *Plyler v. Doe*, the Supreme Court struck down the Texas law on the ground that denial of public funding for the children of undocumented migrants violated the Equal Protection Clause (Blokhuis et al. 2021: 378). For a majority on the Court, Justice Brennan rejected the claim that undocumented aliens, because of their immigration status, lacked equal protection rights. "We reject this argument," he wrote. "Aliens, even aliens whose presence in this country is unlawful, have long been recognized as 'persons' guaranteed due process of law by the Fifth and Fourteenth Amendments."

Writing for the majority, Justice Brennan explained that the total denial of education to this group of children violated the Equal Protection Clause. Denying the children of undocumented migrants the benefits of public education furthered no substantial state interest, and could very well lead to "the creation and perpetuation of a subclass of illiterates within our boundaries, surely adding to the problems and costs of unemployment, welfare, and crime." Justice Brennan then described at length the aims and purposes of education in American jurisprudence, from *Rodriguez* to *Brown* and beyond:

Public education is not a "right" granted to individuals by the Constitution [citing *San Antonio v. Rodriguez*]. But neither is it merely some governmental "benefit" indistinguishable from other forms of social welfare legislation. Both the importance of education in maintaining our basic institutions, and the lasting impact of its deprivation on the life of the child, mark the distinction. The "American people have always regarded education and [the] acquisition of knowledge as matters of supreme importance" [citing *Meyer v. Nebraska*, 262 U.S. 390 (1923)]. We have recognized "the public schools as a most vital civic institution for the preservation of a democratic system of government," [citing *Abington School District v. Schempp*, 374 U.S. 203 (1963)] and as the primary vehicle for transmitting "the values on which our society rests" [citing *Ambach v. Norwick*, 441 U.S. 68 (1979)].

"[A]s ... pointed out early in our history, ... some degree of education is necessary to prepare citizens to participate effectively and intelligently in our open political system if we are to preserve freedom and independence" [citing *Wisconsin v. Yoder*]. And these historic "perceptions of the public schools as inculcating fundamental values necessary to the maintenance of a democratic political system have been confirmed by the observations of social scientists" [citing *Ambach v. Norwick*]. In addition, education provides the basic tools by which individuals might lead economically productive lives to the benefit of us all. In sum, education has a fundamental role in maintaining the fabric of our society. We cannot ignore the significant social costs borne by our Nation when select groups are denied the means to absorb the values and skills upon which our social order rests.

In addition to the pivotal role of education in sustaining our political and cultural heritage, denial of education to some isolated group of children poses an affront to one of the goals of the Equal Protection Clause: the abolition of governmental barriers presenting unreasonable obstacles to advancement on the basis of individual merit. Paradoxically, by depriving the children of any disfavored group of an education, we foreclose the means by which that group might raise the level of esteem in which it is held by the majority. But more directly, "education prepares individuals to be self-reliant and self-sufficient participants in society" [citing *Wisconsin v. Yoder*].

Illiteracy is an enduring disability. The inability to read and write will handicap the individual deprived of a basic education each and every day of his life. The inestimable toll of that deprivation on the social, economic, intellectual, and psychological well-being of the individual, and the obstacle it poses to individual achievement, make it most difficult to reconcile the cost or the principle of a status-based denial of basic education with the framework of equality embodied in the Equal Protection Clause. What we said 28 years ago in *Brown v. Board of Education*, still holds true.

Justin Driver observes that the *Plyler* decision "single-handedly enabled innumerable children to use education to expand both their minds and their horizons" (2018: 354). Clearly, population growth and diversity have implications for the purposes of public education in American jurisprudence. Five justices agreed that denial of education to students who are undocumented would not serve anyone's interests.

"SOME MODICUM OF DISCIPLINE AND ORDER"

In addition to the Court's recognition of the civic purposes of education for students in the American constitutional context, it has also recognized the need for order and control for school officials. As its membership has changed over the years, the Court has at times construed citizenship broadly (in favor of students) and at times narrowly (in favor of school officials).

In terms of both the constitutional rights of students and the purposes of education in American jurisprudence, the Court has taken an increasingly narrow view since the "War on Drugs" initiated by President Nixon in 1971 moved into public schools. By 1989, school districts in California and New York had implemented policies mandating automatic expulsion for any student found in possession of drugs on school property. "Zero tolerance" policies concerning the possession and use of drugs, including tobacco and alcohol, were quickly adopted by school districts nationwide. In the wake of the federal Gun-Free Schools Act of 1994, students found in possession of firearms and other weapons on school property were also subject to mandatory expulsion (Black 2016). By the year 2000, 94 percent of all schools in the United States had implemented zero tolerance policies for weapons and firearms, 87 percent for alcohol, and 79 percent for tobacco. By 2014, 46 percent of high schools, 42 percent of middle schools, and 18 percent of elementary schools nationwide reported having at least one law enforcement officer on site, with higher rates in urban schools (Karteron 2018: 872; Blokhuis et al. 2021: 262).

In seven significant cases involving constitutional rights claims by and on behalf of students in public schools after 1975, the Supreme Court described the purposes of education in the United States in increasingly narrow terms, with an initial focus on obedience and order and a later focus on preventing illegal drug use: *Goss v. Lopez* (1975), *New Jersey v. T.L.O.* (1985), *Bethel v. Fraser* (1986), *Hazelwood v. Kuhlmeier* (1988), *Vernonia School District 47J v. Acton* (1995), *Board of Education v. Earls* (2002), and *Morse v. Frederick* (2007). We will consider each of these cases in turn.

Goss v. Lopez, 419 U.S. 565 (1975)

The Due Process Clause of the Fourteenth Amendment prohibits government agents and officials from depriving "any person of life, liberty, or property without due process of law." As mentioned above, in the Civil Rights era, the Supreme Court issued a trilogy of decisions extending limited constitutional rights to minors in custodial contexts. In *Kent v. United States*, 383 U.S. 541 (1966), the Court recognized that the exercise of unchecked discretionary authority in juvenile justice proceedings could have serious disadvantages, observing that young offenders were "[getting] neither the [constitutional] protections accorded to adults nor the solicitous care and regenerative treatment postulated for children." In *In re Gault*, 387 U.S. 1 (1967), the Court held that the Due Process Clause of the Fourteenth Amendment applies to juvenile court proceedings, finding that "departures from established principles of due process [in the juvenile courts] have frequently resulted not in enlightened procedure, but in arbitrariness." And in *Tinker v. Des Moines*, discussed earlier in this chapter, the Court ascribed limited First Amendment rights to students in public schools to engage in nondisruptive speech and expressive conduct.

In the American criminal justice system, the adjudication of guilt is guided by principles of natural justice including a presumption of innocence and a burden of proof on the state to establish guilt beyond a reasonable doubt. Whatever the accusation, the defendant has the right to a fair and impartial trial. These same principles apply to disciplinary actions in public schools. Both the Fifth Amendment and the Fourteenth Amendment include clauses stating that no person shall "be deprived of life, liberty, or property, without due process of law." Although the concept of due process has never been fully defined, it embodies a principle of even-handedness. And in its procedural sense, it includes a right to be heard. At the minimum, it requires that individuals not be punished or deprived of their rights by the state without first being given a chance to tell their side of the story. Another important due process principle is proportionality. The greater the contemplated deprivation of life, liberty, or property, the more extensive the procedures must be to guard against injustice (Blokhuis et al. 2021: 230).

Until 1975, there was confusion and disagreement in the federal courts over exactly how much process public school officials were required to provide when investigating student misconduct (Blokhuis et al. 2021: 237). In *Goss v. Lopez*, nine students from marginalized communities were accused of destroying school property and disrupting the learning environment. They were suspended for ten days without a hearing, in accordance with an Ohio law. In finding this law unconstitutional, the Supreme Court recognized that students in public schools could not be deprived of their property interest in receiving a public education without basic due process protections including notice and an opportunity to be heard. The *Goss* decision remains the due process touchstone whenever suspension or expulsion is contemplated in public schools. For a slim majority of the Court, Justice White aligned disciplinary processes consistent with due process as an important purpose of education in the United States:

> Our schools are vast and complex. Some modicum of discipline and order is essential if the educational function is to be performed. Events calling for discipline are frequent occurrences, and sometimes require immediate, effective action. Suspension is considered not only to be a necessary tool to maintain order, but a valuable educational device. The prospect of imposing elaborate hearing requirements in every suspension case is viewed with great concern, and many school authorities may well prefer the untrammeled power to act unilaterally, unhampered by rules about notice and hearing. But it would be a strange disciplinary system in an educational institution if no communication was sought by the disciplinarian with the student in an effort to inform him of his dereliction and to let him tell his side of the story in order to make sure that an injustice is not done.

Goss resolved the major questions concerning the application of the Fourteenth Amendment in public schools, accommodating both the right to fair treatment for students and the need to act quickly and without undue expenditure of resources for school officials. Because all states had made public school attendance a statutory right, students had a corresponding property interest in receiving an education, and any nontrivial deprivation of this interest would require due process. For short-term suspensions, defined by the court as ten days or less, due process requires oral or written notice of the charges, followed by an opportunity to be heard and to refute the charges (Blokhuis et al. 2021: 241).

In a dissenting opinion (joined by three other members of the Court), Justice Powell adopted respect for law and order as a primary purpose of education in the United States:

> The State's generalized interest in maintaining an orderly school system is not incompatible with the individual interest of the student. Education in any meaningful sense includes the inculcation of an understanding in each pupil of the necessity of rules and obedience thereto. This understanding is no less important than learning to read and write. One who does not comprehend the meaning and necessity of discipline is handicapped not merely in his education but throughout his subsequent life. In an age when the home and church play a diminishing role in shaping the character and value judgments of the young, a heavier responsibility falls upon the schools. When an immature student merits censure for his conduct, he is rendered a disservice if appropriate sanctions are not applied or if procedures for their application are so formalized as to invite a challenge to the teacher's authority – an invitation which rebellious or even merely spirited teenagers are likely to accept.

> The lesson of discipline is not merely a matter of the student's self-interest in the shaping of his [*sic*] own character and personality; it provides an early understanding of the relevance to the social compact of respect for the rights of others. The classroom is the laboratory in which this lesson of life is best learned. Mr. Justice Black [dissenting in *Tinker*] summed it up: "School discipline, like parental discipline, is an integral and important part of training our children to be good citizens – to be better citizens."

New Jersey v. T.L.O., 469 U.S. 325 (1985)

Ten years after *Goss*, the Supreme Court was called upon to resolve conflicting lower court decisions on the nature and scope of Fourth Amendment protections in public school contexts. When school officials believe a student has committed a criminal act or violated a school rule, they have both a common law duty of care and a statutory duty to investigate. The investigation of student misconduct in American public schools today often involves surveillance, searches of students' persons and effects, including bags, vehicles, and electronic devices, and questioning by school officials and police (Ahranjani 2017: 1098; Blokhuis et al. 2021: 172).

New Jersey v. T.L.O. involved a high school student whose purse was searched by an assistant vice-principal after a teacher reported finding her and another student smoking in a restroom. The search revealed marijuana and evidence that the student had been dealing marijuana, leading to charges in juvenile court. The Supreme Court determined that the Fourth Amendment applied to searches by public school officials. However, unlike police officers, school officials do not need to have probable cause or obtain a warrant before searching a student. Instead, they must have a "reasonable suspicion" that a particular student has violated the law or school rules. Writing for the majority, Justice White rejected the claim that public school officials stand *in loco parentis* to students:

> Such reasoning is in tension with contemporary reality and the teachings of this Court. We have held school officials subject to the commands of the First Amendment, see *Tinker v. Des Moines Independent Community School District*, 393 U. S. 503 (1969), and the Due Process Clause of the Fourteenth Amendment, see *Goss v. Lopez*, 419 U. S. 565 (1975). If school authorities are state actors for purposes of the constitutional guarantees of freedom of expression and due process, it is difficult to understand why they should be deemed to be exercising parental rather than public authority when conducting searches of their students ... Today's public school officials do not merely exercise authority voluntarily conferred on them by individual parents; rather, they act in furtherance of publicly mandated educational

> and disciplinary policies. In carrying out searches and other disciplinary functions pursuant to such policies, school officials act as representatives of the State, not merely as surrogates for the parents, and they cannot claim the parents' immunity from the strictures of the Fourth Amendment.

In a concurring opinion, Justice Powell again emphasized the maintenance of order and respect for rules as educational aims:

> The special relationship between teacher and student also distinguishes the setting within which schoolchildren operate ... The attitude of the typical teacher is one of personal responsibility for the student's welfare as well as for his [*sic*] education.
>
> The primary duty of school officials and teachers, as the Court states, is the education and training of young people. A State has a compelling interest in assuring that the schools meet this responsibility. Without first establishing discipline and maintaining order, teachers cannot begin to educate their students. And apart from education, the school has the obligation to protect pupils from mistreatment by other children, and also to protect teachers themselves from violence by the few students whose conduct in recent years has prompted national concern. For me, it would be unreasonable and at odds with history to argue that the full panoply of constitutional rules applies with the same force and effect in the schoolhouse as it does in the enforcement of criminal laws.

Bethel School District v. Fraser, 478 U.S. 675 (1986)

Bethel School District v. Fraser involved a high school senior suspended for delivering a nomination speech filled with sexual innuendo and lewd gestures, in violation of a school policy against disruptive behavior and despite warnings from his teachers. "I know a man who is rock hard," Matt Fraser declared, adding, "he's firm in his pants, he's firm in his shirt, his character is firm – but most of all, his belief in you the students of Bethel, is firm. Jeff Kuhlman is a man who takes his point and pounds it in."

According to Driver (2018: 94), the Supreme Court in *Fraser* construed citizenship thinly, focusing on "decorum, etiquette and politesse" and held that school officials could suspend Fraser without violating his free speech rights under the First Amendment. Writing for the Court, Chief Justice Burger invoked historical conceptions of the purposes of education in the United States, citing work by Charles A. Beard and Mary R. Beard (1968):

> The role and purpose of the American public school system were well described by two historians, who stated: "[P]ublic education must prepare

pupils for citizenship in the Republic. ... It must inculcate the habits and manners of civility as values in themselves conducive to happiness and as indispensable to the practice of self-government in the community and the nation."

In *Ambach v. Norwick*, 441 U.S. 68, 441 U.S. 76-77 (1979), we echoed the essence of this statement of the objectives of public education as the "inculcat[ion of] fundamental values necessary to the maintenance of a democratic political system." These fundamental values of "habits and manners of civility" essential to a democratic society must, of course, include tolerance of divergent political and religious views, even when the views expressed may be unpopular. But these "fundamental values" must also take into account consideration of the sensibilities of others, and, in the case of a school, the sensibilities of fellow students. The undoubted freedom to advocate unpopular and controversial views in schools and classrooms must be balanced against the society's countervailing interest in teaching students the boundaries of socially appropriate behavior. Even the most heated political discourse in a democratic society requires consideration for the personal sensibilities of the other participants and audiences.

Hazelwood School District v. Kuhlmeier, 484 U.S. 260 (1988)

In *Hazelwood v. Kuhlmeier*, a school principal censored stories about teenage pregnancy and divorce from the student-run school newspaper. The students alleged that in exercising prior restraint, the principal had violated their First Amendment rights. In a decision that remains a benchmark for school-sponsored or curricular speech, the Supreme Court held that public school officials "do not offend the First Amendment by exercising editorial control over the style and content of student speech in school-sponsored expressive activities so long as their actions are reasonably related to legitimate pedagogical concerns." Writing for a majority on the Court, Justice White invoked both *Bethel v. Fraser* and *Brown v. Board of Education* in discussing the purposes of education in the United States:

> A school must also retain the authority to refuse to sponsor student speech that might reasonably be perceived to advocate drug or alcohol use, irresponsible sex, or conduct otherwise inconsistent with "the shared values of a civilized social order," or to associate the school with any position other than neutrality on matters of political controversy. Otherwise, the schools would be unduly constrained from fulfilling their role as "a principal instrument in awakening the child to cultural values, in preparing him for later professional training, and in helping him [*sic*] to adjust normally to his [*sic*] environment."

Dissenting, Justice Brennan noted that the purposes of education in the United States included an appreciation of civil rights, including the First Amendment guarantee of freedom of the press:

> When the young men and women of Hazelwood East High School registered for Journalism II, they expected a civics lesson. *Spectrum*, the newspaper they were to publish, "was not just a class exercise in which students learned to prepare papers and hone writing skills, it was a … forum established to give students an opportunity to express their views while gaining an appreciation of their rights and responsibilities under the First Amendment to the United States Constitution … ."
>
> "[A]t the beginning of each school year," the student journalists published a Statement of Policy—tacitly approved each year by school authorities—announcing their expectation that "*Spectrum*, as a student-press publication, accepts all rights implied by the First Amendment. … Only speech that 'materially and substantially interferes with the requirements of appropriate discipline' can be found unacceptable and therefore prohibited."…
>
> In my view the principal broke more than just a promise. He violated the First Amendment's prohibitions against censorship of any student expression that neither disrupts classwork nor invades the rights of others, and against any censorship that is not narrowly tailored to serve its purpose.
>
> Public education serves vital national interests in preparing the Nation's youth for life in our increasingly complex society and for the duties of citizenship in our democratic Republic. The public school conveys to our young the information and tools required not merely to survive in, but to contribute to, civilized society. It also inculcates in tomorrow's leaders the "fundamental values necessary to the maintenance of a democratic political system." All the while, the public educator nurtures students' social and moral development by transmitting to them an official dogma of "community values."

Vernonia School District 47J v. Acton, 515 U.S. 646 (1995)

Students in public schools are routinely told by teachers and school officials to be quiet, to turn off their phones, and to refrain from criticizing authorities, praying, proselytizing, and using vulgar and offensive words and gestures. Government officials could not require such things of adults in other contexts, much less punish them for noncompliance, without violating the Constitution. But because most K–12 students are legal minors subject to custody and because of the special characteristics of the public school environment, students enjoy watered-down versions of the constitutional protections afforded to adults (Blokhuis 2015).

In *Vernonia School District v. Acton*, a case involving a seventh-grade student who challenged a school policy mandating random drug testing of all interscholastic athletes, Justice Scalia identified "deterring drug use by our Nation's schoolchildren" as an important aim of education while defining the "special characteristics of the school environment" in terms of the "custodial and tutelary" relationship between public school officials and students:

> Traditionally at common law, and still today, unemancipated minors lack some of the most fundamental rights of self-determination—including even the right of liberty in its narrow sense, i.e., the right to come and go at will. They are subject, even as to their physical freedom, to the control of their parents or guardians. …
>
> In *T.L.O.*, we rejected the notion that public schools, like private schools, exercise only parental power over their students, which of course is not subject to constitutional constraints. Such a view of things, we said, "is not entirely 'consonant with compulsory education laws,'" and is inconsistent with our prior decisions treating school officials as state actors for purposes of the Due Process and Free Speech Clauses. But while denying that the State's power over schoolchildren is formally no more than the delegated power of their parents, *T.L.O.* did not deny, but indeed emphasized, that the nature of that power is custodial and tutelary, permitting a degree of supervision and control that could not be exercised over free adults.

Board of Education of Pottawatomie County v. Earls, 536 U.S. 822 (2002)

In the wake of *Vernonia*, some school districts began testing all students engaged in extracurricular activities beyond athletics, including members of musical clubs and debate teams. In *Board of Education v. Earls*, the Supreme Court held that suspicionless drug searches furthered the aim articulated by Justice Scalia in *Vernonia*: preventing drug use by students. For the Court, Justice Thomas noted,

> This Court has already articulated in detail the importance of the governmental concern in preventing drug use by schoolchildren. The drug abuse problem among our Nation's youth has hardly abated since *Vernonia* was decided in 1995. In fact, evidence suggests that it has only grown worse. As in *Vernonia*, "the necessity for the State to act is magnified by the fact that this evil is being visited not just upon individuals at large, but upon children for whom it has undertaken a special responsibility of care and direction." The health and safety risks identified in *Vernonia* apply with equal force to Tecumseh's children. Indeed, the nationwide drug epidemic makes the war against drugs a pressing concern in every school.

Notably, in *Earls,* Justice Ginsburg changed her stance from *Vernonia*, where she had joined the majority. In her *Earls* dissent, she and the other dissenters seemed concerned about the expansion of suspicionless searches, pointing out, "the government is nowhere more a teacher than when it runs a public school" (Ahranjani 2021: 287). Her dissenting view was adopted by a majority in *Safford Unified School District No. 1 v. Redding*, 557 U.S. 364 (2009). In that case, the Court found the strip search of a thirteen-year-old student by school officials looking for an Ibuprofen tablet to be unreasonable, in violation of the Fourth Amendment.

Morse v. Frederick, 551 U.S. 393 (2007)

Five years after *Earls*, the Supreme Court recognized a school principal's interest in censoring drug-related speech. Joseph Frederick was eighteen years of age when he unfurled a "BONG HiTS 4 JESUS" banner on a city sidewalk during an Olympic torch relay. Any other adult in Juneau, Alaska was at liberty to hoist the same banner on the same sidewalk, yet Principal Morse could suspend Frederick without violating the First Amendment because Frederick was cast as (a) a pupil (b) promoting illegal drug use (c) at a school-sponsored event (Blokhuis et al. 2021: 137). Writing for the Court, Chief Justice Roberts held the material and substantial disruption standard enunciated in *Tinker* would not apply in cases involving the promotion of illegal drug use by students, as this was contrary to the purposes of education in the United States:

> Congress has declared that part of a school's job is educating students about the dangers of illegal drug use. It has provided billions of dollars to support state and local drug-prevention programs, and required that schools receiving federal funds under the *Safe and Drug-Free Schools and Communities Act* of 1994 certify that their drug prevention programs "convey a clear and consistent message that … the illegal use of drugs [is] wrong and harmful." Thousands of school boards throughout the country— including JDHS— have adopted policies aimed at effectuating this message. … Student speech celebrating illegal drug use at a school event, in the presence of school administrators and teachers, thus poses a particular challenge for school officials working to protect those entrusted to their care from the dangers of drug abuse.
>
> The "special characteristics of the school environment," and the governmental interest in stopping student drug abuse—reflected in the policies of Congress and myriad school boards, including JDHS—allow schools to restrict student expression that they reasonably regard as promoting illegal drug use.

As these Supreme Court decisions clearly illustrate, there has been a marked shift over time in terms of how the aims and purposes of education have been construed in American jurisprudence. The broad, student-focused conceptions of the Civil Rights era have given way to a narrower conception more attuned to the interests of school and governmental authorities.

EVERY STATE CONSTITUTION PROVIDES A FRAMEWORK FOR PUBLIC EDUCATION

In the United States, each of the fifty states has an education clause in its constitution. These clauses typically articulate the civic aims and moral purposes of education (Tyack, James, and Benavot 1987: 30). Some state constitutions contain vague language requiring legislatures to support or encourage public education. For example, Article IX, Section 1 of the California constitution provides simply that, "A general diffusion of knowledge and intelligence being essential to the preservation of the rights and liberties of the people, the Legislature shall encourage by all suitable means the promotion of intellectual, scientific, moral, and agricultural improvement" (Parker 2016: 6). Other state constitutions contain provisions requiring the legislature to establish and maintain "common schools for all children." Article XI, Section 1 of the New York constitution says, "The legislature shall provide for the maintenance and support of a system of free common schools, wherein all the children of this state may be educated" (Parker 2016: 16).

A number of state constitutions describe the aims and purposes of the public education legislatures are to provide. For example, Article VII, Section 1 of the Texas constitution says, "A general diffusion of knowledge being essential to the preservation of the liberties and rights of the people, it shall be the duty of the Legislature of the State to establish and make suitable provision for the support and maintenance of an efficient system of public free schools." Article X, Section 1 of the Illinois constitution provides that, "A fundamental goal of the People of the State is the educational development of all persons to the limits of their capacities" (Parker 2016: 10).

Some states constitutions offer guarantees of equality of educational opportunities, or describe public educational duties as basic obligations. For example, Part X, Section 1 of the Montana constitution requires "a system of education which will develop the full educational potential of each person. Equality of educational opportunity is guaranteed to each person of the state" (Parker 2016: 14). Article XIII, Section 1 of the Georgia constitution says, "The provision of an adequate public education for the citizens shall be a primary obligation of the State of Georgia. Public education for the citizens prior to the college or postsecondary level shall be free and shall be provided for by taxation" (Parker 2016: 8). And some state constitutions go even further, offering specific guarantees concerning efficiency, safety, security, quality, and even maximum class sizes. For example, Article IX, Section 1 of the Florida constitution provides as follows:

> The education of children is a fundamental value of the people of the State of Florida. It is, therefore, a paramount duty of the state to make adequate provision for the education of all children residing within its borders. Adequate provision shall be made by law for a uniform, efficient, safe, secure, and high quality system of free public schools that allows students to obtain a high quality education and for the establishment, maintenance, and operation of institutions of higher learning and other public education programs that the needs of the people may require.

The exact language in state constitutional documents concerning the purposes of education matters. On the front end, the language establishes specific obligations for legislatures and state officials and corresponding rights for all children in the state. At the back end, the constitutional language serves as a basis for legal action when necessary to vindicate a right to a public education delivered in particular ways, funded at particular levels, and designed with particular aims and purposes in view (Blokhuis and Curren 2021).

Broadly speaking, the education clauses in state constitutions require either "adequate" education or "equitable" education (Dunn and West 2009: 98, 145; Robinson 2019: 269–71). After the Supreme Court determined there was no federal constitutional right to education in *San Antonio v. Rodriguez*, school finance reformers shifted their attention to the educational purposes and the corresponding rights of students in state constitutions. Litigation has resulted in major reforms. In about half of all states, plaintiffs have succeeded in convincing the court to order the state legislature to change the educational finance system, but implementation and enforcement of these court orders has often been challenging (Blokhuis et al. 2021: 381).

The constitution of New Jersey states that "The Legislature shall provide for the maintenance and support of a thorough and efficient system of free public schools for the instruction of all the children in the State between the ages of five and eighteen years" (Art. VIII, § 4, para. 1). In 1990, the Supreme Court of New Jersey provided a detailed analysis of the constitutional mandate to provide for "a thorough and efficient system of free public schools" in *Abbott v. Burke*, 575 A.2d 359 (N.J. 1990). Using the spending patterns of wealthier districts as a benchmark for the state's funding obligations, the court attempted to address both equity and adequacy with a broad interpretation of the constitutional purposes of education. For the court, Chief Justice Wilentz wrote:

> "Thorough and efficient" means more than teaching the skills needed to compete in the labor market, as critically important as that may be. It means being able to fulfill one's role as a citizen, a role that encompasses far more than merely registering to vote. It means the ability to participate fully in society, in the life of one's community, the ability to appreciate music, art, and literature, and the ability to share all of that with friends. As plaintiffs point out in so many ways, and tellingly, if these courses are not integral to a thorough and efficient education, why do the richer districts invariably offer them? The disparity is dramatic. Alongside these basic-skills districts are school systems offering the broadest range of courses, instruction in numerous languages, sophisticated mathematics, arts, and sciences at a high level, fully equipped laboratories, hands-on computer experience, everything parents seriously concerned for their children's future would want, and everything a child needs. In these richer districts, most of which have some disadvantaged students, one will also find the kind of special attention and educational help so badly needed in poorer urban districts that offer only basic-skills training. If absolute equality were the constitutional mandate, and 'basic skills' sufficient to achieve that mandate, there would be little short of a revolution in the suburban districts when parents learned that basic skills is what their children were entitled to, limited to, and no more.

Fourteen years later, in *Hoke County Board of Education v. North Carolina*, 599 S.E.2d 365 (N.C. 2004), the Supreme Court of North Carolina likewise defined constitutional "adequacy" in terms of the broad purposes of education. "An education that does not serve the purpose of preparing students to participate and compete in the society in which they live and work is devoid of substance and is constitutionally inadequate," wrote the court:

> A sound basic education ... provides students with at least: (1) sufficient knowledge of fundamental mathematics and physical science to enable the student to function in a complex and rapidly changing society; (2) sufficient fundamental knowledge of geography, history, and basic economic and political systems to enable the student to make informed choices with regard to issues that affect the student personally or affect the student's community, state, and nation; (3) sufficient academic and vocational skills to enable the student to successfully engage in post-secondary education or vocational training; and (4) sufficient academic and vocational skills to enable the student to compete on an equal basis with others in formal education or gainful employment in contemporary society.

Two years later, the Court of Appeals of New York affirmed the right of public school children to the "sound basic education" described in the New York state constitution. In *Campaign for Fiscal Equity, Inc. v State of New York*, 29 AD3d 175 (N.Y. App. 2006), the court established a threshold for funding schools in New York City at a level adequate to the task of fulfilling the aims and purposes of education, broadly construed:

> More than a decade ago, we held that the Education Article of the New York State Constitution requires the State "to offer all children the opportunity of a sound basic education." Plaintiffs had sought a declaratory judgment against the State, claiming that students in New York City public schools were not receiving a basic education and that the State's public school financing system was unconstitutional.
>
> Mindful of the fundamental value of education in our democratic society, we agreed with plaintiffs' interpretation of the Education Article. The State must ensure that New York's public schools are able to teach "the basic literacy, calculating, and verbal skills necessary to enable children to eventually function productively as civic participants capable of voting and serving on a jury." In assessing adequacy of education, this standard is the constitutional minimum or floor that we had acknowledged earlier...
>
> In 2003, we decided that this trial record supports the conclusion that, because of inadequate funding for their public schools, children in New York City "are not receiving the constitutionally-mandated opportunity for a sound basic education." In CFE I, we had understood a sound basic education as teaching skills that enable students to undertake civil responsibilities meaningfully. In CFE II, we defined "sound basic education" more exactly, as the "opportunity for a meaningful high school education, one which prepares [children] to function productively as civic participants."

CONCLUSION

From the 1940s to the 1970s, the Supreme Court's characterization of the aims and purposes of American public education tended to favor students, with expansive new conceptions of individual rights and liberties for children in public schools including limited due process and free speech rights under the US Constitution. Broadly pro-student decisions include *West Virginia v. Barnette* (1943), *Brown v. Board of Education* (1954), *Tinker v. Des Moines* (1969), *Wisconsin v. Yoder* (1972), *San Antonio v. Rodriguez* (1973), and *Plyler v. Doe* (1982). The Supreme Court's characterization of the aims and purposes of public education and has since tended to favor the interests of school officials in maintaining order and efficiency. Broadly pro-government decisions include *Goss v. Lopez* (1975), *New Jersey v. T.L.O.* (1985), *Bethel v. Fraser* (1986), *Hazelwood v. Kuhlmeier* (1988), *Vernonia v. Acton* (1995), *Board of Education v. Earls* (2002), and *Morse v. Frederick* (2007).

These decisions reveal several common themes. First, the Court has clearly recognized the importance of public education for fostering republican citizenship and democratic traditions, as *Barnette* and *Plyler* illustrate. Second, the Court has acknowledged a legal duty on the part of school officials to maintain order, as *Tinker*, *Goss*, *Fraser*, *T.L.O.*, *Kuhlmeier*, and *Morse* indicate. Third, the Court has held that if students are to become engaged and active citizens, they must be able to learn about and exercise in school at least some of the rights they will enjoy as adults, as *Brown* and *Yoder* show. Balancing these interests is no easy task, particularly in a country as large and diverse as the United States.

Over the last two centuries, the United States has grown from a population of less than 10 million to over 330 million. The country's diversity contributes to its strength and to the strength of its public schools and educational systems. As described early in the chapter, and as the Supreme Court noted in *Keyishian v. Board of Regents,* 385 U.S. 589 (1967), "The Nation's future depends upon leaders trained through wide exposure to that robust exchange of ideas which discovers truth out of a multitude of tongues." As much as the growth in population and diversity enhances the "marketplace of ideas," it also certainly introduces challenges. Disaffection with government institutions that have mistreated Black and Latinx students, students with disabilities, and students from other vulnerable groups has long affected American public schools. While some justices have focused on order and assimilation and on public schools as training grounds for "good" citizens, this may be read as patronizing and even oppressive to marginalized people. If the purposes of education set forth by a largely homogenous group of settlers in a relatively small country are to stand the test of time, both courts and schools must continue to reflect the interests of an increasingly large and diverse American population in securing the unalienable right of every individual to "life, liberty and the pursuit of happiness."

REFERENCES

Ahranjani, Maryam (2017), "The Prisonization of America's Public Schools," *Hofstra Law Review*, 45 (4): 1097–117.

Ahranjani, Maryam (2021), "School 'Safety' Measures Jump Constitutional Guardrails," *Seattle University Law Review*, 44 (2): 273–306.

Beard, Charles A. and Mary R. Beard (1968), *New Basic History of the United States*, New York: Doubleday.

Black, Derek W. (2016), *Ending Zero Tolerance: The Crisis of Absolute School Discipline*, New York: New York University Press.

Blokhuis, J.C. (2015), "Student Rights and the Special Characteristics of the School Environment in American Jurisprudence," *Journal of Philosophy of Education*, 49 (1): 65–85.

Blokhuis, J.C. and Randall Curren (2021), "The Judicialization of American Education," in Kathy Hytten (ed.), *Oxford Encyclopedia of Philosophy of Education*, New York: Oxford University Press. https://doi.org/10.1093/acrefore/9780190264093.013.1602.

Blokhuis, J.C., Jonathan Feldman, Michael Imber, and Tyll van Geel (2021), *Education Law*, 6th edn., New York: Routledge.

Brighouse, Harry (2005), *On Education*, New York: Routledge.

Callan, Eamonn (1997), *Creating Citizens*, Oxford: Oxford University Press.

Curren, Randall and J.C. Blokhuis (2011), "The Prima Facie Case against Homeschooling," *Public Affairs Quarterly*, 25 (1): 1–19.

Curren, Randall (2000), *Aristotle on the Necessity of Public Education*, Lanham, MD: Rowman & Littlefield.

Curren, Randall (2006), "Developmental Liberalism," *Educational Theory*, 56 (4): 451–68.

Dewey, John (1966), *Democracy and Education: An Introduction to the Philosophy of Education*, New York: Free Press.

Driver, Justin (2018), *The Schoolhouse Gate: Public Education, the Supreme Court, and the Battle for the American Mind*, New York: Pantheon.

Dunn, Joshua M. and Martin R. West, eds. (2009), *From Schoolhouse to Courthouse: The Judiciary's Role in American Education,* Washington, DC: Brookings Institute.

Feinberg, Joel (2007), "The Child's Right to an Open Future," in Randall Curren (ed.), *Philosophy of Education: An Anthology*, 112–23, London: Blackwell.

Fuller, Bruce and Arun Rasiah (2005), "Schooling Citizens for Evolving Democracies," in Susan Fuhrman and Marvin Lazerson (eds.), *The Institutions of American Democracy: The Public Schools*, 81–106, New York: Oxford University Press.

Gutmann, Amy (1999), *Democratic Education*, Princeton, NJ: Princeton University Press.

Karteron, Alexis (2018), "Arrested Development: Rethinking Fourth Amendment Standards for Seizures and Uses of Force in Schools," *Nevada Law Journal*, 18 (3): 863–918.

Parker, Emily (2016), "Constitutional Obligations for Public Education," Education Commission of the States, March 1. Available online: http://www.ecs.org/wp-content/uploads/2016-Constitutional-obligations-for-public-education-1.pdf (accessed April 2, 2021).

Robinson, Kimberly J. (2019), *A Federal Right to Education: Fundamental Questions for Our Democracy*, New York: New York University Press.

Tyack, David, Thomas James, and Aaron Benavot (1987), *Law and the Shaping of Public Education, 1785–1954*, Madison: University of Wisconsin Press.

CHAPTER THREE

Curriculum

The First Amendment and Enduring Curricular Controversies

J.C. BLOKHUIS AND DAVID HÒA KHOA NGUYỄN

Throughout the world, public schooling shapes the cultural, ideological, and religious identities of future adults. In the United States, public schools influence what millions of American children know, value, and believe. Thus, debates over the public school curriculum have a long history in American politics and jurisprudence. For evangelical Christians and other religious conservatives, American public schools are "a central battlefield in the so-called culture wars, which they fight with the hope of turning the nation back in what they believe to be a more godly direction" (Bindewald 2015b: 88).

In this chapter, we review significant judicial opinions establishing constitutional limits on prayer, Bible reading, religious observances, and the use of religious books and music in the American public school curriculum, focusing on three clauses within the First Amendment—the Free Speech Clause, the Free Exercise Clause, and the Establishment Clause. We then consider "released time" policies in a growing number of American states. These policies allow students in public schools to earn credits for private religious instruction received offsite without violating the First Amendment. "Public schools may legally establish released time programs anywhere in the U.S. so long as they obtain parental permission for student participation, meet off-campus, and are not supported by public funds or school resources," notes Bindewald (2015b: 81). We then review persistent religious objections to aspects of the science curriculum in American public schools and explore how state legislatures, local school districts, and individual teachers have turned to the courts over the course of an enduring cultural conflict over the theory of evolution.

EDUCATION IN THE US CONSTITUTIONAL CONTEXT

In the American constitutional context, the independent welfare and developmental interests of children have long been held to include access to public knowledge, to diverse formative influences, and to opportunities beyond what their parents might be willing or able to provide (Blokhuis 2015). Under the Due Process Clause of the Fourteenth Amendment, which prohibits government agencies from depriving any person of "life, liberty, or property, without due process of law," American parents may claim a substantive right to direct (but not *control*) the upbringing of their children. Yet the federal Constitution does not specifically address public education or curricular matters. Congress has no direct control over what is taught in American public schools, though the federal government can influence the curriculum by funding specific programs.

Education is a state responsibility in the US constitutional context. Under the constitution of each state, children are entitled to receive a public education at public expense, and it falls to each state legislature to establish a curriculum for its public schools. In practice, the public school curriculum in each state is a collaborative effort between the legislature, local school districts, and parents. While a modicum of discontinuity between what children experience at home and what they experience in public schools may be theoretically desirable (see Brighouse 2005), some religious parents would prefer as much continuity between home and school as possible in terms of religious beliefs and practices. As a result, American courts have frequently been called upon to balance the competing curricular interests of children, their parents, and state legislatures (Shulman 2014; Blokhuis and Curren 2021).

Under the First Amendment of the US Constitution, "Congress shall make no law respecting an establishment of religion, or prohibiting the free exercise thereof." The first part is the Establishment Clause, which prohibits the federal and state governments from using public funds to promote or sponsor any specific faith or religion, from advancing or inhibiting religion in general, or privileging one faith over another. The second part is the Free Exercise Clause, which prohibits governments from interfering with individual religious beliefs. In *Everson v. Board of Education*, 330 U.S. 1 (1947), a New Jersey school district policy of reimbursing parents for the costs associated with busing their children to private and public schools was challenged under the Establishment Clause of the First Amendment. In his majority opinion, Supreme Court Justice Hugo Black wrote:

> The "establishment of religion" clause of the First Amendment means at least this: Neither a state nor the Federal Government can set up a church. Neither can pass laws which aid one religion over another. Neither can force nor influence a person to go to or to remain away from church

> against his [*sic*] will or force him [*sic*] to profess a belief or disbelief in any religion. No person can be punished for entertaining or professing religious beliefs or disbeliefs, for church attendance or nonattendance. No tax in any amount, large or small, can be levied to support any religious activities or institutions whatever they may adopt to teach or practice religion. Neither a state nor the Federal Government can, openly or secretly participate in the affairs of any religious organizations or groups and vice versa. In the words of Jefferson, the clause against establishment of religion bylaws was intended to erect a "wall of separation between church and state."

Until the 1960s, there did not seem to be much of a "wall of separation between church and state" in American public schools. Bible readings, organized prayers, and a variety of other religious observances and ceremonies were part of the public school curriculum in every state. In *Engel v. Vitale*, 370 U.S. 421 (1962), the Supreme Court held that the daily recital of a brief prayer composed by the New York Board of Regents for public schools in that state violated the Establishment Clause, concluding that "it is no part of the business of government to compose official prayers for any group of the American people to recite as a part of a religious program carried on by government." The prayer in question read as follows: "Almighty God, we acknowledge our dependence upon Thee, and we beg Thy blessings upon us, our parents, our teachers and our country. *Amen.*" For the majority, Justice Hugo Black wrote:

> There can be no doubt that New York's state prayer program officially establishes the religious beliefs embodied in the Regents' prayer. The respondents' argument to the contrary, which is largely based upon the contention that the Regents' prayer is "nondenominational" and the fact that the program, as modified and approved by state courts, does not require all pupils to recite the prayer, but permits those who wish to do so to remain silent or be excused from the room, ignores the essential nature of the program's constitutional defects. Neither the fact that the prayer may be denominationally neutral nor the fact that its observance on the part of the students is voluntary can serve to free it from the limitations of the Establishment Clause, as it might from the Free Exercise Clause, of the First Amendment, both of which are operative against the States by virtue of the Fourteenth Amendment. Although these two clauses may, in certain instances, overlap, they forbid two quite different kinds of governmental encroachment upon religious freedom.
>
> The Establishment Clause, unlike the Free Exercise Clause, does not depend upon any showing of direct governmental compulsion and is violated by the enactment of laws which establish an official religion whether

> those laws operate directly to coerce non-observing individuals or not. This is not to say, of course, that laws officially prescribing a particular form of religious worship do not involve coercion of such individuals. When the power, prestige and financial support of government is placed behind a particular religious belief, the indirect coercive pressure upon religious minorities to conform to the prevailing officially approved religion is plain. But the purposes underlying the Establishment Clause go much further than that. Its first and most immediate purpose rested on the belief that a union of government and religion tends to destroy government and to degrade religion. The history of governmentally established religion, both in England and in this country, showed that whenever government had allied itself with one particular form of religion, the inevitable result had been that it had incurred the hatred, disrespect and even contempt of those who held contrary beliefs.

The following year, the Court found that nondenominational prayers and Bible readings in public schools had both the purpose and primary effect of advancing religion in *School District of Abington Township v. Schempp*, 374 U.S. 203 (1963). Though student participation in the prayers and Bible readings was voluntary, the Court nonetheless found a violation of the Free Exercise Clause:

> [The Free Exercise Clause] recognizes the value of religious training, teaching and observance and, more particularly, the right of every person to freely choose his [*sic*] own course with reference thereof, free of any compulsion from the state ... The Free Exercise Clause, likewise considered many times here, withdraws from legislative power, state and federal, the exertion of any restraint on the free exercise of religion. Its purpose is to secure religious liberty in the individual by prohibiting any invasions thereof by civil authority. Hence it is necessary in a free exercise case for one to show the coercive effect of the enactment as it operates against him [*sic*] in the practice of religion.

In *Lemon v. Kurzman*, 403 U.S. 602 (1971), the constitutionality of subsidy programs for the salaries of teachers of secular subjects in Catholic schools in Pennsylvania and Rhode Island was challenged under the Establishment Clause. In this case, the Court established a three-part test to help determine the constitutionality of such programs. According to the first prong of the *Lemon* test, an impugned program or policy or statute must have a secular legislative purpose. Under the second prong, its primary effect must neither advance nor inhibit religion. And under the third prong, it must not result in "excessive government entanglement" with religion. Distinguishing public funding for secular textbooks in parochial schools, which the Court had found constitutional three years earlier in *Board of Education v. Allen*, 392 U.S. 236 (1968), Chief Justice Burger felt subsidizing the salaries of teachers in parochial schools went too far:

> We need not and do not assume that teachers in parochial schools will be guilty of bad faith or any conscious design to evade the limitations imposed by the statute and the First Amendment. We simply recognize that a dedicated religious person, teaching in a school affiliated with his or her faith and operated to inculcate its tenets, will inevitably experience great difficulty in remaining religiously neutral. Doctrines and faith are not inculcated or advanced by neutrals. With the best of intentions, such a teacher would find it hard to make a total separation between secular teaching and religious doctrine. What would appear to some to be essential to good citizenship might well for others border on or constitute instruction in religion. Further difficulties are inherent in the combination of religious discipline and the possibility of disagreement between teacher and religious authorities over the meaning of the statutory restrictions.
>
> We do not assume, however, that parochial school teachers will be unsuccessful in their attempts to segregate their religious belief from their secular educational responsibilities. But the potential for impermissible fostering of religion is present.

In *Lee v. Weisman*, 505 U.S. 577 (1992), the practice of inviting clerics to offer prayers at school graduation ceremonies was challenged under the Establishment Clause. The Court added a "coercion analysis" to the *Lemon* test, noting that "state-sponsored and state-directed religious exercise[s]" create "subtle coercive pressures" for participation and conformity of belief. Because students themselves have limited First Amendment rights in public school contexts, some school officials hoped student-led prayers might pass constitutional muster. In *Santa Fe Independent School District v. Doe*, 530 U.S. 290 (2000), students were permitted to deliver invocations of their own choosing before football games. The Court rejected this approach, noting the invocations were authorized by a government policy and that their primary purpose was to preserve the long-standing practice of opening football games with prayer.

In *Doe v. Indian River School District*, 653 F.3d 256 (3d Cir. 2011), the Third Circuit applied the enhanced *Lemon* test to find that moments of silence at school board meetings regularly attended by students violated the Establishment Clause. According to the Court, student attendance at board meetings was similar to attendance at sporting events and graduation ceremonies. Moments of silence were akin to prayers. Seven years later, in *Freedom from Religion Foundation v. Chino Valley Unified School District Board of Education*, 896 F.3d 1132 (9th Cir. 2018), the Ninth Circuit likewise prohibited prayers at school board meetings attended by students.

RELIGIOUS CURRICULAR CONTENT

In *School District of Abington Township v. Schempp*, 374 U.S. 203 (1963), the Supreme Court held that if religious texts or materials were studied as part of a literature, history, world culture, or comparative religion course, the Establishment Clause would not be violated. In American jurisprudence, Bible study programs in public schools are unconstitutional when they involve instructors or materials selected by outside religious groups (Blokhuis et al. 2021: 93).

In recent years, the federal courts have heard constitutional challenges to curricular content with ties to religious traditions or texts, including a yoga in schools program, a "Bible in the Schools" program, and the inclusion of material on Islam in a history program. In *Sedlock v. Baird*, 235 Cal. App. 4th 874 (2015), parents in California unsuccessfully challenged a public school yoga program under the Establishment Clause, claiming that yoga is a spiritual practice closely tied to Hinduism. Applying the *Lemon* test, the court found the yoga program had a secular purpose and that it did not advance or inhibit Hinduism or excessively entangle the school district in religion.

Three years later, in *Deal v. Mercer County Board of Education*, 911 F.3d 183 (4th Cir. 2018), *cert. denied*, 2019 U.S. LEXIS 5658 (2019), the Fourth Circuit upheld an Establishment Clause challenge to a "Bible in the Schools" program that had been operating for eight decades in West Virginia. The privately funded program included thirty minutes of weekly Bible instruction for elementary school students and forty-five minutes of weekly Bible instruction for middle school students, including lessons about Moses, the Ten Commandments, and the death and resurrection of Jesus.

The following year, in *Wood v. Arnold*, 915 F.3d 308 (4th Cir. 2019), *cert. denied*, 2019 U.S. LEXIS 6431 (2019), the same court deployed the *Lemon* test to determine whether statements about Islam and an assignment in a high school world history class on the *Shahadah* (an Islamic oath acknowledging the Prophet Muhammad as a messenger of God) violated the Establishment Clause. For a unanimous court, Justice Barbara Milano Keenan found no constitutional violation, noting:

The student, Caleigh Wood, contends that school officials Evelyn Arnold and Shannon Morris (the defendants) used the statements about Islam to endorse that religion over Christianity, and compelled Wood against her will to profess a belief in Islam…

In this case, the comparative faith statement was part of an academic unit in which students studied Middle Eastern empires and the role of Islam. The unit did not focus exclusively on Islam's core principles, but explored "among other things, formation of Middle Eastern empires including the basic concepts of the Islamic faith and how it along with politics, culture, economics, and geography contributed to the development of those empires." Nothing in the record indicates that the comparative faith statement was made with a subjective purpose of advancing Islam over Christianity, or for any other predominately religious purpose. Nor does the record show that the proffered secular purpose of teaching about Muslim empires in the context of world history was pretextual. Thus, on its face, the comparative faith statement was introduced for a genuine secular purpose.

Similarly, the *shahada* assignment was a tool designed to assess the students' understanding of the lesson on Islam. In total, the worksheet included 17 questions with 27 blank entries to be completed by the students on the history of Islam, "beliefs and practices" of Muslims, and links between Islam, Judaism, and Christianity. The students were not required to memorize the *shahada*, to recite it, or even to write the complete statement of faith. Instead, the worksheet included a variety of factual information related to Islam and merely asked the students to demonstrate their understanding of the material by completing the partial sentences. This is precisely the sort of academic exercise that the Supreme Court has indicated would not run afoul of the Establishment Clause. Because the school had a predominately secular purpose in teaching world history, we conclude that both the comparative faith statement and the *shahada* assignment satisfy the first prong of *Lemon*.

RELIGIOUS HOLIDAYS AND OBSERVANCES IN PUBLIC SCHOOLS

In American jurisprudence, public schools have long struggled with religious holidays and observances. In *Florey v. Sioux Falls School District 49–5*, 619 F.2d 1311 (8th Cir. 1980), a school district adopted a rule that "music, art, literature and drama having a religious theme or basis" could be included in the school curriculum only if "presented in a prudent and objective manner and as a traditional part of the cultural and religious heritage of the particular holiday." The Eighth Circuit found this rule did not violate the Establishment

Clause. "We view the thrust of these rules to be the advancement of the students' knowledge of society's cultural and religious heritage," wrote the court, "as well as the provision of an opportunity for students to perform a full range of music, poetry and drama that is likely to be of interest to the students and their audience."

In *Doe v. Duncanville Independent School District*, 70 F.3d 402 (5th Cir. 1995), the Fifth Circuit approved the performance of *The Lord Bless You and Keep You* by a high school choir, finding that "repeated singing of a particular religious song [did not amount] to an endorsement of religion." And in *Bauchman v. West High School*, 132 F.3d 542 (10th Cir. 1997), the Tenth Circuit observed that the First Amendment did not forbid all mention of religion in public schools. Applying the *Lemon* test, the court found two religious songs performed at a graduation ceremony had been selected for secular purposes, including the promotion of friendship and goodwill (Blokhuis et al. 2021: 89).

RELEASED TIME POLICIES

Benjamin Bindewald (2015b: 83) traces the origins of released time policies in American public schools to an interdenominational church conference in New York City in 1905. There, Dr. George U. Wenner suggested students be released from school for one afternoon each week for religious instruction (citing Gorham 1934). This was a particularly attractive proposition for Protestants concerned about the loss of their dominant status as industrialization and mass immigration profoundly changed American cities and schools: "Protestantism could return to the public schools only if it was accompanied by Catholicism and Judaism," Bindewald notes (2015b: 84, quoting Pfeffer 1975: 181), "and out of this realization came the released-time program."

In 1914, the official start date for release time policies, Dr. William Wirt, the Superintendent of Public Schools in industrial Gary, Indiana, "established a program through which elementary students were released from public-school supervision to religious leaders for instruction in the Protestant, Catholic, or Jewish religion" (Bindewald 2015b: 84; citing Berrett 1998). The "Gary Plan" became the template for school districts across the Midwest and later, the United States as a whole. By the 1940s, Bindewald notes, "the explosive growth of these programs had reached 2,000 communities in 49 states, enrolling over two million students" (citing Shaver 1956).

In *McCollum v. Board of Education*, 333 U.S. 203 (1948), the Supreme Court found a released time program enabling an interfaith group to offer religious instruction to students *on campus* to be unconstitutional. The classes were taught by local clerics at no expense to the schools. Students whose parents had signed consent forms attended for thirty minutes to forty-five minutes each week. Others were required to pursue their studies elsewhere in the building. Relying on the "no aid" principle in *Everson v. Board of Education*, 330 U.S. 1 (1947) the previous year, the Court held that the program violated the Establishment Clause:

> To hold that a state cannot, consistently with the First and Fourteenth Amendments, utilize its public school system to aid any or all religious faiths or sects in the dissemination of their doctrines and ideals does not, as counsel urge, manifest a governmental hostility to religion or religious teachings. A manifestation of such hostility would be at war with our national tradition as embodied in the First Amendment's guaranty of the free exercise of religion. For the First Amendment rests upon the premise that both religion and government can best work to achieve their lofty aims if each is left free from the other within its respective sphere. Or, as we said in the *Everson* case, the First Amendment has erected a wall between Church and State which must be kept high and impregnable.
>
> Here not only are the State's tax-supported public school buildings used for the dissemination of religious doctrines. The State also affords sectarian groups an invaluable aid in that it helps to provide pupils for their religious classes through use of the State's compulsory public school machinery. This is not separation of Church and State.

Four years later, in *Zorach v. Clauson*, 343 U.S. 306 (1952), the Court found a released time program allowing public school students to receive religious instruction *off campus* to be constitutional. Attendance was taken on behalf of the public school, and students attended with parental consent. To reach its conclusion, the Court chipped away at the "wall of separation" in *Everson* and *McCollum*:

> The First Amendment, however, does not say that, in every and all respects there shall be a separation of Church and State. Rather, it studiously defines the manner, the specific ways, in which there shall be no concert or union or dependency one on the other. That is the common sense of the matter. Otherwise the state and religion would be aliens to each other – hostile, suspicious, and even unfriendly. Churches could not be required to pay even property taxes. Municipalities would not be permitted to render police or fire protection to religious groups. Policemen [*sic*] who helped parishioners into their places of worship would violate the Constitution. Prayers in our legislative halls; the appeals to the Almighty in the messages of the Chief Executive; the proclamations making Thanksgiving Day a holiday; "so help me God" in our courtroom oaths – these and all other references to the

> Almighty that run through our laws, our public rituals, our ceremonies would be flouting the First Amendment. A fastidious atheist or agnostic could even object to the supplication with which the Court opens each session: "God save the United States and this Honorable Court."

Finding that it "would have to press the concept of separation of Church and State to these extremes to condemn the present law on constitutional grounds," the Court treated the released time policy in *Zorach* as an accommodation of sorts for parents and students seeking religious instruction.

In the wake of *Zorach*, American courts have consistently upheld the constitutionality of released time programs when classes are held (a) off campus; (b) with parental permission; and (c) without government assistance. But as Bindewald (2015a: 3) has noted, a profound shift in released time policies has taken place in recent years. By his account, the "Gary Plan" programs of a century ago allowed Protestant, Catholic, Jewish, and Mormon instructors to offer lessons off campus consistent with what Protestant, Catholic, Jewish, and Mormon parents were offering their children at home without seeking to convert anyone to a different faith tradition. "Christian activists have recently revitalized this previously diminishing phenomenon and reconceptualized it as an 'open door' through which to proselytize public school students," notes Bindewald (2015a: 3; citing Ericsson et al. 1996). "This reconceptualization of released time as a means of winning religious converts differentiates contemporary evangelical programs from the original programs … established with the primary purpose of providing moral instruction to children within the religious tradition of their parents."

In addition to federal court rulings permitting release time programs (Nguyen 2019), a growing number of states have passed legislation allowing such programs (including Alabama, Arizona, California, Florida, Hawaii, Idaho, Indiana, Iowa, Kentucky, Maine, Massachusetts, Michigan, Minnesota, Montana, New Mexico, New York, North Dakota, Ohio, Oregon, Pennsylvania, South Carolina, South Dakota, Tennessee, Vermont, West Virginia, and Wisconsin). Some states permit school boards to adopt release time program policies (including Alabama, California, Idaho, Indiana, and Iowa), while others require school boards to adopt such policies (including Arizona, Florida, Hawaii, and Kentucky).

In 2006, evangelical Christians lobbied successfully for the passage of the South Carolina Released Time Credit Act, SC Code Ann. § 59-39-112. This would allow credits received in released time programs in that state to count toward a high school degree or diploma. The legislation made South Carolina "a center of operations for a growing movement of evangelical Christians to establish these reconceptualized released time programs throughout the United

States" (Bindewald 2015a: 3). While proponents cast the legislation as a means of accommodating religious diversity, opponents including the Freedom from Religion Foundation (a non-profit group advocating for the separation of church and state) challenged the legislation, arguing that it goes far beyond accommodation.

In *Moss v. Spartanburg County School District Seven*, 683 F.3d 599 (4th Cir. 2012), *cert. denied*, 568 U.S. 1011 (2012), the Fourth Circuit held that a released time policy allowing public school students to earn credit for courses taught off campus by private instructors did *not* violate the Establishment Clause (Blokhuis et al. 2021: 86). The decision, authored by Circuit Judge Paul V. Niemeyer, merits exposition at some length:

> Early in 2007, a private, unaccredited religious education organization, Spartanburg County Bible Education in School Time ("Spartanburg Bible School"), approached a number of South Carolina school districts, including Spartanburg County School District Seven, requesting that they allow students to participate in a released time religious course—a two-semester Christian worldview class—for academic credit. In discussions with School District Seven, the school officials conveyed their preference that administrators receive grades under the released time program as transfer credits from accredited private schools, rather than from unaccredited education providers, such as Spartanburg Bible School. This arrangement would be consistent with the School District's practice of receiving grades awarded by a private school, including grades for religious courses, when a private school student transfers into public school. ...
>
> The Mosses concede that off-campus released time initiatives are generally constitutional, as allowed by *Zorach v. Clauson,* 343 U.S. 306 (1952) [and] *Smith v. Smith,* 523 F.2d 121 (4th Cir. 1975). They contend, however, that the School District's released time program in this case is different from that approved in *Zorach* because it provides academic credit for released time coursework, whereas such credit was not part of the off-campus educational program approved in *Zorach*. ...
>
> The School District contends that its released time policy is constitutional under the holdings of *Zorach* and *Smith*, and the fact that the School District gives credit for the released time course is, it argues, no different than the widely accepted practice of giving course credit to students who transfer from private religious schools to public schools. ...
>
> In *McCollum*, 333 U.S. 203 (1948) the public school brought religious instructors into the school to conduct classes in the school's classrooms, while students normally occupying those classrooms for secular courses

> went elsewhere, and the School District's superintendent approved and supervised each of the religious instructors brought into the school. …
>
> By contrast, in *Zorach* and *Smith*, the public school permitted students to leave school grounds to receive religious instruction off campus and agreed to receive reports of the students' attendance at those classes. Under these circumstances, the Supreme Court and this court concluded that the public schools did "no more than accommodate their schedules to a program of outside religious instruction." Indeed, the Court suggested that if public schools were not permitted to accommodate the religious desires of students and parents in this fashion, the result would be an unconstitutionally hostile environment toward religion.
>
> Here, the School District's released time policy takes place off campus and expressly prohibits any use of public staff or funds for its execution. The circumstances before us are therefore far more similar to those in *Zorach* and *Smith* than those in *McCollum*. …
>
> We see no evidence that the program has had the effect of establishing religion or that it has entangled the School District in religion. As was the General Assembly and School District's purpose, the program properly accommodates religion without establishing it, in accordance with the First Amendment.

The *Spartanburg* decision paved the way for states to grant academic credit to public school students participating in released time programs. As noted earlier, South Carolina passed its released time credit legislation in 2006, allowing school boards to count up to two credit hours of released time instruction toward a high school diploma. Ohio followed suit in 2014, and Indiana, Tennessee, and Alabama followed in 2019. In each state, academic credit is granted based on criteria including the number of hours of instruction, the course syllabus, the methods of assessment, and the qualifications of course instructor. Given the popularity of release time programs, more states are likely to follow suit (Nguyen 2019).

RELIGIOUS OBJECTIONS TO THE SCIENCE CURRICULUM

Every year, science teachers in American public schools find themselves in the horns of an enduring cultural dilemma. Should creationism be taught alongside evolution? The form of creationism most heavily promoted for inclusion in the public school science curriculum is the fundamentalist Christian variety. Fundamentalism stresses that everything in the Bible is literally true, including the account of creation from the Book of Genesis. "Young-earth creationism" aligns with the biblical account of the sudden appearance of the Earth and all living things (Pennock 2006: 541).

Two decades ago, 44 percent of Americans shared the view that "human beings were created pretty much in their present form about 10,000 years ago" (cited by Pennock 2006: 544; Laats and Siegel 2016: 3).

Proponents of creationism have accordingly claimed that their beliefs should be reflected in the science curriculum. Yet Robert Pennock points out, "It does not matter what the poll figures are because matters of empirical fact are not appropriately decided by majority rule" (2006: 544–5). Nevertheless, the content of the science curriculum in American public schools varies from state to state, and policies on the teaching of evolution and creationism can change as governments come and go. Thus, for example, from 2001 to 2016, science textbooks in Alabama contained the following disclaimer (addressed to students) from the State Board of Education (Schlanger 2015):

> This textbook discusses evolution, a controversial theory some scientists present as a scientific explanation for the origin of living things, such as plants, animals and humans.
>
> No one was present when life first appeared on earth. Therefore, any statements about life's origins should be considered as theory, not fact.
>
> The word "evolution" may refer to many types of change. Evolution describes changes that occur within a species. (White moths, for example, may "evolve" into gray moths.) This process is microevolution, which can be observed and described as fact. Evolution may also refer to the change of one living thing to another, such as reptiles into birds. This process, called macroevolution, has never been observed and should be considered a theory. Evolution also refers to the unproven belief that random, undirected forces produced a world of living things.
>
> There are many unanswered questions about the origin of life which are not mentioned in your textbook, including:
>
> - Why did the major groups of animals suddenly appear in the fossil record (known as the "Cambrian Explosion")?
> - Why have no new major groups of living things appeared in the fossil record for a long time?
> - Why do major groups of plants and animals have no transitional forms in the fossil record?
> - How did you and all living things come to possess such a complete and complex set of "Instructions" for building a living body?
>
> Study hard and keep an open mind. Someday, you may contribute to the theories of how living things appeared on earth.

In 2016, the State Board of Education updated its disclaimer for science textbooks in Alabama (National Center for Science Education [NCSE] 2015):

> The word "theory" has many meanings. Theories are defined as systematically organized knowledge, abstract reasoning, a speculative idea or plan, or a systematic statement of principles. Scientific theories are based on both observations of the natural world and assumptions about the natural world. They are always subject to change in view of new and confirmed observations.
>
> Many scientific theories have been developed over time. The value of scientific work is not only the development of theories but also what is learned from the development process. The Alabama Course of Study: Science includes many theories and studies of scientists' work. The work of Copernicus, Newton, and Einstein, to name a few, has provided a basis of our knowledge of the world today.
>
> The theory of evolution by natural selection is a controversial theory that is included in this textbook. It is controversial because it states that natural selection provides the basis for the modern scientific explanation for the diversity of living things. Since natural selection has been observed to play a role in influencing small changes in a population, it is assumed that it produces large changes, even though this has not been directly observed. Because of its importance and implication, students should understand the nature of evolutionary theories. They should learn to make distinctions between the multiple meanings of evolution, to distinguish between observations and assumptions used to draw conclusions, and to wrestle with the unanswered questions and unresolved problems still faced by evolutionary theory.
>
> There are many unanswered questions about the origin of life. With the explosion of new scientific knowledge in biochemical and molecular biology and exciting new fossil discoveries, Alabama students may be among those who use their understanding and skills to contribute to knowledge and to answer many unanswered questions. Instructional materials associated with controversy should be approached with an open mind, studied carefully, and critically considered.

Politics may be fickle, but science is not. "Science is, first and foremost, non-dogmatic; it is open to evidential support and falsification," notes Harvey Siegel (1981: 96). Because scientific hypotheses can be confirmed or disconfirmed by evidence, a scientific theory is legitimate "only if it meets the criteria of testability, explanatory power, and predictive power." Religion, on the other hand, is "a system of beliefs that has, as its most prominent feature, some conception of a divine creator or of a supernatural order in the universe and that requires the [uncritical] acceptance of some doctrine on faith" (97).

Evolution is a scientific theory closely associated with Charles Darwin, who concluded that national selection based on chance variations explains the adaptation of living organisms to their environments. As with all scientific theories, evolutionary theory is based on empirical evidence, including observable characteristics of living organisms and of fossilized remains (see Evans and Selina 2010; Pennock 2011). Empiricism is a theory of knowledge by which complex ideas are abstracted from observation and experience. Creationism, by contrast, is based on the presumed truth of biblical accounts of the genesis of earth (Shreve 2010). "In general," notes Pennock (2006: 541), "creationism is the rejection of evolution in favor of special creation of some form." Because creationists typically accept biblical accounts of the origins of life as *a priori* truths, their stance is fundamentally at odds with the scientific method, which requires that hypotheses and theories be tested against empirical observations of the natural world.

A handful of states allow creationism or the pseudoscientific theory of intelligent design to be taught in public schools as part of the science curriculum (including Arkansas, Louisiana, and Tennessee). In other states, especially those with expansive voucher and charter school laws (such as Indiana, Florida, and Texas), public funds are channeled to private schools that teach creationism or intelligent design.

Cultural and religious conflicts over the teaching of evolution in American public schools began over a century ago (Superfine 2009). In the 1920s, anti-evolution bills were introduced in twenty states in the wake of the notorious "Scopes Monkey Trial." The case arose in 1925, after the Tennessee legislature enacted the Tennessee Anti-Evolution Act (commonly referred to as the Butler Act, after the legislator who sponsored it). The Act stated in part:

> That it shall be unlawful for any teacher in any of the Universities, normal [schools] and all other public schools of the state which are supported in whole or in part by the public school funds of the state, to teach any theory that denies the story of the divine creation of man as taught in the Bible and to teach instead that man has descended from a lower order of animals.

In *Scopes v. State*, 154 Tenn. 105 (1925), biology teacher John Scopes was found guilty of violating the Butler Act and fined $100. The Tennessee Supreme Court reversed the trial court on a technicality, finding that the jury ought to have set the fine. More importantly, however, the court rejected claims that the Butler Act violated the Establishment Clause in the Tennessee state constitution:

> We are not able to see how the prohibition of teaching the theory that man has descended from a lower order of animals gives preference to any religious establishment or mode of worship. So far as we know, there is no

> religious establishment or organized body that has in its creed or confession of faith any article denying or affirming such a theory. So far as we know, the denial or affirmation of such a theory does not enter into any recognized mode of worship. Since this cause has been pending in this court, we have been favored, in addition to briefs of counsel and various *amici curiae*, with a multitude of resolutions, addresses, and communications from scientific bodies, religious factions, and individuals giving us the benefit of their views upon the theory of evolution. Examination of these contributions indicates that Protestants, Catholics, and Jews are divided among themselves in their beliefs, and that there is no unanimity among the members of any religious establishment as to this subject. Belief or unbelief in the theory of evolution is no more a characteristic of any religious establishment or mode of worship than is belief or unbelief in the wisdom of the prohibition laws. It would appear that members of the same churches quite generally disagree as to these things.

The sensational *Scopes* trial embarrassed religious conservatives, who kept a low profile for decades. Moreover, the term "evolution" itself largely disappeared from public view as textbook authors deployed less controversial terms such as "change" or "development." By the mid-1960s, most Americans were unfamiliar with evolution as a basic organizing principle in biology (Laats and Siegel 2016: 29). With the Sputnik crisis came federally funded Biological Sciences Curriculum Study (BSCS) textbooks, bringing evolution back into public schools just as the Supreme Court was taking prayer out in *Engel v. Vitale*, 370 U.S. 421 (1962), and *Abington v. Schempp*, 374 U.S. 203 (1963).

Having passed constitutional muster in 1926, the Butler Act was repealed one year before the US Supreme Court in *Epperson v. Arkansas*, 393 U.S. 97 (1968), found the state's ban on the teaching of evolution to be unconstitutional. In a firm rejection of the reasoning in *Scopes*, the Court held that the Establishment Clause prohibits state action requiring that teaching and learning in public schools be tailored to the principles of any religion:

> Arkansas' law cannot be defended as an act of religious neutrality. Arkansas did not seek to excise from the curricula of its schools and universities all discussion of the origin of man. The law's effort was confined to an attempt to blot out a particular theory because of its supposed conflict with the Biblical account, literally read. Plainly, the law is contrary to the mandate of the First, and in violation of the Fourteenth Amendment of the Constitution.

The *Epperson* decision galvanized supporters of creationism, who regrouped and cast themselves as an oppressed religious minority seeking equitable treatment in public schools. In response, some states began implementing "balanced treatment" laws requiring that creationism be taught *alongside* evolution as a competing theory. In *Segraves v. California*, No. 278978 (1981), a proponent of creationism claimed that exclusively teaching evolutionary theory in public schools violated the free exercise rights of fundamentalist Christian students. Judge Irving H. Perluss found no free exercise violation if evolutionary theory were taught nondogmatically and ruled, much as Chief Justice Grafton Green had in *Scopes*, that it was unnecessary to establish the scientific legitimacy of creationism to resolve the case (Blokhuis 2017: 347).

In *Wright v. Houston Independent School District*, 366 F. Supp. 1208 (S.D. Tex. 1972), aff 'd, 486 F.2d 137 (5th Cir. 1973), the plaintiffs claimed that public schools established the religion of secularism by teaching evolution uncritically and without reference to the biblical account of creation. "In the case at bar, the offending material is peripheral to the matter of religion," wrote the court. "Teachers of science in the public schools should not be expected to avoid the discussion of every scientific issue on which some religion claims expertise."

Fourteen years later, in *Edwards v. Aguillard*, 482 U.S. 578 (1987), the Supreme Court struck down the Creationism Act, a "balanced treatment" law in Louisiana. Writing for the majority, Justice William Brennan found that

> the purpose of the *Creationism Act* was to restructure the science curriculum to conform with a particular religious viewpoint. Out of many possible science subjects taught in the public schools, the legislature chose to affect the teaching of the one scientific theory that historically has been opposed by certain religious sects. As in *Epperson,* the legislature passed the Act to give preference to those religious groups which have as one of their tenets the creation of humankind by a divine creator. The "overriding fact" that confronted the Court in *Epperson* was "that Arkansas' law selects from the body of knowledge a particular segment which it proscribes for the sole reason that it is deemed to conflict with … a particular interpretation of the Book of Genesis by a particular religious group."
>
> Similarly, the *Creationism Act* is designed *either* to promote the theory of creation science which embodies a particular religious tenet by requiring that creation science be taught whenever evolution is taught *or* to prohibit the teaching of a scientific theory disfavored by certain religious sects by forbidding the teaching of evolution when creation science is not also taught. The Establishment Clause, however, "forbids *alike* the preference of a religious doctrine *or* the prohibition of theory which is deemed antagonistic to a particular dogma." Because the primary purpose of the *Creationism Act* is to advance a particular religious belief, the Act endorses religion in violation of the First Amendment.

Disappointed with the outcome in *Edwards*, a school board in Louisiana adopted a policy that required its teachers to read the following "disclaimer" every time evolution was mentioned in one of its classrooms:

> It is hereby recognized by the Tangipahoa Board of Education that the lesson to be presented, regarding the origin of life and matter, is known as the Scientific Theory of Evolution and should be presented to inform students of the scientific concept and is not intended to influence or dissuade the Biblical version of Creation or any other concept. It is further recognized by the Board of Education that it is the basic right and privilege of each student to form his/her own opinion or maintain beliefs taught by parents on this very important matter of the origin of life and matter. Students are urged to exercise critical thinking and gather all information possible and closely examine each alternative toward forming an opinion.

In *Freiler v. Tangipahoa Parish Board of Education*, 185 F.3d 337 (5th Cir. 1999) the Fifth Circuit found this disclaimer violated the Establishment Clause by promoting particular religious beliefs. Six years later, in *Selman v. Cobb County School District*, 390 F. Supp. 2d 1286 (N.D. Ga. 2005), a district court in Georgia found a similar sticker unconstitutional because it misconstrued the "theory" of evolution as "a questionable opinion or hunch." The sticker in that case read as follows: "This textbook contains material on evolution. Evolution is a theory, not a fact, regarding the origin of living things. This material should be approached with an open mind, studied carefully, and critically considered." The court concluded "that an informed, reasonable observer would interpret the Sticker to convey a message of endorsement of religion" (Blokhuis et al. 2021: 91).

In *Kitzmiller v. Dover*, 400 F. Supp. 2d. 707 (M.D. Pa. 2005), the Dover School Board in Pennsylvania required ninth grade science teachers to read the following "Statement on Intelligent Design":

> The Pennsylvania Academic Standards require students to learn about Darwin's theory of evolution and eventually to take a standardized test of which evolution is a part. Because Darwin's theory is a theory, it continues to be tested as new evidence is discovered. The theory is not a fact. Gaps in the theory exist for which there is no evidence. A theory is defined as a well-tested explanation that unifies a broad range of observations. Intelligent design is an explanation of the origin of life that differs from Darwin's view. The reference book, *Of Pandas and People*, is available in the library along with other resources for students who might be interested in gaining an understanding of what intelligent design actually involves.

> With respect to any theory, students are encouraged to keep an open mind. The school leaves the discussion of the origins of life to individual students and their families. As a standards-driven district, class instruction focuses upon preparing students to achieve proficiency on standards-based assessments.

Science teachers in the district resisted the board's mandate, claiming that reading such a statement would mislead students. The court found that because intelligent design is a form of creationism, the board's statement violated the Establishment Clause:

> Professor Haught, who as noted was the only theologian to testify in this case, explained that in Western intellectual tradition, non-natural causes occupy a space reserved for ultimate religious explanations. Robert Pennock, [the] Plaintiffs' expert in the philosophy of science, concurred with Professor Haught and concluded that because its basic proposition is that the features of the natural world are produced by a transcendent, immaterial, non-natural being, ID [intelligent design] is a religious proposition regardless of whether that religious proposition is given a recognized religious label.
>
> It is notable that not one defense expert was able to explain how the supernatural action suggested by ID could be anything other than an inherently religious proposition. Accordingly, we find that ID's religious nature would be further evident to our objective observer because it directly involves a supernatural designer. A "hypothetical reasonable observer," adult or child, who is "aware of the history and context of the community and forum" is also presumed to know that ID is a form of creationism. The evidence at trial demonstrates that ID is nothing less than the progeny of creationism.

Supporters of intelligent design (ID) claim it is an alternative theory to evolution, not grounded in religious beliefs, as creationism is, and should therefore not be barred by the Establishment Clause from the public school science curriculum (Beckwith 2003). Proponents further claim that censoring ID might be considered viewpoint discrimination, a violation of state neutrality under the Free Exercise Clause of the First Amendment. Opponents maintain that ID is not valid since it is not grounded in the scientific method (Ravitch 2011). Since falsifiability is one of the key elements of any scientific theory, Ravitch argues that ID cannot be considered part of the scientific realm. Its underlying assumptions cannot be verified through experiment or observation, and are not subject to being rejected or modified if evidence shows that they are wrong (Sprackland 2006). Evolutionary theory, however, is readily verifiable and capable of modification since it has been subjected to innumerable tests for more than 150 years.

"To be scientific, a theory [or] hypothesis must be open to empirical confirmation or disconfirmation; it must yield testable predictions; it must explain; it must be held non-dogmatically; and it must be tentative, fallible, and self-correcting," note Adam Laats and Harvey Siegel (2016: 51). "The methodological constraints that science puts on itself serve to provide just this sort of knowledge, and thus it is scientific knowledge that is appropriate to teach in public schools," says Pennock (2006: 546).

Religion, on the other hand, "has as its most prominent feature some conception of a divine creator or of a supernatural or transcendent order in the universe" (Laats and Siegel 2016: 59–60). "Creationists are ideologues who 'know' in advance what is the 'absolutely true' answer to the question of origins … [and] it is simply not intellectually honest or professionally responsible to teach as though scientific conclusions were simply a matter of opinion," adds Pennock (2006: 548).

WHITHER THE *LEMON* TEST?

In recent years, as its conservative wing has grown, the US Supreme Court has become less committed to government neutrality vis-à-vis religion. As a result, it has been receptive to arguments for expanded government assistance to nonpublic schools and to the use of government-funded vouchers for children to attend private schools where creationism and its variants, including intelligent design, are taught as science (McCarthy 2001). In *American Legion v. American Humanist Association* (2019), a nonschool case involving the constitutionality of a 1925 war memorial in the shape of a cross originally built on private land, members of the conservative wing of the Supreme Court openly criticized the *Lemon* test. Justice Brett Kavanaugh (nominated by Donald Trump) noted that "the Court's decisions over the span of several decades demonstrate that the *Lemon* test is not good law and does not apply to Establishment Clause cases." Justice Clarence Thomas (nominated by George H.W. Bush) indicated his wish to "overrule the *Lemon* test in all contexts," while Justice Neil Gorsuch (nominated by Donald Trump) called for *Lemon* to be "shelved."

In *Kennedy v. Bremerton School District*, 597 U.S. ___ (2022), a football coach who routinely engaged in prayer on the field at the conclusion of each game filed suit after the school district declined to renew his contract. Overturning *Lemon v. Kurtzman* and with it, the *Lemon* test, the Court found the coach's prayers were private religious observance protected by the First Amendment.

CONCLUSION

In this chapter, we reviewed watershed opinions in which the US Supreme Court established constitutional limits on prayer, Bible reading, religious observances, and the use of religious books and music in American public schools. Curricular controversies in the US constitutional context tend to rely on claims based on the Free Speech Clause, the Free Exercise Clause, and the Establishment Clause of the US Constitution. To illustrate, we considered "released time" policies which allow students in public schools to earn credits for private religious instruction received offsite without violating the First Amendment.

We then explored how state legislatures, school districts, teachers, students and their parents have turned to the courts for over a hundred years in an enduring cultural conflict over the theory of evolution in public schools. American courts have blurred the lines between science and religion and between knowledge and belief in their attempts to balance children's interests in access to scientific knowledge with the First Amendment claims of fundamentalist Christian parents in an increasingly judicialized American public education system (see Curren and Blokhuis 2011; Blokhuis and Curren 2021).

As Justice Niemeyer noted in *Moss v. Spartanburg County School District Seven*, 683 F.3d 599 (4th Cir. 2012), "it is a governing principle that private religious education is an integral part of the American school system." In the American constitutional context, Justice Niemeyer continued, parents have a right to choose "whether to fulfill their compulsory education obligations by attending a secular public school or a religious private school." This right traces its origins to *Pierce v. Society of Sisters*, 268 U.S. 510 (1925), a constitutional challenge to an Oregon law that would have required parents to enroll their children in public schools only. In response, the Supreme Court famously declared that "the fundamental theory of liberty upon which all governments of this Union rest excludes any general power of the State to standardize its children by forcing them to accept instruction from public teachers only."

While US Supreme Court rulings have made it clear that biblical accounts of creation are unlikely to find their way back onto the public school science curriculum, controversies over religious curricular content will undoubtedly keep public schools at the center of American culture wars as conservative Christians turn to the courts in the hope of "turning the nation back in what they believe to be a more godly direction" (Bindewald 2015b: 88).

REFERENCES

Beckwith, Francis J. (2003), *Law, Darwinism, and Public Education*, Lanham, MD: Rowman & Littlefield.

Berrett, William E. (1998), *A Miracle in Weekday Religious Education*, Salt Lake City, UT: Salt Lake Printing.

Bindewald, Benjamin J. (2015a), "Evangelical Released Time for Religious Education in South Carolina: A Normative Case Study," *Theory and Research in Education*, 13 (1): 105–20.

Bindewald, Benjamin J. (2015b), "The Good, the Bad, and the Ugly of Released Time for Religious Education: Reflections on the Program's 100th Anniversary," *Journal of Philosophy and History of Education*, 65 (1): 81–94.

Blokhuis, J.C. (2015), "Student Rights and the Special Characteristics of the School Environment in American Jurisprudence," *Journal of Philosophy of Education*, 49 (1): 65–85.

Blokhuis, J.C. (2017), "*Teaching Evolution in a Creation Nation*, by A. Laats & H. Siegel," *Theory and Research in Education*, 15 (3): 346–9.

Blokhuis, J.C. and Randall Curren (2021), "The Judicialization of American Education," in Kathy Hytten (ed.), *Oxford Encyclopedia of Philosophy of Education*, New York: Oxford University Press. https://doi.org/10.1093/acrefore/9780190264093.013.1602.

Blokhuis, J.C., Jonathan Feldman, Michael Imber, and Tyll van Geel (2021), *Education Law*, 6th edn., New York: Routledge.

Brighouse, H. (2005), "Channel One, the Anti-Commercial Principle, and the Discontinuous Ethos," *Educational Policy*, 19 (3): 528–49.

Curren, Randall and J.C. Blokhuis (2011), "The Prima Facie Case against Homeschooling," *Public Affairs Quarterly*, 25 (1): 1–19.

Ericsson, Samuel, Kimberlee Colby, Robert Payne, and Stephen Crawford (1996), *Religious Released Time Education: The Overlooked Open Door in Public Schools*, Oak Park, IL: Center for Law and Religious Freedom of the Christian Legal Society.

Evans, Dylan and Howard Selina (2010), *Evolution: A Graphic Guide*, London: Icon Books.

Gorham, Donald R. (1934), *A Study of the Status of Weekday Church Schools in the United States*, Philadelphia: University of Pennsylvania Press.

Laats, Adam and Harvey Siegel (2016), *Teaching Evolution in a Creation Nation*, Chicago: University of Chicago Press.

McCarthy, Martha (2001), "Preserving the Establishment Clause: One Step Forward and Two Steps Back," *Brigham Young University Education and Law Journal*, 2001 (2): 271–98.

National Center for Science Education (NCSE) (2015), "Alabama Retains Its Evolution Disclaimer," March 15. Available online: https://ncse.ngo/alabama-retains-its-evolution-disclaimer (accessed August 13, 2021).

Nguyen, David H.K. (2019), "Reviving the Debate: The Constitutionality of Granting Academic Credit for Religious Instruction in Public Schools," 65th Annual Conference of the Education Law Association, Norfolk, VA.

Pennock, Robert T. (2006), "Should Creationism Be Taught in the Public Schools?" in Randall Curren (ed.), *Philosophy of Education: An Anthology*, 539–52, Malden, MA: Wiley-Blackwell.

Pennock, Robert T. (2011), "Can't Philosophers Tell the Difference between Science and Religion?" *Synthese*, 178: 177–205.

Pfeffer, Leo (1975), *God, Caesar, and the Constitution*, Boston: Beacon.

Ravitch, Frank S. (2011), *Marketing Intelligent Design: Law and Creationist Agenda*, Cambridge: Cambridge University Press.

Schlanger, Zoë (2015), "Here's the Evolution-Questioning 'Sticker' Alabama Puts on Its Biology Textbooks," *Newsweek*, September 18. Available online:https://www.newsweek.com/alabama-biology-textbooks-evolution-sticker-373662 (accessed August 13, 2021).
Shaver, Erwin L. (1956), *The Weekday Church School*, Boston: Pilgrim.
Shreve, Gene (2010), "Religion, Science, and the Secular State: Creationism in American Public Schools," *American Journal of Comparative Law*, 58 (1): 51–8.
Shulman, Jeffrey (2014), *The Constitutional Parent: Rights, Responsibilities, and the Enfranchisement of the Child*, New Haven, CT: Yale University Press.
Siegel, Harvey (1981), "Creationism, Evolution, and Education: The California Fiasco," *Phi Delta Kappan*, 63 (October): 96–7.
Sprackland, Robert George (2006), "A Scientist Tells Why 'Intelligent Design' Is NOT Science," *Education Digest*, 71 (5): 29–34.
Superfine, Benjamin Michael (2009), "The Evolving Role of the Courts in Educational Policy: The Tension between Judicial, Scientific, and Democratic Decision Making in *Kitzmiller v. Dover*," *American Educational Research Journal*, 46 (4): 898–923.

CHAPTER FOUR

Schools and Education Systems

At the Vanguard of a Rights Revolution

JONATHAN FELDMAN AND J.C. BLOKHUIS

In the United States, where the judicialization of education is most advanced (Blokhuis and Curren 2021), the federal courts have long been called upon to assess the constitutionality of state laws and policies governing schools and education systems. Because public school districts are state-funded governmental agencies, the Constitution and federal civil rights statutes regulate the relationships between public school officials, teachers, and students. Parochial and other private schools are not state agencies, so the Constitution does not apply. However, teachers and students in private schools may claim protection under federal civil rights statutes, particularly if their schools receive federal assistance.

In this chapter, we review the history of constitutional and federal civil rights litigation in American schools and education systems. Dr. Martin Luther King Jr. (1968) proclaimed that "the arc of the moral universe is long, but it bends toward justice." On the one hand, the limitations imposed by the Constitution and federal civil rights statutes on the operation of public schools and the decisions of public school officials are now quite significant. On the other hand, teachers in parochial schools can only rarely rely upon anti-discrimination laws, and one section of the Americans with Disabilities Act of 1990 (Title III) does not apply to parochial schools at all. De facto school segregation in the nation's metropolitan regions remains a huge problem. These are just a few examples of the limited scope of civil rights guarantees.

THE CONSTITUTIONAL CONTEXT

On paper, the authority of the federal government over schools and education systems in the United States is limited. The Tenth Amendment stipulates that "powers not delegated to the United States by the Constitution, nor prohibited by it to the States, are reserved to the States respectively, or to the people." Because the power to create and operate schools and education systems has never been delegated to the federal government from state governments, there is no centralized educational governance or policy-making structure in the United States. Congress has used its taxing and spending authority to impose regulations on public and nonpublic schools in exchange for federal funding. The result is an exceptionally complex system of state and local control (van Geel 1976). Rules, policies, and standards can vary from state to state, from district to district, and since the advent of charter schools, from one building (or part of a building) to the next (Blokhuis et al. 2021: 2).

Most state constitutions contain provisions requiring legislatures to establish, maintain, and support common schools. For example, Article XI, Section 1 of the New York constitution says, "The legislature shall provide for the maintenance and support of a system of free common schools, wherein all the children of this state may be educated." Article VIII, Section 201 of the Mississippi constitution indicates, "The Legislature shall, by general law, provide for the establishment, maintenance and support of free public schools upon such conditions and limitations as the Legislature may prescribe." Over the course of the common school movement in the nineteenth century, state constitutions were adopted or amended to require legislatures to establish and maintain public school systems (Butts 1978; Cremin 1980; Kaestle 1983). State legislatures created local public school districts and granted school officials the authority to raise taxes and borrow money, to acquire property, to construct buildings, to hire and fire teachers and other personnel, to purchase supplies, to prescribe the curriculum, and to discipline students. Although the specifics vary from state to state, legislation generally requires most parents to enroll their children in an approved educational program of some sort. Most states also prescribe learning aims; establish minimum requirements for high school graduation; and regulate aspects of nonpublic, charter, online, and home-based education systems (Blokhuis et al. 2021: 4). According to the National Center for Education Statistics (NCES), 47.3 million children (82 percent) attended traditional public schools in 2016, 5.8 million (10 percent) attended parochial and other private schools, three million (5 percent) attended charter schools, and 1.7 million (3 percent) were homeschooled (Wang, Rathbun, and Musu 2019).

THE FIRST AMENDMENT

In much of the English-speaking world, public funding for parochial schools is commonplace. About a third of all state-funded schools in the United Kingdom are "faith schools" (in England and Wales) or "denominational schools" (in Scotland and Northern Ireland). Apart from religious studies, students enrolled in these schools follow the national curriculum (Humanists UK 2021). In Canada, Section 93 of the Constitution Act of 1867 gives each province exclusive jurisdiction over schools and education systems, with specific rights for certain religious and linguistic minority groups (Brown et al. 2019: 8–9). Thus, in Ontario, the most populous province in Canada, there are seventy-two publicly funded school districts, including twenty-nine English-speaking Catholic boards, eight French-speaking Catholic boards, thirty-one English-speaking public boards, and four French-speaking public boards (Pardy 2016).

In the United States, the First Amendment states that Congress—the *federal* government—"shall make no law respecting an establishment of religion" (the Establishment Clause). In the early days of the American Republic, *state* government funding for parochial schools was both commonplace and widely regarded as a practical way to foster an educated citizenry (Justice and Macleod 2016). In *Cantwell v. Connecticut*, 310 U.S. 296 (1940), however, the Supreme Court found the Establishment Clause applicable to state governments. A number of Establishment Clause challenges to state support for parochial schools quickly ensued.

In *Everson v. Board of Education*, 174 330 U.S. 1 (1947), the Supreme Court considered the constitutionality of a state-funded transportation program for students enrolled in parochial schools. In this seminal case, the Court for the first time employed Thomas Jefferson's metaphor that the Establishment Clause erected "a wall of separation between Church and State." Governments could not pass laws that aided one religion, aided all religions, or preferred one religion over another. Nevertheless, the Court concluded that the transportation program was intended to help parents get their children to accredited schools and not aid for private schools per se. The following year, in *McCollum v. Board of Education*, 333 U.S. 203 (1948), the Court found a program allowing clergy members to offer religious instruction to students in public schools unconstitutional. Relying on the "no aid" principle it had enunciated in *Everson* the previous year, the Court found the program provided "sectarian groups an invaluable aid."

In *Zorach v. Clauson*, 343 U.S. 306 (1952), the Court found no constitutional violation in a program that allowed public school students to receive religious instruction offsite during school hours. To reach its conclusion, the Court abandoned the strict separation of church and state used in *Everson* and *McCollum*. Instead, the Court held that the Establishment Clause prohibited "concert or union or dependency [of] one on the other."

In *Board of Education v. Allen*, 177 392 U.S. 236 (1968), the Court established yet another standard for analyzing challenges to programs of state aid to parochial schools. The Court found that a state program through which secular textbooks were made available to students in parochial schools had neither the purpose nor the primary effect of aiding religion. Three years later, in a case involving state subsidies for the salaries of teachers employed in parochial schools, the Court developed a framework for analyzing alleged violations of the Establishment Clause in *Lemon v. Kurtzman*, 178 403 U.S. 602 (1971). Combining elements of the doctrines used in *Zorach* and *Allen*, the three-part *Lemon* test holds that a government policy or practice violates the Establishment Clause if (a) its purpose is to endorse or disapprove of religion; (b) its primary effect is to aid or inhibit religion; or (c) it creates "excessive entanglement" between church and state.

VOUCHER PROGRAMS AND THE ESTABLISHMENT CLAUSE

State-funded voucher programs that help parents defray tuition costs in parochial and other nonpublic schools have a long history in the United States. Three years after *Zorach*, influential free-market economist Milton Friedman (1955) claimed vouchers would facilitate competition among schools and better educational outcomes for all (Ben-Porath and Johanek 2019). In *Zelman v. Simmons-Harris*, 536 U.S. 639 (2002), the Supreme Court held that a voucher program in Cleveland did not violate the Establishment Clause, even though forty-six of the fifty-six nonpublic schools participating in the voucher program were parochial schools. The Court found the voucher program consistent with state neutrality under the three-prong *Lemon* test:

> In sum, the Ohio [voucher] program is entirely neutral with respect to religion. It provides benefits directly to a wide spectrum of individuals, defined only by financial need and residence in a particular school district. It permits such individuals to exercise genuine choice among options public and private, secular and religious. The program is therefore a program of true private choice. In keeping with an unbroken line of decisions rejecting challenges to similar programs, we hold that the program does not offend the Establishment Clause.

In the wake of the *Zelman* decision, some state courts ruled that their own state constitutions prohibited vouchers as governmental aid to parochial schools. In *Bush v. Holmes*, 919 So. 2d 392 (Fla. 2006), the Florida Supreme Court ruled that a voucher program violated a state constitutional requirement that education be provided through a "uniform" system of public schools. In *Cain v. Horne*, 202 P.3d 1178 (Ariz. 2009), the Arizona Supreme Court ruled that a voucher program permitting students with disabilities to attend parochial and other nonpublic schools violated its state constitution.

Voucher programs in the United States have expanded to include education tax credits and donation tax credits to offset tuition fees at nonpublic schools. Education savings accounts (ESAs) are perhaps the most complex of so-called "neo-voucher" programs, allowing parents who withdraw their children from public schools to receive a deposit of public funds into special savings accounts to defray tuition costs and incidental expenses (Blokhuis et al. 2021: 55). Traditional voucher programs such as those in *Zelman* exist in at least fifteen states, while "neo-voucher" programs including tax credits and ESAs exist in nineteen states and the District of Columbia (National Education Policy Center [NEPC] 2019).

In 2016, in *Schwartz v. Lopez*, 382 P.3d 886 (Nev. 2016), the Nevada Supreme Court found the state had improperly directed funds appropriated for K–12 public education to ESAs, in violation of the state constitution. Two years later, the Montana Supreme Court found the state's dollar-for-dollar tax credit program for donations of up to $150 to organizations offering tuition scholarships for students in parochial schools violated its state constitution. In *Espinoza v. Montana Department of Revenue*, 591 U.S. ___ (2020), the Supreme Court overruled the Montana Supreme Court, holding that the tax credit program allowing students to attend private schools could not discriminate against parochial schools. Two years later, in *Carson v. Makin*, 596 U.S. ___ (2022), the Supreme Court ruled that the exclusion of sectarian schools from a tuition assistance program in Maine violated the Free Exercise Clause.

THE FOURTEENTH AMENDMENT

In American jurisprudence, the first ten amendments to the Constitution (known collectively as the Bill of Rights) were made applicable to state governments and agencies, including public school districts, through the Fourteenth Amendment. Thus the Fourteenth Amendment is particularly important in understanding the trajectory of civil rights litigation in American schools and education systems. The Fourteenth Amendment prohibits states and state agencies from making or enforcing any law that deprives "any person of life, liberty, or property without due process of law" (the Due Process Clause), or which denies "any person the equal protection of the laws" (the Equal Protection Clause).

PARENTAL RIGHTS AND THE DUE PROCESS CLAUSE

For almost a century, the Supreme Court has been called upon to balance the interests of states in ensuring that *all* children have similar opportunities to receive the public education to which they are independently entitled against the interests of parents in directing the upbringing of *their* children. In the Progressive era, as the period from roughly 1890 to 1925 was known, freedom of contract was a substantive due process right under the Fourteenth Amendment. In *Lochner v. New York*, 198 U.S. 45 (1905), the Supreme Court struck down legislation limiting working hours for bakers based on freedom of contract principles—right of individuals to contract for goods and services and employment without government interference.

After the First World War, a number of states sought to foster the exclusive use of the English language in private and public schools. In *Meyer v. Nebraska*, 262 U.S. 390 (1923), the Supreme Court struck down a Nebraska law requiring that all instruction in private schools be in English and barring the teaching of any modern foreign language until after the eighth grade. The Court held that teachers had substantive due process rights to pursue their profession, and parents were free to contract with them for their services. The Fourteenth Amendment protected "the right of the individual to contract, to engage in any of the common occupations of life, to acquire useful knowledge, to marry, establish a home and bring up children, to worship God according to the dictates of his [*sic*] own conscience, and generally to enjoy those privileges long recognized at common law as essential to the orderly pursuit of happiness." Two years later, in *Pierce v. Society of Sisters*, 268 U.S. 510 (1925), a case involving constitutional challenge under the Fourteenth Amendment by a Catholic school and a military academy, the Supreme Court struck down a proposed Washington statute that would have violated freedom of contract principles by requiring all parents in the state to enroll their children in public schools only. The law would have put private schools out of business, depriving parents of their right to contract for private educational services.

Although the Court repudiated its *Lochner*-era decisions in *West Coast Hotel v. Parrish*, 300 U.S. 379 (1937), many American parents have continued to assert an unlimited right to direct the upbringing of their children. In *Prince v. Massachusetts*, 321 U.S. 158 (1944), the Court declared, "It is cardinal with us that the custody, care and nurture of the child reside first in the parents, whose primary function and freedom include preparation for obligations the state can neither supply nor hinder." And in *Wisconsin v. Yoder*, 406 U.S. 205 (1972), the Court declared, "However read, the Court's holding in *Pierce* stands as a charter of the rights of parents to direct the religious upbringing of their children." But the Court in *Pierce* did not recognize an exclusive or unfettered parental right. On the one hand, if states had no authority to regulate nonpublic schools, some students might be denied a quality education. On the other hand, if states had too much authority to regulate nonpublic schools, they could become indistinguishable from public schools and thus limit parental choice (Blokhuis et al. 2021: 36).

RACIAL DISCRIMINATION AND THE EQUAL PROTECTION CLAUSE

The quest for civil rights in the United States has long focused on ensuring equal treatment for members of historically disadvantaged groups in schools and education systems. Lawsuits seeking to advance civil rights focused first on desegregating public schools. These desegregation efforts served as a model for later civil rights movements based on gender, national origin, disability, sexual orientation, and first language. For teachers, the quest for equality has also included efforts to outlaw age discrimination.

Civil rights litigants seeking to desegregate publicly funded schools initially proceeded under the Equal Protection Clause of the Fourteenth Amendment, and later under a number of federal civil rights statutes, including the Civil Rights Act of 1964, Title IX of the Education Amendments of 1972, and the Americans with Disabilities Act of 1990.

Adopted in the wake of the Civil War in 1868, the Fourteenth Amendment was intended to protect the legal and political rights of African Americans. Later in the nineteenth century, in *Strauder v. West Virginia*, 100 U.S. 303 (1879), the Supreme Court invoked the Amendment for the first time to invalidate a law preventing African Americans from serving on juries. The ruling made sense because the law was obviously discriminatory. Seven years later, however, in *Plessy v. Ferguson*, 163 U.S. 537 (1896), the Supreme Court upheld a Louisiana statute requiring "separate but equal" accommodations on trains. In the wake of *Plessy*, there was no clear basis for challenging the strict racial segregation enforced on a similar basis in public schools and education systems throughout the American South.

In the 1930s, Thurgood Marshall and the National Association for the Advancement of Colored People (NAACP) challenged segregated higher education systems in a number of states. In *Sweatt v. Painter*, 339 U.S. 629 (1950), the Supreme Court agreed that white and African American law schools in Texas were unequal in terms of the reputation of their faculties, the experience of their administrations, and the employment prospects of their alumni and ordered the law school at the University of Texas to admit the African American plaintiff. In *McLaurin v. Oklahoma State Regents*, 339 U.S. 637 (1950), decided the same year, the Court found in favor of an African American plaintiff who had been assigned to a desk in an anteroom, restricted to the mezzanine of the library, and required to eat at a separate table in the cafeteria, noting that these restrictions "impair[ed] and inhibit[ed] his ability to study, to engage in discussion and exchange views with other students, and, in general, to learn his profession."

Encouraged by the success of its challenges to segregation in publicly funded colleges and universities, the NAACP turned its attention to elementary and secondary schools. The original plan was to bring suits in various states to demonstrate that white public schools had more resources than African American public schools and were therefore unequal. But in *Brown v. Board of Education*, 347 U.S. 483 (1954) (*Brown I*), the Court overruled *Plessy*, finding that segregated schools were *inherently* unequal.

RACIAL DISCRIMINATION AND THE CIVIL RIGHTS ACT OF 1964

De jure segregation occurs by law. De facto segregation occurs for individual, social, or systemic reasons. After declaring that de jure segregation violated the Equal Protection Clause in *Brown I*, the Supreme Court had to face the practical question of what remedy to order. Clearly, states with dual education systems and long histories of white supremacy would resist Supreme Court rulings mandating desegregation. In *Brown v. Board of Education*, 349 U.S. 294 (1955) (*Brown II*), the Court simply ordered local authorities to make a "good faith" effort to comply, "with all deliberate speed." The ensuing years brought very little movement toward desegregation in public schools and school systems. However, the *Brown* decision galvanized the civil rights movement, which led to the adoption of the most sweeping reform since Reconstruction, the Civil Rights Act of 1964. This federal statute prohibited race-based discrimination in programs receiving federal assistance and barred discrimination in employment on the basis of race, gender, and religion. To enforce this law, the Department of Justice filed lawsuits to integrate school systems nationwide (Blokhuis and Curren 2021). States refusing to desegregate would be denied federal education funds.

Following the enactment of the Civil Rights Act of 1964, the Supreme Court decided that states could no longer delay complying with *Brown*. In *Green v. County School Board of New Kent County*, 391 U.S. 430 (1968), the Court invalidated a "freedom of choice" attendance plan in a Virginia district because it had not worked. Virtually all students in the district continued to attend the same segregated schools. The following year, the Court effectively declared the *Brown II* era "of all deliberate speed" over in *Alexander v. Holmes County Board of Education*, 396 U.S. 19 (1969). Segregated school systems were required to make desegregation plans that were meaningful.

Though potentially effective in school districts with diverse student populations, desegregation plans would not produce diverse student populations in predominantly African American districts unless they were combined with predominantly white school districts. In *Milliken v. Bradley*, 418 U.S. 717 (1974) (*Milliken I*), a lower court attempted to impose just such an interdistrict remedy in Detroit, then as now a mostly African American urban school district surrounded by mostly white suburban districts. As only about 33 percent of students in Detroit at the time were white, the lower court sought to include suburban districts in its desegregation plan. The Supreme Court rejected this plan, holding that cross-district remedies could only be implemented where one school district had caused segregation in an adjacent district, or where district boundaries had been intentionally drawn on the basis of race. Justice Thurgood Marshall dissented, predicting that the Supreme Court's decision would hasten white flight and further divide the community. This observation proved prescient, as by 1990 metropolitan Detroit had the highest residential segregation in the nation. Its public schools and education systems continue to rank among the most segregated in the United States. Nearly seven decades after *Brown*, de facto segregation persists (Blokhuis et al. 2021: 289).

The Equal Protection Clause requires that states and state agents (including public school officials) treat students equally. Accordingly, *Brown I* prohibited de jure segregation in public schools only. It did not apply to parochial or other nonpublic schools. In the aftermath of *Brown I*, officials in some states sought to exploit this loophole by closing public schools and paying tuition for white students in private academies (Anderson 2016). In the wake of federal civil rights laws, as explained below, nonpublic schools can no longer discriminate on the basis of race in this manner. Nonetheless, when devising a school desegregation plan for a given area, courts cannot include parochial or other private schools in the remedy.

GENDER DISCRIMINATION AND THE EQUAL PROTECTION CLAUSE

While the Supreme Court's jurisprudence on race-based discrimination evolved dramatically after *Brown I*, its application of the Equal Protection Clause in gender-based discrimination cases lagged behind. This was due in large part to the Court's use of a low-level "rational basis" test in gender discrimination cases. In *Goesaert v. Cleary*, 335 U.S. 464 (1948), a Michigan law prevented women from bartending unless they were the wives or daughters of bar owners. The Court found the discriminatory law had a "rational" basis, as bar owners would surely protect their wives and daughters from the dangers any other women would face on the job.

A quarter century later, the Court abandoned "rational basis" for "close scrutiny" in *Frontiero v. Richardson*, 411 U.S. 677 (1973), recognizing that discrimination based on gender, like discrimination based on race, was "inherently suspect." To trigger close scrutiny, a plaintiff must first establish the existence of either *overt* gender discrimination (e.g., when a law or policy explicitly treats males and females differently) or *covert* gender discrimination (e.g., silent preferential treatment of men or women). If the plaintiff succeeds, the government must prove that its policy serves a compelling purpose and that treating males and females differently is substantially related to that purpose. The law or policy will be declared unconstitutional if the government cannot do so.

Gender discrimination in pay is illegal both under Title VII and the Equal Pay Act of 1963, a federal statute mandating equal pay for equal work. Differences in pay can be justified with a seniority system, a merit pay system, a system that measures pay by quality and quantity of production, or any other factor not based on sex. The most common equal pay issues in American schools and education systems concern male and female coaches.

GENDER DISCRIMINATION AND FEDERAL CIVIL RIGHTS LAWS

Several federal statutes supplement the Equal Protection Clause by prohibiting various forms of discrimination, including Title VI of the Civil Rights Act of 1964, which deals with race and ethnicity in many settings, and Title IX of the Education Amendments of 1972, which deals with gender discrimination. The Title VI statute and its implementing regulations mandate that public school officials not discriminate on the basis of race, color, or national origin. A school district that violates this law faces the loss of all federal funds. Title VI applies to all school activities, even if only one program or activity receives federal funds.

Title IX of the Education Amendments of 1972 closely parallels Title VI, and bars discrimination in public schools and education systems receiving federal aid. Like Title VI, Title IX applies to *everything* a school does, even if only one activity or program receives federal funds. Title IX permits lawsuits by both federal agencies and individuals and applies to any school that receives federal funds. Students may use Title IX to seek a court order ending the discrimination and monetary damages from the offending school district. In *Franklin v. Gwinnett County Public Schools*, 503 U.S. 60 (1992), for example, the plaintiff alleged that a former teacher had signed her out of class and sexually assaulted her on three occasions. The Supreme Court found that damages under Title IX were appropriate.

Title IX is routinely invoked in cases seeking gender equity in athletic programs in public schools. For example, in *Myers v. Board of Education of the Batavia City School District*, No. 13-CV-342S (W.D.N.Y. 2016), a federal district court approved a consent decree in a case involving a group of students alleging that their school district had provided superior facilities and equipment for its baseball programs (for boys) than it had for its softball programs (for girls). The baseball team played its home games at a professional minor league stadium, while the softball team played on a poorly maintained field with no fencing, scoreboard, dugouts, or stands. The school district agreed to build a brand new varsity softball facility and promised to ensure that boys' and girls' sports would receive equal benefits (Empire Justice 2013).

The reach of Title IX is much broader than sports, however. The extensive regulations issued to enforce Title IX prohibit gender-based admission tests, codes of conduct, counseling materials, and rules concerning marriage or pregnancy. Title IX regulations now permit sex-segregated classes and even single-sex schools under certain specified conditions. To be permissible, single-sex programs must be undertaken to improve educational achievement, meet identified educational needs, and be voluntary. "Substantially equal" single-sex programs must be offered to students of the excluded gender, and substantially equal coeducational programs must also be provided.

Nonbinary and Transgender Students

In recent years, Title IX has been invoked by nonbinary and transgender students to challenge discriminatory policies in public schools. Such policies often focus on bathrooms and locker rooms, and decree that only students who are biologically male or female may use designated facilities. In defense of such policies, school districts have argued that the legislative history of Title IX was concerned with expanding educational opportunities for girls and women, not nonbinary or transgender students. However, because the plain language of Title IX prohibits discrimination "on the basis of sex," transgender plaintiffs in *Whitaker v. Kenosha Unified School Dist. No. 1 Board of Education*, 858 F.3d 1034 (7th Cir. 2017), and *Dodds v. United States Department of Education*, 845 F.3d 217 (6th Cir. 2016), have successfully invoked Title IX protections.

In *Grimm v. Gloucester County School Board*, 972 F.3d 586 (4th Cir. 2020), a transgender male student was allowed to use the boys' room until other parents complained. Grimm then filed a Title IX suit. The Fourth Circuit affirmed transgender student rights under both Title IX and the Equal Protection Clause: "The proudest moments of the federal judiciary have been when we affirm the burgeoning values of our bright youth, rather than preserve the prejudices of the past," wrote the court. "How shallow a promise of equal protection that would not protect Grimm from the fantastical fears and unfounded prejudices of his adult community. It is time to move forward."

The following year, Grimm's school district asked the Supreme Court to decide whether public schools must allow transgender students to use restrooms consistent with their gender identity, citing an executive order signed by President Joe Biden declaring that Title IX protects students from discrimination on the basis of gender identity. The district claims both the Fourth Circuit ruling and the executive order have created a "nationwide policy" that prevents it from tailoring restroom and locker room policies that would protect cisgender students (Walsh 2021).

RACIAL AND SEXUAL HARASSMENT AND FEDERAL CIVIL RIGHTS LAWS

Racial and sexual harassment were first prohibited in the context of employment law in the United States. The implementing regulations of Title VII of the Civil Rights Act of 1964 provide that an employee may not be subjected to a racially or sexually hostile, intimidating, or offensive work environment. In addition to hostile-environment harassment, the regulations also outlaw "*quid pro quo* harassment," under which an employee is asked to exchange sexual favors for employment or benefits.

According to guidelines published by the federal Department of Education (ED), racial or sexual harassment occurs when a student experiences race-based or gender-based conduct "by an employee, by another student, or by a third party that is sufficiently severe, persistent, or pervasive to limit a student's ability to participate in or benefit from an education program or activity, or to create a hostile or abusive educational environment." Courts in recent decades have increasingly found that students may not be subjected to racial or sexual harassment by public school personnel, or even by other students. Students may seek redress for racial or sexual harassment under the Constitution, but in most cases, federal statutes offer the most effective protection. The federal courts view the racial harassment of students as a violation of Title VI and the sexual harassment of students as a violation of Title IX.

There has been more litigation over sexual harassment than racial harassment in American schools and education systems, so the law regarding sexual harassment is far more developed. The ED guidelines state that "sexually harassing conduct … can include unwelcome sexual advances, requests for sexual favors, and other verbal and nonverbal, or physical conduct of a sexual nature." If the conduct is sufficiently severe, even "a single or isolated incident of sexual harassment may … create a hostile environment." However, Title IX does not prohibit nonsexual touching or other nonsexual conduct.

Sexual conduct by one student toward another may constitute harassment if the conduct is unwelcome and persistent or severe. In *Davis v. Monroe County Board of Education*, 526 U.S. 629 (1999), the Supreme Court explained that a single act of student-on-student harassment will usually not amount to a Title IX violation. Four conditions must be met by plaintiffs in peer sexual harassment cases. The harassment must have been so severe and pervasive that it undermined the plaintiff's educational experience. It must have occurred during school hours and on school grounds. And school officials must have had actual knowledge of the harassment and been deliberately indifferent to it. In *Gabrielle M. v. Park Forest-Chicago Heights, Illinois School District 163*, 315 F.3d 817 (7th Cir. 2003), a boy harassed a kindergarten student by leaning against her while holding his crotch, unzipping and lowering his pants, and kissing, groping, and inappropriately touching her. Although the girl required counseling, neither her attendance nor her grades suffered, so the court ruled she had not been denied educational opportunities.

ENGLISH LANGUAGE LEARNERS AND FEDERAL CIVIL RIGHTS LAWS

In 1970, the Office for Civil Rights (OCR) issued a memorandum interpreting Title VI's prohibition against discrimination on the basis of "national origin" to include children unable to speak and understand English, requiring public school districts to take affirmative steps to rectify language deficiencies or risk losing all federal funds (Office for Civil Rights 1970). In *Lau v. Nichols*, 414 U.S. 563 (1974), English language learners (ELL) from China claimed that the complete lack of language assistance they had received in school violated both the Equal Protection Clause and Title VI. The Supreme Court ruled for the students, based on the OCR interpretation of Title VI. Later that year, Congress adopted the Equal Educational Opportunity Act (EEOA), which requires districts to take appropriate action to enable students to overcome language barriers.

TEACHERS AND FEDERAL CIVIL RIGHTS LAWS

In addition to students, teachers and school employees are empowered to challenge discrimination under a variety of federal statutes. Title IX of the Education Amendments of 1972 prohibits gender discrimination by schools receiving federal funding, including employment discrimination. A number of statutes address employment discrimination more explicitly. Title VII of the Civil Rights Act of 1964 forbids discrimination in public and private employment on the basis of race, gender, color, religion, or national origin. The Pregnancy

Discrimination Act of 1978 prohibits employers from discriminating on the basis of pregnancy and specifies that Title VII's prohibition of discrimination on the basis of gender includes discrimination on the basis of "pregnancy, childbirth, or related medical conditions."

Sexual and Racial Harassment

In *quid pro quo* harassment cases, an employee is asked to exchange sex for job benefits, continued employment, or promotion. In hostile-environment harassment cases, either sexual or racial, an employee is subjected to an intimidating, hostile, or offensive working environment because of the employee's sex or race. Although there have been more lawsuits involving sexual than racial harassment, the principles governing both kinds of cases are similar. To determine whether conduct is sufficiently pervasive or severe to constitute harassment, courts consider the nature of the conduct (touching is worse than verbal abuse), the frequency or repetitiveness of the conduct, and the period of time over which the conduct occurred. Thus, an isolated joke, inappropriate remark, or lewd comment is not usually sufficient to establish a hostile environment. However, ongoing sexist jokes or gender- or race-based comments about a person's appearance or behavior may constitute hostile-environment harassment (Blokhuis et al. 2021: 440).

According to the Title VII regulations, only behaviors of a sexual nature can constitute sexual harassment. In *Vermett v. Hough*, 627 F. Supp. 587 (W.D. Mich. 1986), a district court concluded that if the work atmosphere in a school or school system is unpleasant in general, or if nonsexual practical jokes are played on all faculty members regardless of gender, Title VII is not violated. Behavior by a member of the same sex is covered by Title VII as long as it fits the definition of harassment. So is harassment that is based on the victim's failure to conform to a sex-stereotype or sexual orientation. In *Bostock v. Clayton County,* 590 U.S. ___ (2020), an official with the juvenile court system in Georgia claimed he had been accused of misspending funds and fired in retaliation for joining a gay softball league. The Supreme Court held that Title VII protects employees against discrimination because of their sexual orientation or gender identity.

Teachers with Disabilities

School employees with disabilities are protected by two of the same federal laws that protect students with disabilities. The Rehabilitation Act of 1973 (Section 504) provides that "no otherwise qualified individual with a disability" shall be excluded from participation "solely by reason of her or his disability." This law applies only to programs receiving federal financial assistance. The Americans with Disabilities Act (ADA) of 1990 prohibits schools and education systems with more than fifteen employees from engaging in disability discrimination in any aspect of employment, whether or not they receive federal assistance. Both of these laws apply to people who have "a physical or mental impairment which substantially limits one or more such person's major life activities," have a record of such an impairment, or are regarded as having such an impairment.

Hostile Work Environments

A number of federal courts have ruled that the ADA protects teachers and other school personnel from harassment or a "hostile work environment" related to their disability. However, as is the case with Title IX, a plaintiff claiming disability harassment cannot prevail unless he or she can show that the harassment is pervasive and severe. Even where the alleged disability-related harassment would appear to be pervasive and severe, plaintiffs have still lost if their disability falls outside the ADA.

AGE DISCRIMINATION AND FEDERAL CIVIL RIGHTS LAWS

Intentionally treating employees differently on the basis of age is addressed by the Age Discrimination in Employment Act of 1978 (ADEA). This federal statute protects people above the age of forty from discrimination on the basis of age with regard to hiring, firing, and other terms and conditions of employment. Thus, mandatory retirement for teachers is prohibited by law. Although the ADEA recognizes that age may sometimes be a bona fide occupational qualification, it is unlikely to apply to a teaching position. In *Alberty v. Columbus Township*, 730 F. App'x 352 (6th Cir. 2018), the township replaced a 74-year-old clerk with a thirty-year-old clerk. The Sixth Circuit held this did not amount to age discrimination because the township's actions were founded upon legitimate budgetary concerns. A school charged with age discrimination may defend itself by showing that an adverse employment decision was based on considerations other than age.

STUDENTS WITH DISABILITIES AND FEDERAL CIVIL RIGHTS LAWS

By law, students with disabilities in the United States are entitled to a meaningful education. Three federal laws work in tandem: the Rehabilitation Act of 1973 (Section 504), the Americans with Disabilities Act (ADA), and the Individuals with Disabilities Education Act (IDEA).

Both Section 504 and the IDEA guarantee children with disabilities a "free appropriate public education" (FAPE) designed to meet their individual educational needs. Once these needs are ascertained, the educational services to be provided are memorialized in an "individualized educational program" (IEP). Services must be provided in the "least restrictive environment" (LRE), which means that disabled and nondisabled students should be educated together to the greatest extent possible. The input of parents is both highly desirable and legally required.

Under Section 504, if a school receives federal dollars, it must not engage in disability discrimination. This sweeping prohibition protects teachers and other school employees, as well as students. Under certain circumstances, even parents with disabilities may be covered. In *Rothschild v. Grottenthaler*, 907 F.2d 286 (2d Cir. 1990), the court found that Section 504 requires schools to provide Deaf parents with a sign-language interpreter at school-based events. Unlike the IDEA, which only covers students who need special education, Section 504 protects children who merely have "impairments," whether or not they have any difficulties with learning. Students with epilepsy, severe allergies, or attention deficit hyperactivity disorder (ADHD) are covered by Section 504 even if they might not qualify for special education under the IDEA (Blokhuis et al. 2021: 328).

Like Section 504, the ADA covers all persons who have substantial physical or mental "impairments." While Section 504 only applies to recipients of federal aid, the ADA applies to any entity that provides goods or services to the public. This includes most public and nonpublic schools.

Title II of the ADA protects individuals with disabilities from discrimination by public schools. It requires that public schools remove "architectural, communication or transportation barriers" and that they provide "auxiliary aids and services" for accessibility. Title III of the ADA prohibits discrimination by private entities that operate in the public sphere, including nonreligious private schools. Apart from employment matters, however, private religious schools are specifically excluded.

Before 2008, the Supreme Court interpreted ADA eligibility narrowly—even ruling, in one infamous case, that a truck driver who was blind in one eye was not "disabled" for ADA purposes. However, by passing the ADA Amendments Act of 2008 (ADAAA), Congress explicitly rejected these decisions and expanded eligibility for elementary and secondary students under both the ADA and Section 504 (Weber 2010).

Disability-Based Harassment

Some courts view disability-based harassment of students as analogous to racial or sexual harassment, and school officials who are "deliberately indifferent" to such harassment may be vulnerable to lawsuits. However, in *Long v. Murray County School District*, 522 Fed. Appx. 576 (11th Cir. 2013), a case involving insults and physical assaults, the court found that school officials had investigated each incident and had made a good-faith effort to adopt and implement an anti-bullying policy. Thus, the school district was not liable.

Under both Section 504 and the ADA, individuals with disabilities are not to be treated differently solely because of their disability. For example, schools cannot impose a surcharge on students with disabilities for attending after-school programs or a surcharge on parents with disabilities for the cost of making school functions accessible. Moreover, a school may not treat a student differently because of the student's association with someone who has a disability. Thus, for example, a child may not be excluded from a sports team because a sibling is HIV positive (Blokhuis et al. 2021: 334).

In addition to its nondiscrimination mandate, Section 504 (as explained above) guarantees FAPE. Although there is no requirement that a child's "Section 504 education plan" be committed to writing, Section 504 does provide for some meaningful educational rights. Under Section 504, students with disabilities are entitled to thorough evaluations of their educational needs and they must be educated to the maximum extent possible with their nondisabled peers. Consistent with its anti-discrimination focus, Section 504 requires that school facilities be made accessible. It also mandates modifications in classrooms; "reasonable accommodations" in courses (including modified teaching techniques and exam procedures); and the provision of auxiliary aids and devices (such as communication aids).

THE INDIVIDUALS WITH DISABILITIES EDUCATION ACT

In enacting the Individuals with Disabilities Education Act of 1975 (IDEA), Congress sought to go beyond anti-discrimination measures, and provide for positive rights to education for students with disabilities. The IDEA provides federal funding to help states offer a meaningful education for students with disabilities. To be eligible for IDEA funds, a state must ensure that all children with disabilities are afforded a "free, appropriate public education [FAPE] which emphasizes special education and related services designed to meet their unique needs." The FAPE requirement covers students in public schools (including charter schools) and even students who have been suspended or expelled. FAPE is not mandated, however, if parents choose to enroll a child with a disability in a parochial or other nonpublic school.

The meaning of an "appropriate" education has been tested in the courts. In *Board of Education of Hendrick Hudson Central School District v. Rowley*,

458 U.S. 176 (1982), a Deaf kindergarten student had been provided with a sign language interpreter for a two-week trial period. When the trial period was over, her parents sued, alleging that she needed the interpreter to receive a "free appropriate public education." Because the student had been making adequate progress, the Supreme Court ruled that she was not entitled to a sign language interpreter under the IDEA. *Rowley* made it clear that students with disabilities are not entitled to maximize their potential. In short, the Supreme Court rejected an "equality standard" in favor of an "adequacy standard" (Bagenstos 2017; Blokhuis et al. 2021: 343). In *Endrew F. v. Douglas County School District*, 137 S. Ct. 988 (2017), the parents of a student with autism sought reimbursement from their local school district for fees charged by a private school, claiming the district had not fulfilled its duties under the IDEA. The Supreme Court agreed, and held that "every child should have the chance to meet challenging objectives." Although students still have no right to "maximize" their potential, *Endrew F.* raised the bar beyond the level required by *Rowley* (Bagenstos 2017; Blokhuis et al. 2021: 346).

The ADA and the IDEA intersect in a number of ways. For example, the parties to an IDEA dispute must undertake a lengthy dispute resolution process. Until recently, most federal courts held that these same time-consuming procedures also applied to school-based claims under the ADA. The Supreme Court addressed this issue in *Fry v. Napoleon Community Schools*, 137 S. Ct. 743 (2017), a case involving a student who wished to bring her service dog to school. The Court held that if the essence of the case does not address FAPE issues, a plaintiff can go directly to court on her ADA claim and bypass the IDEA's time-consuming dispute resolution procedures.

The two laws may also intersect regarding the communication needs of Deaf students. In *K.M.* ex rel. *Bright v. Tustin Unified School District*, 725 F.3d 1088 (9th Cir. 2013), students who were hard of hearing were denied real-time transcriptions of class discussions by their schools. However, because the students already received a meaningful educational program, they could not argue that they had been denied FAPE under the IDEA. So they argued under the ADA instead. The Ninth Circuit agreed, citing the ADA's mandate that people with disabilities be afforded equal access and effective communication.

CONCLUSION

Progress on civil rights has not proceeded in a linear fashion in American schools and education systems, though the arc has ultimately bent toward justice. In nonpublic schools, the civil rights of students and teachers remain circumscribed. In public schools, the civil rights landscape has improved dramatically since Thurgood Marshall first began the push for equality under law in the 1930s. Racial and sexual harassment can be vigorously challenged by students and school employees in public schools. The reach of the ADA has been expanded by recent congressional amendments, while protections for LGBTQ employees and transgender students have dramatically improved in recent years. "The proudest moments of the federal judiciary have been when we affirm the burgeoning values of our bright youth, rather than preserve the prejudices of the past," wrote Justice Henry F. Floyd in *Grimm v. Gloucester County School Board*, 972 F.3d 586 (4th Cir. 2020). Thanks to the efforts of civil rights lawyers from Thurgood Marshall to Ruth Bader Ginsburg, the arc of jurisprudence in American education law continues to bend toward justice.

REFERENCES

Anderson, Carol (2016), "Burning 'Brown' to the Ground," LearningforJustice.org. Available online: https://www.tolerance.org/magazine/fall-2016/burning-brown-to-the-ground (accessed February 20, 2021).

Bagenstos, Samuel R. (2017), "Educational Equality for Children with Disabilities: The 2016 Term Cases," University of Michigan Public Law Research Paper No. 563, August 7. Available online: https://papers.ssrn.com/sol3/papers.cfm?abstract_id=3015033 (accessed February 20, 2021).

Ben-Porath, Sigal R. and Michael C. Johanek (2019), *Making Up Our Mind: What School Choice Is Really About*, Chicago: University of Chicago Press.

Blokhuis, J.C. and Randall Curren (2021), "The Judicialization of American Education," in Kathy Hytten (ed.), *Oxford Encyclopedia of Philosophy of Education*, New York: Oxford University Press. https://doi.org/10.1093/acrefore/9780190264093.013.1602.

Blokhuis, J.C., Jonathan Feldman, Michael Imber, and Tyll van Geel (2021), *Education Law*, 6th edn., New York: Routledge.

Brown, Anthony F., Marvin A. Zuker, Nicola Simmons, and Robert G. Keel (2019), *Education Law*, 5th edn., Toronto: Thomson Reuters Canada.

Butts, Robert Freeman (1978), *Public Education in the United States: From Revolution to Reform*, New York: Holt, Rinehart and Winston.

Cremin, Lawrence A. (1980), *American Education: The National Experience, 1783–1876*, New York: HarperCollins.

Empire Justice (2013), "*Myers v. Batavia City Board of Education*," EmpireJustice.org, April 5. Available online: https://empirejustice.org/resources_post/5827/ (accessed March 2, 2021).

Friedman, Milton (1955), "The Role of Government in Education," in R.A. Solo (ed.), *Economics and the Public Interest*, 123–44, New Brunswick, NJ: Rutgers University Press.

Humanists UK (2021), "State-Funded Faith Schools," Humanists UK. Available online: https://humanism.org.uk/campaigns/schools-and-education/faith-schools/ (accessed February 21, 2021).

Justice, Benjamin and Colin Macleod (2016), *Have a Little Faith: Religion, Democracy, and the American Public School*, Chicago: University of Chicago Press.

Kaestle, Carl F. (1983), *Pillars of the Republic: Common Schools and American Society, 1780– 1860*, New York: Hill and Wang.

King, Martin Luther, Jr. (1968), "Remaining Awake Through a Great Revolution," Speech given at the National Cathedral, March 31. Available online: https://kinginstitute.stanford.edu/king-papers/publications/knock-midnight-inspiration-great-sermons-reverend-martin-luther-king-jr-10 (accessed February 20, 2021).

National Education Policy Center (NEPC) (2019), "Has the Tide Turned Against Vouchers?" February 21. Available online: https://nepc.colorado.edu/publication/newsletter-vouchers-022119 (accessed February 21, 2021).

Office for Civil Rights (1970), "Identification of Discrimination and Denial of Services on the Basis of National Origin," US Department of Education, July 10. Available online: https://www2.ed.gov/about/offices/list/ocr/docs/nationaloriginmemo.html (accessed March 2, 2021).

Pardy, Bruce (2016), "Does Constitutional Protection Prevent Education Reform in Ontario?" Fraser Institute, December 1. Available online: https://www.fraserinstitute.org/sites/default/files/does-constitutional-protection-prevent-education-reform-in-ontario.pdf (accessed February 21, 2021).

van Geel, Tyll (1976), *Authority to Control the School Program*, Lexington, MA: Lexington Books.

Walsh, Mark (2021), "School District Asks U.S. Supreme Court to Decide Scope of Transgender Student Rights," *Education Week*, February 19. Available online: https://www.edweek.org/policy-politics/school-district-asks-u-s-supreme-court-to-decide-scope-of-transgender-student-rights/2021/02?ct=t (accessed March 2, 2021).

Wang, Ke, Amy Rathbun, and Lauren Musu (2019), *School Choice in the United States: 2019*, National Center for Education Statistics, September 1. Available online: https://nces.ed.gov/pubs2019/2019106.pdf (accessed February 21, 2021).

Weber, Mark C. (2010), "A New Look at Section 504 and the ADA in Special Education Cases," *Texas Journal on Civil Liberties and Civil Rights 16*, July 8. Available online: https://papers.ssrn.com/sol3/papers.cfm?abstract_id=1636483 (accessed February 20, 2021).

CHAPTER FIVE

Learning and Human Development

The Influence of the United Nations Convention on the Rights of the Child

R. BRIAN HOWE AND KATHERINE COVELL

Learning and human development are affected not only by domestic law but also by international law. This is seen clearly in the implementation of the United Nations Convention on the Rights of the Child (UNCRC) and its influence on children's learning and development in schools. The purpose of this chapter is to show how the application of the UNCRC promotes learning and human development worldwide. Our analysis proceeds as follows. First, we describe the content and significance of the UNCRC, emphasizing its role in elevating the status of children and advancing their human rights. Second, we explain the application of the UNCRC to schools. Using the framework of children's rights *to* education, *in* education, and *through* education, we analyze the meaning of these rights and review problems in their implementation. Third, after describing initiatives in education on children's rights and studies of its general effects, we examine its impact on children's learning and development. Finally, we conclude with a brief look at various countries' compliance with their legal obligations to incorporate children's rights education in schools, the obstacles to its comprehensive inclusion, and prospects for change.

THE UN CONVENTION ON THE RIGHTS OF THE CHILD

A major event occurred in 1989. The UN Convention on the Rights of the Child, the product of an international children's rights movement that had grown before and expanded significantly after the Second World War, was unanimously approved by the UN General Assembly (Becker 2020). The UNCRC was then signed and ratified by virtually all UN Member States, making it the most quickly and most widely ratified convention in modern world history. It was remarkable that so many countries, with different cultures, religions, and histories, agreed to recognize and affirm the inherent human rights of children.

The approval and ratification of the UNCRC is significant for several reasons. First, it elevates the moral and legal status of children by recognizing that children have human rights (Freeman 2020). With the endorsement of the world community, the UNCRC represents a new conception of children much different from older conceptions. In the distant past, children were regarded as the property and responsibility of their parents (Hart 1991). In the more recent past, in a more progressive vein, children were regarded as a vulnerable population of "not yets" in need of protection and care, if not by their parents then by the state (Verhellen 2015). Although their status improved, children were not yet seen as persons in their own right, with agency, value, and dignity. In the UNCRC, however, the status of children—defined as young persons under age eighteen—was elevated. Children now were conceived as bearers of rights deserving respect and support, not out of pity or compassion, but because they are persons with inherent rights (Verhellen 2015; Freeman 2020). The claim that children have human rights, and that these rights should be given priority in public policy and law, has greater force than claims based on pity or compassion.

Second, the UNCRC is significant because it provides a systematic statement on children's rights that did not previously exist in international law, and of general principles to guide in the implementation of these rights. Specific meanings would have to be worked out over time with interpretations of the UNCRC by the UN Committee on the Rights of the Child, the body responsible for monitoring implementation and issuing reports. Within the UNCRC, there are three categories of children's rights: (a) rights of provision (e.g., health care, education), (b) rights of protection (e.g., from abuse and violence), and (c) rights of participation and expression (e.g., the right to be heard, freedom of thought and expression) (Hammarberg 1990). In addition, there are four general principles to guide the application of children's rights: (a) nondiscrimination (Article 2), whereby children are to be protected from all forms of discrimination, (b) the best interests of the child (Article 3), whereby a primary consideration in all actions concerning children is their best interests, (c) the right to survival and development (Article 6), whereby children are to be supported in their overall development, not merely kept alive, and (d) participation (Article 12), whereby children have the right to express their views and their views given weight in accordance with their age and maturity. That these rights and principles are understood and endorsed by the world community is a major advance. States that have ratified the UNCRC may try to explain their shortcomings by saying they need more time or resources. But they cannot deny their official support for children's rights.

Third, the UNCRC is significant because it is legally binding (Verhellen 2015). Unlike a declaration, which is an aspirational document, a convention requires action on the part of signatory states. By ratifying the UNCRC, states parties commit to implement its provisions (if not already implemented) and to ensure that domestic laws, policies, and practices are in compliance (Article 4). Education laws and practices, for example, must ensure that children can enjoy the substance of their rights to provision, protection, and participation in schools and education systems. Implementation may be effected immediately or, as is commonly the case, it may be done progressively over time. States parties are required to demonstrate compliance or progress through a reporting system. In this system, periodic reports are sent by governments for review to the UN Committee on the Rights of the Child. The committee, in turn, upon reviewing government reports together with shadow reports from civil society organizations, provides feedback in reports called Concluding Observations. These committee reports are to be used by states parties for improving their children's rights records. The committee also provides feedback and appraisal on particular issues in a document known as General Comments, which again is to be used to move the children's rights agenda forward.

International law is not a system of "hard law" in which rights are capable of immediate enforcement through domestic courts (Abbott and Snidal 2000). Rather, it is a system of "soft law" in which rights are enforced indirectly and over time through a process of appraisal, criticism, moral goading, and political pressure. Governments typically do not want to be embarrassed by international or domestic criticism. So it is in their interests to act, if only slowly. Inadequate though their actions might be, with the UNCRC a system has been put in place to encourage governments in advancing the rights for children that did not exist before.

Finally, the UNCRC is significant because it provides social guarantees that were not present before to safeguard and promote the welfare and developmental interests of children. As philosopher Henry Shue observes, "Enjoyment of the substance of a right is socially guaranteed ... only if all social institutions, as well as individual persons, avoid depriving people of the substance of the right and some provide, if necessary, aid to anyone who has nevertheless been deprived of the substance of the right" (2020: 75). At a symbolic level, the UNCRC sends out the important message that children are persons with rights and that these rights, like all human rights, should be prioritized in schools and other social institutions. At an advocacy level, the UNCRC provides child advocacy groups with a tool and a standard for reviewing and criticizing government failings, and for pressuring governments into fuller implementation of children's rights.

And at the legal level, though far from ideal, the UNCRC requires governments to account for their effort or lack of effort on behalf of children's rights. That government authorities are required to explain themselves is a process that did not exist previously. This is a major advance for children.

One country has not yet ratified the UNCRC—the United States. Although President Clinton signed the UNCRC in 1995, it has not been ratified by the Senate, depriving American children of a major means of advancing their rights. Ratification would require a two-thirds majority vote in the Senate, which is unlikely given fears among conservative voters that the UNCRC would override national sovereignty while undermining parental authority (Todres 2006). However, states such as Vermont, cities such as Chicago, and professional organizations such as the American Psychological Association have passed resolutions in support of the UNCRC (Howe and Covell 2013). Teachers, although on a very limited basis, provide education on human rights, including children's human rights, in subjects such as social studies, which is recommended or required in forty-two states (Sirota 2017).

Although the UNCRC has not been incorporated into American law, principles found in the UNCRC are aligned with education practices in the United States. The principle of nondiscrimination, for instance, informs the practice of equal protection rights in schools and treatment of students with disabilities (Blokhuis et al. 2021); the principle of the best interests of the child guides school placement decisions such as ones for children in foster care (Legal Center for Foster Care and Education 2011). So to a certain extent, despite the failure of the Senate to ratify the treaty, the principles reflected in the UNCRC serve as standards in parts of the United States.

CHILDREN'S RIGHTS IN SCHOOLS

By ratifying the UNCRC, states parties commit themselves to the implementation of the rights of the child in schools and education systems. Following Eugeen Verhellen (2001), we can analyze the obligations of government authorities responsible for education as comprising the following three intertwined tasks.

The Right to *Education*

The first task is to provide for the child's right *to* education (Articles 28 and 29). Article 28 affirms that the child has the right to education and that authorities have the responsibility to achieve this right progressively and on the basis of equal opportunity. Primary education is to be compulsory and made available at no cost to all, and secondary education is to be made accessible to all children, with financial support if necessary. Moreover, Article 28 calls for educators to take measures to encourage regular school attendance and reduce dropout rates. But it is not simply the right *to* education that is articulated in the UNCRC, it is the right to education that promotes the learning and human development of every child.

Article 29 requires that the education of the child be directed to the: (a) "development of the child's personality, talents and mental and physical abilities to their fullest potential," (b) "development of respect for human rights and fundamental freedoms," (c) "development of respect for the child's parents, his or her own cultural identity, language and values, for the national values of the country in which the child is living, the country from which he or she may originate, and for civilizations different from his or her own," (d) "preparation of the child for responsible life in a free society, in the spirit of understanding, peace, tolerance, equality of sexes, and friendship among all peoples, ethnic, national and religious groups and persons of indigenous origin," and (e) "development of respect for the natural environment." These provisions, together with other articles in the UNCRC, point to the need for effective human rights, citizenship, and environmental education (Howe and Covell 2013: 36–7).

In its review and interpretation of Article 29, as part of *General Comment No. 1*, the UN Committee on the Rights of the Child (2001) has made a number of important comments on the aims of education. The primary aim, says the committee, is to provide for children's learning and human development in the broadest sense. Learning is to encompass not only the cultivation of the intellect but also the development of the child's personality, talents, abilities, and respect for human rights. This entails building a sense of identity and affiliation, socializing for tolerance and the appreciation of others, and broadening respect for the environment. Education is to promote personal, social, and emotional development as well as academic achievement, and the empowerment of children through enhanced self-esteem and self-confidence. This requires child-centered education within which recognition is given to the uniqueness of each child, to special needs, to the importance of relevance to their learning, and to teaching that is tailored to their evolving capacities. Finally, says the committee, learning and development require an educational process that affirms the child's rights and dignity through curricula, pedagogical methods, and school environments that support and model children's rights.

Rights in *Education*

A second task is to provide for children's rights *in* education (Articles 2, 12–15, 19, 23, 24, 27, 30, 31, 33, and 34). As notably stated by the UN Committee on the Rights of the Child (2001), the rights of children do not stop at the schoolhouse door. These rights include the "three Ps" of protection, provision, and participation. Under the UNCRC, children have the right to be protected from discrimination of any kind (Article 2), from abuse and violence (Article 19) from the illicit use of drugs (Article 33), and from sexual abuse and exploitation (Article 34); the right to be provided with health care (Article 24), material welfare (Article 27), and opportunities for play and recreation (Article 31). In addition, children with disabilities have the right to be provided with special care and education (Article 23) and minority and Indigenous children have the right to enjoy their own culture, practice their own religion, and use their own language (Article 30). And importantly, participation rights are also to be respected in schools, including the right to express views freely (Article 12) along with freedom of thought, conscience, religion, association, and peaceful assembly, subject to reasonable limits (Articles 13–15).

As emphasized by the UN Committee on the Rights of the Child (2009) in *General Comment No. 12*, and in studies of education rights (Howe and Covell 2005; Lundy, Orr, and Shier 2017), consistency with the UNCRC requires that children be provided systematically with opportunities to participate in their classrooms and their schools. In classrooms, facilitated by democratic (or authoritative) teaching styles, children should be actively involved in their learning, including the design of classroom rules. At the level of the school, children should have meaningful input—directly or indirectly through elected representatives—on committees and councils and into school planning, curricula, policies, and regulations. In line with Article 12 of the UNCRC, the focus needs to be on participatory learning that enables children to acquire knowledge and skills as valued coequal members of their learning communities.

Rights through *Education*

A third task is to implement children's rights *through* education (Articles 29 and 42). This means an education that enables children to learn about their rights, to understand their rights, and to claim their rights. Under Article 29 of the UNCRC, children's education shall be directed to the "development of respect for human rights and fundamental freedoms." This presupposes that children have knowledge and understanding of human rights, including children's rights under the UNCRC (Howe and Covell 2005: 29–35). And under Article 42, states parties have agreed "to undertake to make the principles of the Convention widely known, by appropriate and active means, to adults and children alike." In light of these two articles, the Committee on the Rights of the Child has pressed countries repeatedly to take measures to implement education on children's rights in schools (Hodgkin and Newell 2007; Howe and Covell 2013, 2020). Schools are where children can be reached on a systematic and comprehensive basis. It is insufficient merely to send messages by way of websites, social media, informational brochures, or speeches during events such as national child day. Required by the term "appropriate and active means" is comprehensive and effective rights education in schools.

HUMAN RIGHTS EDUCATION (HRE) AND CHILDREN'S RIGHTS EDUCATION (CRE)

The UN Committee on the Rights of the Child (2001) has called upon political authorities to integrate children's rights education (CRE) into all schools and education systems, including curricula, policies, practices, teaching materials, and teacher training. This call is part of a more general call by the United Nations for human rights education (HRE), as expressed in the UN Declaration of Human Rights Education and Training (UN General Assembly, Human Rights Council 2011). HRE is broader than CRE. Where CRE refers to education on the rights of the child as described in the UNCRC, the focus of HRE is on human rights more generally, as described in international human rights treaties. As explained by Howe and Covell (2020), because the subject of children's rights is of particular relevance to them, children are more engaged by education on their own human rights than on human rights in the abstract. Therefore, CRE is a useful way to introduce the general subject of rights, providing a good foundation for later HRE. However, according to the UN, *all* HRE is a positive undertaking and a key place to start is in schools, a primary setting (along with families) for socialization and for the inculcation of values and beliefs. Thus, as called for in the UN World Program for Human Rights Education (United Nations Educational, Scientific and Cultural Organization [UNESCO] 2006) in its action plan, HRE needs to be implemented throughout primary and secondary schools in all policies and practices. This is required because, under the UNCRC, it is an obligation, and under the UN Declaration of Human Rights Education and Training, it is a right.

Components of HRE

In addition to the above, the United Nations has specified that HRE should encompass education *about*, *through*, and *for* human rights, directed at "the building and promotion of a universal culture of human rights" (UN General Assembly, Human Rights Council 2011). Education *about* human rights describes the cognitive component where learners are provided with knowledge and understanding of human rights, legal mechanisms for protecting rights, values that underpin rights (such as equality and inclusion), and threats to the realization of rights (such as racism, sexism, poverty, and xenophobia). Education *through* human rights describes the process dimension: it must occur in a rights-respecting learning environment in which rights are practiced and modeled and in which the rights of all are respected. Education *for* human rights describes the empowerment dimension in which the focus is on motivating action and promoting a sense of social responsibility in support of human rights. Schools that provide such education contribute to fostering attitudes, values, and behavior in support of building a culture of human rights. Whereas education *about*, *through*, and *for* human rights has been defined as key components of HRE, they are equally important components of CRE.

Initiatives in HRE and CRE

Although initiatives to provide education *about*, *through*, and *for* human rights have been few, efforts have been made to introduce and implement HRE or CRE in some schools and classrooms. Initiatives have been undertaken by individual teachers and schools such as those working with Human Rights Education Associates in the United States; by the county of Hampshire in England, where CRE was introduced across the entire district; and nongovernmental organizations (NGOs) such as Amnesty International, with its Human Rights Friendly Schools project.

In general, evaluations of such initiatives have shown positive outcomes on children's learning or behavior (Covell and Howe 2001; Tibbitts and Kirchschlaeger 2010; Wallberg and Kahn 2011; Bajaj 2012; Činčera, Skalík, and Binka 2018; Dunhill 2018; Howe and Covell 2020; Naser et al. 2020; Quennerstedt and Moody 2020). Overall, there is evidence that CRE and HRE can impel a broader understanding of human rights, support for human rights values such as nondiscrimination, tolerance, and diversity, and more empathy and sensitivity to human rights violations. Nowhere is this more evident than in the countywide CRE initiative implemented in Hampshire.

THE RIGHTS, RESPECT AND RESPONSIBILITY (RRR) INITIATIVE

Most studies have been of individual classrooms, grades, or schools, at a particular point in time. Findings have been even more positive when comprehensive education on rights is incorporated throughout schools and sustained over time. A good illustration of the whole-school approach is the Rights, Respect and Responsibility initiative undertaken by the county of Hampshire, England, in the early 2000s (Howe and Covell 2013: 167–84). The aim of the RRR (now called Rights Respecting Education) was to improve educational outcomes for children by building a positive school climate and a shared values framework based on the UNCRC. Knowledge and understanding of children's rights and social responsibility were to provide the values framework for all classroom practices, school policies, codes of conduct, mission statements, teaching materials, and school curricula. The framework was to be put into effect across the whole school—across classrooms, across grade levels, and across school practices and policies.

Following a period of planning, pilot-testing, teacher training, and the development of resource materials, the RRR was implemented in schools with children aged four to fourteen years. The initiative was sustained over a decade during which its implementation and impact were independently evaluated. Full implementation was not accomplished in all schools. Some schools did not integrate children's rights fully into the curricula and school practices. However, those that did implement the whole-school approach provided strong evidence of success, as shown in RRR evaluation data collected over a decade (Covell, Howe, and McNeil 2008; Covell 2010; Howe, Covell, and McNeil 2010; Covell, Howe, and Polegato 2011) and as summarized by Covell (2014) and Howe and Covell (2013, 2020). Teaching materials and curricula were infused with children's rights, opportunities for the practice of participation were expanded, and school policies were adjusted to reflect and respect the rights of the child. In building a shared values framework based on rights and responsibilities, the initiative was shown to be successful in improving outcomes for children and advancing the goals of educating *about*, *through*, and *for* human rights.

Educating about, through, *and* for *Rights*

In the RRR initiative, children were educated *about* their human rights in several ways (Howe, Covell, and McNeil 2010). One was through incorporating the rights described in the UNCRC into teaching materials and curricula. This was done not only in social studies and history but in a variety of subjects. For example, the right to clean water and its necessity to health were discussed as part of a science unit on microorganisms, and the right to nutritious food was taught in mathematics by graphing distances between food supply and access. Another way was through placing posters on rights in classrooms and around the school. For instance, posters in the library explained the right to access information, and posters in the playground described the right to play and leisure. In addition, classroom charters of rights and corresponding responsibilities were developed by students and teachers together. Examples in the charters included "we have the right to be heard" and "we have the responsibility to listen to and respect other people's ideas." These charters were used to guide classroom behaviors.

The RRR evaluation data showed that the children acquired broad knowledge and a good understanding of the nature of human rights, of social responsibility as a corollary of rights, and of the importance of rights (Covell 2014; Howe and Covell 2020: 707–8). They understood their rights not as opportunities to do whatever they might wish—as many children without HRE believe—but very much as those described in the UNCRC. They also understood social responsibility as an accompaniment of rights—when every child has a right, they also have a duty to respect and uphold the rights of others. And they understood the importance of rights and rights-related values such as equality, nondiscrimination, tolerance, and inclusion. Even children as young as four demonstrated this. When interviewed, they did not talk, like older children did, about abstract concepts such as equality and justice, but their answers indicated that they had grasped the fundamental meanings. Rights, they said, mean that you "have clean water and healthy food," "play nicely," "stay safe," and get "treated properly." Across ages, children understood they were equally entitled to protection, provision, and participation; that rights were important to positive interpersonal relations; and that they, as a matter of principle, should not violate the rights of other children.

Children were educated *through* rights by a process of education, in line with the UN Declaration of Human Rights Education and Training (UN General Assembly, Human Rights Council 2011), aiming to be respectful of the rights of learners and educators (Covell 2014). RRR educators were well aware that children are educated not only through the curriculum but also the hidden curriculum. Children's rights must be practiced as well as taught. Otherwise, children will detect hypocrisy, undermining effective HRE. So the educators took measures to ensure rights-respecting schools. Some children's rights already were in practice such as through a ban on corporal punishment and a policy of inclusion for children with disabilities. But other rights such as participation were only partially provided for. So in line with Article 12 of the UNCRC, major efforts were made to expand opportunities for meaningful participation in classrooms and throughout schools. In classrooms, extensive use was made of small group discussions of issues, interactive exercises, role-play, self-directed learning, and project-based learning. In schools, participation was increased through wider student involvement on school councils, in school newspapers, and on committees, including ones dealing with budgetary allocations, spending and hiring, disciplinary decisions, and planning.

As shown in the evaluation data, the efforts had a positive impact (Covell 2010). The children made use of the expanded opportunities for participation and, as they did, they became more engaged in school. With more engagement, the rates of absenteeism and early school leaving decreased. Moreover, as reported by teachers, higher levels of participation were associated with the building of greater skills in decision-making, problem-solving, collaboration, making persuasive arguments, and critical thinking, qualities important in the practice of democratic citizenship (Howe and Covell 2005). Over time, as the children experienced participation, their levels of self-confidence, self-esteem, and feelings of efficacy increased, qualities discussed by the UN Committee on the Rights of the Child (2001) in its comments on the aims of education. Thus through a process of rights-respecting education, children developed a greater sense of value as members of their school and were enabled to exercise their rights.

Finally, children were educated *for* human rights, in line with the Declaration of Human Rights Education and Training (Covell 2014; Howe and Covell 2020). The aim of RRR educators was not only to advance knowledge and values. It was also to empower children to act and motivate them to be supportive of the rights of others. The third R in the RRR initiative was *responsibility*, a duty to speak up when rights are violated. The intention was not to achieve behavior control and obedience through a heavy emphasis on responsibility (Howe and Covell 2010). Rather, it was to advance the understanding that with rights comes social responsibility. Cultivating this understanding came through the values framework highlighted in RRR schools. It came not only through codes of behavior and the classroom charters of rights and responsibilities, but also through exercises, projects, and role-playing activities designed to raise social consciousness and increase sensitivity about the effects of rights violations on people. Role-play, for example, was used to show the effects of discrimination on immigrants with limited language skills and on persons with disabilities. Understanding the effects, the children were encouraged to think about what should be done in response. Cultivating a sense of social responsibility was also effected through the modeling of children's rights in the school. Social responsibility was modeled through the educators taking it upon themselves to facilitate children's voices and provide rights-respecting education.

The RRR evaluation data showed the initiative succeeded in raising children's social consciousness and empowering them to act *for* human rights (Howe and Covell 2020: 708–9). As reported by the teachers, the children over time were more cooperative in their behavior, more supportive of inclusion, more sensitive to the needs of other children such as those with learning difficulties, and more respectful of others in general. It was particularly noteworthy that incidents of bullying, teasing, and other inappropriate behaviors decreased significantly and were fully eliminated in some schools. This led children in increasing numbers to report a respectful, fair, and safe school climate. Thus children's understanding of social responsibility was having an effect. This was revealed also in children's advocacy outside the school. Some were motivated to contact their members of parliament for greater action on behalf of human rights, some invited politicians into their schools to be interviewed on rights-related issues, and some made rights-based presentations at city council meetings and at school board meetings. Some even became involved in organizing a well-publicized movement to declare their nearby town a rights-respecting community, with endorsements from local churches and newspapers, the police, a nearby college and university, and the Children's Commissioner for England (Covell 2014: 835). This was a remarkable demonstration of educating *for* human rights.

LEARNING AND DEVELOPMENT

Accompanying education *about*, *through*, and *for* human rights, the UN Committee on the Rights of the Child (2001) has called for a style of learning consistent with the UNCRC. As shown in studies of the impact of HRE and CRE in schools, when initiatives and programs are well designed and fully implemented, and when they have outcomes in line with the UNCRC, the style of learning is child-centered, participatory, and transformative (Tibbitts and Kirchschlaeger 2010; Wallberg and Kahn 2011; Bajaj 2012; Činčera, Skalík, and Binka 2018; Dunhill 2018; Howe and Covell 2020; Naser et al. 2020). And with this learning, again consistent with that called for by the committee, is education directed at children's holistic development.

In introducing CRE into schools, educators had to decide which pedagogical approaches to use. They were well aware of the deficiencies of the traditional teacher-centered approach, which Freire (2018) labeled the banking model of education. According to this model, teachers deposit information and children passively receive the deposits, then memorize and repeat the material on tests. This would achieve only a superficial understanding of rights, and be in contradiction to the UNCRC principle of respecting children and their rights. To deepen understanding, and be in accord with the UNCRC, the educators recognized the need for child-centered and participatory learning.

In child-centered education, the child—not the teacher—is at the center of learning (Entwistle 2012). This is premised on the view that to engage children and optimize their learning, it is necessary to focus on the happiness and interests of the child and to allow for the child's creativity and a certain measure of freedom. The aim is to teach students, not subjects. The role of the teacher, while very important, is to facilitate learning, not to control, instruct, and drill material into children's heads. In deciding to use child-centered pedagogy, the CRE educators worked very much in the tradition of earlier advocates of child-centered education. But their reasons for doing so focused less on promoting the child's happiness and more on respecting the child's dignity and rights, the key to more effective learning. The CRE educators also understood the need for participatory learning as part of child-centered education. They understood that respect for the child's dignity and rights requires that opportunities be provided for children's active participation in their learning. It would be a great contradiction—and one noticed by children—to introduce CRE in schools while using authoritarian styles of teaching and learning. So in line with the UNCRC, the educators needed to facilitate participation through such means as interactive exercises and projects in the classroom and involvement in councils and committees in the school.

In HRE and CRE initiatives in schools, student participation did not mean, of course, that children had a right to self-determination or full autonomy in decision-making. But in accordance with Article 12 of the UNCRC, and as a sign of respect, it did mean that children—even very young children—were entitled to be consulted in matters affecting them (Doek 2020: 264–5). Moreover, as a further sign of respect, it meant that the views of children were to be listened to, given weight in accord with age and maturity, and acted upon, where appropriate (Lundy 2007). So for the educators, participatory learning was a necessary part of HRE. It was important also, based on research known to the educators, because of its contribution to positive learning outcomes (Covell 2010). Children learn better when they are engaged in school and experience a respectful and welcoming school environment. Active participation is a vehicle through which children become engaged in school and develop a sense of belonging.

Transformative learning is another part of well-implemented HRE. In her analysis of HRE, Tibbitts (2005, 2017) describes transformative learning as a process of developing critical consciousness and cultivating agency in the learner with the aim of taking action in support of human rights. It is a process that involves inviting the learner to critically reflect on injustice and oppression and, based on this reflection, motivating the learner to take action against injustice and violations of rights. The learner is transformed from a thinker to a doer, and from a neutral observer or mild supporter of human rights to a committed activist. This is very much a case of educating *for* rights. For Tibbitts, this kind of learning rarely occurs in schools and formal education. To the extent that HRE is practiced in schools, it tends to be didactic in nature. In contrast, transformative learning most often occurs in nonformal education settings such as in refugee camps and rural villages in the developing world. Educators are typically members of NGOs or local community groups and learners are adults or youth experiencing marginalization, oppression, and violations of their rights.

However, as some research indicates, transformative learning is possible in schools when HRE is well designed and well implemented. Children in schools need not become full-blown social activists. After all, they are in school to receive an education in preparation for higher education or for work and life as adult members of society. But through HRE, children—including very young children—can be empowered to stand up for the rights of others and take action, when rights are being violated.

In addition to the RRR initiative in Hampshire, there are many illustrations of transformative CRE worldwide. As found in a study of a Canadian preschool, for example, children with CRE shifted from a "me" to a "we" consciousness, developing a sense of social responsibility in support of the rights of others, which was reflected in their social behavior (Wallberg and Kahn 2011). In a primary school in England, children were empowered to protect and promote the rights of other children, as shown in more positive social relations and reduced negative behavior such as exclusionary and violent action against others (Dunhill 2018). In a secondary school in the United States, older youth became engaged in social action projects such as raising human rights consciousness and addressing the problem of homelessness in their local community (Spreen and Monaghan 2017). In secondary schools in the Republic of Georgia, children developed feelings of agency, became more supportive of the rights of others (e.g., children with disabilities), and became more motivated to take action in support of rights (Činčera, Skalík, and Binka 2018). Transformative learning was particularly noticeable in parts of India, as found in a study of schools in the southern state of Tamil Nadu (Bajaj 2012). Inspired by CRE, the children in the study developed a strong sense of agency, empowering them to intervene in situations of abuse or violence (e.g., trying to stop a family from killing a female baby, as traditionally practiced), to report or threaten to report abuse, to spread awareness of human rights in the community, and to undertake personal change (e.g., a brother insisting that he and his sister be given equal chores in the family, contrary to traditional male privilege).

Finally, another outcome of CRE is the broadening of children's development. Historically, the main focus of schools was on children's cognitive development. Although some attention was given to sports and physical education, the primary aim was to promote academic achievement and skills in literacy and numeracy. Little consideration was given to children's personal, social, and emotional development. However, in more recent history, with the influence of child-centered education, greater attention was given to the child's holistic—social, emotional, and academic—development and to their overall well-being. Schools were now urged to incorporate social and emotional learning and focus on the whole child. This was the perspective of the UN Committee on the Rights of the Child (2001) in calling for rights-based schooling and HRE directed at children's holistic development. The committee's perspective was very much in accord with education research showing the interconnection between children's academic, personal, social, and emotional development and the importance of all of these areas to effective learning (Jones and Kahn 2017). There was a consensus in the research that strengths or weaknesses in one area promote or hinder development in other areas. Healthy social development, for example, which includes mutual respect, the ability to cooperate, and the demonstration of compassion, assists with academic progress. Healthy emotional development, which encompasses the ability to control emotions, feelings of empathy, and the ability to understand the emotions and perspectives of others, does the same.

Studies have shown that HRE makes a significant contribution to children's holistic development. To begin with, they show that, with HRE, there is a continuation or even improvement in children's academic development. For example, as reported in the RRR evaluation data, academic achievement among children in Hampshire's RRR schools actually increased (Howe and Covell 2013: 178–9). Engaged by their school and motivated to learn, the children progressed remarkably well academically, as measured by marked increases in their achievement scores on standardized assessment tests since the introduction of the RRR. Furthermore, the greatest academic progress was made by socially disadvantaged children going to schools in lower income areas (Covell, Howe, and Polegato 2011). Contrary to the usual occurrence of a major achievement gap between advantaged and disadvantaged children, the gap was profoundly lessened with the implementation of HRE. Over time, the socially disadvantaged children became more engaged in school, as shown in a marked decline in dropout and absentee rates, and more successful in their academic work.

Studies on HRE have also pointed to positive outcomes in children's personal, social, and emotional development. In furthering personal development, a common finding was increased self-esteem and self-confidence and an enhanced sense of agency and empowerment (Bajaj 2012; Howe and Covell 2013; Činčera, Skalík, and Binka 2018; Dunhill 2018; Spreen and Monaghan 2017; Naser et al. 2020). As evidence of social development, the children were reported to be more cooperative and respectful in their social relationships, and better at settling conflicts. For example, in the Canadian preschool, the children were found to be more socially connected and to use the discourse of rights and responsibilities to solve disputes (Wallberg and Kahn 2011). Similarly, in an American primary school, the children became more comfortable in working out disagreements on group projects (Naser et al. 2020). And as evidence of emotional development, accompanying the positive social relationships, the children were better able to manage their emotions and show appropriate empathy. In the Canadian preschool, for instance, there was a marked improvement in emotion regulation (Wallberg and Kahn 2011). And in the RRR schools, as the children came to understand the importance of rights and the injustice of rights violations, they showed more empathy for victims of injustice and more sensitivity to other children's needs (Covell 2014: 834–5).

Finally, the development of respect for the natural environment was another outcome of HRE for children. Although rare, some CRE programs provide for both the child's participation rights and education on the environment. In the Atlantic provinces of Canada, for instance, there have been successful partnerships between schools and the Brilliant Labs initiative, featuring participatory learning and projects on climate change and environmental degradation (Lingley and Wong 2020). In their classes, children first identified an environmental problem in their school or community that they wished to address. They then were provided with a protocol and supportive learning environment and encouraged to construct a solution. Working in groups, and pursuing their knowledge, interests, and skills, the children worked toward sustainable and environmentally responsible solutions. As reported by Lingley and Wong (2020), the outcomes were impressive. They included a class of children creating a micro business for edible spoons to reduce fast food waste. Another class developed eco-friendly water filtration systems. Another class, having learned about wetland ecosystems, combined drones, 3D design and printing, robotics, and coding to collect water samples in hard-to-reach areas. These were striking examples of the benefits of participatory learning and the development of understanding and respect for the environment.

These studies show that well-designed and well-implemented education on children's rights makes a significant contribution to children's holistic development. Not only do children progress academically but they also progress personally, socially, and emotionally. With this development, the aims of education, as stated by the UN Committee on the Rights of the Child (2001), are closer to being realized. CRE in schools that practice and model rights shows a path forward in education directed at developing the child's personality, talents, and abilities, developing respect for human rights, building a sense of identity and affiliation, socializing for tolerance and the appreciation of others, and enhancing respect for the environment.

COMPLIANCE, OBSTACLES, AND PROSPECTS FOR CHANGE

The one area in which there are signs of states parties' compliance with their legal education obligations is seen in children's rights *to* education. Although there is variation by country, the vast majority of primary school-age children—over 90 percent—are now enrolled in school (United Nations Children's Fund [Unicef] 2019). Even in sub-Saharan Africa, where the challenges are the greatest, the enrollment rate is almost 80 percent. However, even here significant problems remain. One is access to education. Even though primary education is supposed to be free, there are major barriers to enrolling or continuing in school, especially in the developing world. These include poverty, the direct and indirect costs of school, cultural beliefs, disability, and in some cases, violence or the threat of violence (Lundy, Orr, and Shier 2017). Another problem is that contrary to the principle of equal opportunity, there is a significant socioeconomic achievement gap in education. Socially disadvantaged children are less likely to learn and achieve to their fullest potential and more likely to have higher rates of school absenteeism, early school leaving, and school failure (Howe and Covell 2013: 53–9). This gap actually has been increasing globally over the past several decades, assisted by disproportionately fewer resources given to schools in poor areas (Chmielewski 2019).

The continuing practice of corporal punishment in schools also poses a threat to children's access to education that allows for their learning and development (Gershoff 2017). Despite a growing international movement against the practice and a legal ban against its use in a growing number of countries, corporal punishment in schools continues to be lawful in sixty-seven countries (Global Initiative to End All Corporal Punishment of Children 2020).

A further problem, as pointed to by the Committee on the Rights of the Child and in various studies, is the attention given in many education systems to excessive competition, high-stakes testing, rote learning, and grade inflation (Hodgkin and Newell 2007; Howe and Covell 2013; Bjork 2015). The preoccupation with competition and testing, as illustrated in the experience of Japan, generates undue stress in children and compromises the holistic development of the child's personality, talents, and abilities (Bjork 2015). So while there is evidence of some compliance with advancing the right to education, serious problems remain.

The general lack of compliance is seen in the global paucity of rights education. Contrary to the repeated calls of the Committee on the Rights of the Child to fully and appropriately integrate HRE and CRE into schools, and contrary to those of the UN World Program for Human Rights Education, rights education has not been widely implemented in schools. Despite important initiatives on HRE and CRE in classrooms, schools, and school districts, most governments have not developed national plans of action, few have incorporated education on children's rights into education legislation and into school curricula, and few have integrated HRE into teaching materials and teacher training (Jerome et al. 2015; Howe and Covell 2020). In the words of Jonathan Todres (2018), reviewing the situation in the United States, there has been a failure in mainstreaming education on human rights. There has been little effort by governments to develop national plans of action, to incorporate HRE into education legislation and school curricula, and to integrate HRE into teaching materials and teacher training. This global lack of action remains a problem. What exists is a jumble of limited and scattered initiatives in classrooms, schools, and school districts. Most often these are limited to some inclusion of human rights information in existing social studies, history, or civics courses. And importantly to the extent that HRE has been put into practice, methods of teaching have not been consistent with children's rights. Rather, they have been largely didactic and teacher-centered, with the focus on lecturing, rote learning, and memorization for tests (Tibbitts 2017). This approach is unsustainable and antithetical to that called for by the UN Committee on the Rights of the Child (2009).

From the perspective of learning and development, a particularly serious impediment to children's learning and development is evidenced by the lack of compliance with providing for children's participation rights. As noted by the UN Committee on the Rights of the Child (2009), in many classrooms and schools there is continuing authoritarianism, undermining the expression of children's views and their right to be heard. Many teachers persist in authoritarian pedagogy and school authorities deny or minimize children's participation in school decision-making. In addition, education research shows that children continue to be given low status in school hierarchies, to be excluded from decision-making in areas such as discipline and school conduct, and to feel that they are not genuinely respected in school (Lundy and Brown 2020). Finally, as also found in research, even in schools incorporating the principle of giving children a voice, school authorities fail to understand and practice the participation rights of the child (Lundy 2007). They fail to appreciate that "voice is not enough"; participation requires creating opportunities for voice, serious listening to children, giving weight to the views of children in accord with age and maturity, and acting upon the views of children, as appropriate. Many schools have failed to provide participation in its full meaning.

The UN Committee on the Rights of the Child (2001, 2009) also expressed concern about the failure of many schools to build a positive school environment for learning. Problems in the school environment such as abuse, bullying, discrimination, and violence put children's learning and achievement seriously at risk. The problem of violence against children more generally led the committee to request that the United Nations investigate the issue. This resulted in the 2006 UN Study on Violence Against Children, the creation of the Office of the Special Representative of the UN Secretary-General on Violence Against Children, and subsequent reports by the Special Representative on the problem of violence (Pais 2020).

In the report on school violence by the Office of the Special Representative of the UN Secretary-General on Violence Against Children (2012), and in other studies of the issue (UNESCO 2017; Pais 2020), it was found that school violence remains a widespread and serious problem globally. Defined broadly to include physical and verbal bullying, cyberbullying, schoolyard fighting, sexual abuse, gang violence, intimidation, and harassment, it affects children such that they find school an ordeal rather than a positive experience. It also was found that those committing violence are not only peers but also teachers and school personnel in forms such as intimidation, verbal abuse, and corporal punishment. The effect is to create an unwelcoming and negative school environment, a well-known risk factor for learning and development.

Behind the lack of compliance and effort has been the lack of commitment to HRE by political and education authorities (Howe and Covell 2020). Public pressure could be a force in bringing about government action, but such pressure has been largely absent. A reason it has been absent is the influence of beliefs and ideologies at odds with HRE.

First, there is a persistent belief in traditional teacher-centered education (Entwistle 2012). According to its subscribers, child-centered and participatory education, including CRE, is to be resisted because it caters to the whims of children who are in need of authority, discipline, and the direction of teachers. What is required is teacher instruction and a return to the basics in education. Second, there is the belief in parental rights where children's rights and CRE are seen as a danger to parental authority (Covell, Howe, and McGillivray 2017). The influence of this belief is seen especially in the American refusal to ratify the UNCRC, which was based in part on concern that children's rights would override the rights of parents (Todres 2006). Third, there is the ideology of neoliberalism (Hill and Kumar 2009), with its focus on market-based approaches to education, student and school performance, competition, standardized testing, and zero tolerance approaches to student misbehavior. Within the neoliberal framework, initiatives such as CRE are to be rejected because they undermine or distract from realizing these goals.

Fourth, there is the ideology of right-wing populism in the United States, Hungary, Poland, and elsewhere (Howe and Covell 2021). In an ideology that prizes authoritarianism and disparages immigrants and members of other marginalized and minority groups, CRE is unwelcome. Empowering children to take action to support the rights of "others" is anathema to right-wing populists. Together, the influence of these different beliefs and ideologies poses serious obstacles for CRE.

Another obstacle has been the general lack of enthusiasm for CRE within schools and education systems. If governments did decide to consider introducing comprehensive CRE in schools, they would want the support and cooperation of teachers and education authorities, especially in the many decentralized education systems of the world. The fact is there has not been widespread support. Research shows that many teachers in many countries are disinterested or are ambivalent about or even opposed to CRE in schools (Covell 2014; Howe and Covell 2021). One reason for this is a lack of teacher training. Without knowledge and understanding of the importance of children's human rights, teachers are less inclined to be supportive. Another reason, for some teachers, is that CRE would lead to disruption in their classrooms, loss of their authority, and loss of their ability to control students. They have misgivings about participatory pedagogy and children being overly demanding of their rights. A second reason for teacher disinterest is the perceived lack of need. In response to the question of a possible introduction of CRE in schools, teachers sometimes reply, "We're already doing that!" (Flowers 2017: 328).

They see CRE much the same as what they are already doing in education on social justice, citizenship, anti-bullying, or anti-racism. They fail to see CRE as a values framework and a foundation for these other types of social education. A third reason is that many teachers understand CRE as something that would have to be added to an already overwhelming workload. Teacher training could correct this and other misconceptions but it is in very short supply. For example, learning that CRE is to be integrated into existing teaching rather than added to it, and learning that CRE can improve student–teacher relationships and student behavior and achievement must be expected to lessen concerns.

These obstacles pose a formidable challenge to CRE. Thus there is unlikely to be implementation of comprehensive CRE in the near future. But in the long term, the prospects are better. At the end of the Second World War, there was no international requirement for HRE, no global movement for HRE, and virtually no CRE in classrooms and schools. However, over time, a duty to provide CRE has been incorporated into numerous international human rights treaties, including the UNCRC and the Declaration on Human Rights Education and Training. A significant movement for CRE has gathered, and pressure for its implementation has steadily grown. And numerous initiatives provide models and hope for CRE on a wider scale. It is true that developments have been sporadic, imperfect, and sometimes disappointing. But it also is true that education about, through, and for human rights, including children's human rights, is much greater now than it was a few decades ago. Systematic and comprehensive CRE will take considerable time. But momentum continues to build.

REFERENCES

Abbott, Kenneth W. and Duncan Snidal (2000), "Hard and Soft Law in International Governance," *International Organization*, 54 (3): 421–56.

Bajaj, Monisha (2011), "Teaching to Transform, Transforming to Teach: Exploring the Role of Teachers in Human Rights Education in India," *Educational Research*, 53 (2): 207–21.

Bajaj, Monisha (2012), "From 'Time Pass' to Transformative Force," *International Journal of Educational Development*, 32 (1): 72–80.

Becker, Jo (2020), "The Evolution of the Children's Rights Movement," in Jonathan Todres and Shani M. King (eds.), *The Oxford Handbook of Children's Rights Law*, 33–48, Oxford: Oxford University Press.

Bjork, Christopher (2015), *High-Stakes Schooling*, Chicago: University of Chicago Press.

Blokhuis, J.C., Jonathan Feldman, Michael Imber, and Tyll van Geel (2021), *Education Law*, 6th edn., New York: Routledge.

Chmielewski, Anna K. (2019), "The Global Increase in the Socioeconomic Achievement Gap, 1964–2015," *American Sociological Review*, 84 (3): 517–44.

Činčera, Jan, Jan Skalík, and Bohuslav Binka (2018), "One World in Schools," *Cambridge Journal of Education*, 48 (6): 769–86.

Covell, Katherine (2010), "School Engagement and Rights-Respecting Schools," *Cambridge Journal of Education*, 40 (1): 39–51.

Covell, Katherine (2014), "Awareness and Education in Human Rights," in Anja Mihr and Mark Gibney (eds.), *The Sage Handbook of Human Rights*, 821–39, Los Angeles: Sage.

Covell, Katherine and R. Brian Howe (2001), "Moral Education Through the 3 Rs: Rights, Respect and Responsibility," *Journal of Moral Education*, 30 (1): 31–42.

Covell, Katherine, R. Brian Howe, and Anne McGillivray (2017), "Implementing Children's Education Rights in Schools," in Martin D. Ruck, Michele Peterson-Badali, and Michael Freeman (eds.), *Handbook of Children's Rights: Global and Multidisciplinary Perspectives*, 296–311, New York: Routledge.

Covell, Katherine, R. Brian Howe, and Justin K. McNeil (2008), "If There's a Dead Rat, Don't Leave It: Young Children's Understanding of their Citizenship Rights and Responsibilities," *Cambridge Journal of Education*, 38 (30): 321–39.

Covell, Katherine, R. Brian Howe, and Jillian L. Polegato (2011), "Children's Human Rights Education as a Counter to Social Disadvantage: A Case Study from England," *Educational Research*, 53 (2): 193–206.

Doek, Jaap E. (2020), "Child Participation," in Jonathan Todres and Shani M. King (eds.), *The Oxford Handbook of Children's Rights Law*, 257–78, Oxford: Oxford University Press.

Dunhill, Ally (2018), "Does Teaching Children About Human Rights Encourage Them to Practice, Protect and Promote the Rights of Others?" *Education 3–13: International Journal of Primary, Elementary and Early Years Education*, 46 (1): 16–26.

Entwistle, Harold (2012), *Child-Centered Education*, New York: Routledge.

Flowers, Nancy (2017), "Afterword," in M. Bajaj (ed.), *Human Rights Education: Theory, Research, Praxis*, 317–33, Philadelphia: University of Pennsylvania Press.

Freeman, Michael (2020), "Taking Children's Rights Seriously," in Jonathan Todres and Shani M. King (eds.), *The Oxford Handbook of Children's Rights Law*, 49–69, Oxford: Oxford University Press.

Friere, Paulo (2018), *Pedagogy of the Oppressed*, 50th anniversary edn., London: Bloomsbury.

Gershoff, Elizabeth T. (2017), "School Corporal Punishment in Global Perspective: Prevalence, Outcomes, and Efforts at Intervention," *Psychology, Health and Medicine*, 22 (1): 224–39.

Global Initiative to End All Corporal Punishment of Children (2020), "Corporal Punishment in Schools." Available online: https://endcorporalpunishment.org/schools/ (accessed January 20, 2021).

Hammarberg, Thomas (1990), "The U.N. Convention on the Rights of the Child – and How to Make It Work," *Human Rights Quarterly*, 12 (1): 97–105.

Hart, Stuart N. (1991), "From Property to Person Status: Historical Perspective on Children's Rights," *American Psychologist*, 46 (1): 53–9.

Hill, Dave and Ravi Kumar (2009), "Neoliberalism and Its Impacts," in Dave Hill and Ravi Kumar (eds.), *Global Neoliberalism and Education and Its Consequences*, 12–29, New York: Routledge.

Hodgkin, Rachel and Peter Newell (2007), *Implementation Handbook for the Convention on the Rights of the Child*, New York: Unicef.

Howe, R. Brian and Katherine Covell (2005), *Empowering Children: Children's Rights Education as a Pathway to Citizenship*, Toronto: University of Toronto Press.

Howe, R. Brian and Katherine Covell (2010), "Miseducating Children about Their Rights," *Education, Citizenship and Social Justice*, 5 (2): 91–102.

Howe, R. Brian and Katherine Covell (2013), *Education in the Best Interests of the Child: A Children's Rights Perspective on Closing the Achievement Gap*, Toronto: University of Toronto Press.

Howe, R. Brian and Katherine Covell (2020), "Human Rights Education: Education About Children's Rights," in Jonathan Todres and Shani M. King (eds.), *The Oxford Handbook of Children's Rights Law*, 699–717, Oxford: Oxford University Press.

Howe, R. Brian and Katherine Covell (2021), "Meeting the Challenge of Populism to Children's Rights: The Value of Human Rights Education," *Journal of Human Rights Practice*, 13 (1): 45–66.

Howe, R. Brian, Katherine Covell, and Justin K. McNeil (2010), "Implementing Children's Human Rights Education in Schools," *Improving Schools*, 13 (2): 117–32.

Jerome, Lee, Lesley Emerson, Laura Lundy, and Karen Orr (2015), *Teaching and Learning about Child Rights: A Study of Implementation in 26 Countries*, Geneva: Unicef.

Jones, Stephanie M. and Jennifer Kahn (2017), "The Evidence Base for How Learning Happens: A Consensus on Social, Emotional, and Academic Development," *American Educator*, 41 (4): 16–43.

Legal Center for Foster Care and Education (2011), "School Stability under Fostering Connections," *Child Law Practice*, 30 (6): 92–4.

Lingley, Jacob and John Wong (2020), "Making Green Solutions, Converging Classroom Projects with the UN Sustainable Development Goals and Canada's 2030 Agenda," *Education Canada*, March 5. Available online: https://www.edcan.ca/articles/green-solutions/ (accessed June 11, 2022).

Lundy, Laura (2007), "Voice is Not Enough: Conceptualizing Article 12 of the United Nations Convention on the Rights of the Child," *British Education Research Journal*, 33 (6): 927–42.

Lundy, Laura and Amy Brown (2020), "Revisiting the Three R's in Order to Realize Children's Educational Rights Relationships, Resources, and Redress," in Jonathan Todres and Shani M. King (eds.), *The Oxford Handbook of Children's Rights Law*, Oxford: Oxford University Press. https://doi.org/10.1093/oxfordhb/9780190097608.013.20.

Lundy, Laura, Karen Orr, and Harry Shier (2017), "Children's Education Rights: Global Perspectives," in Martin D. Ruck, Michele Peterson-Badali, and Michael Freeman (eds.), *Handbook of Children's Rights: Global and Multidisciplinary Perspectives*, 364–80, New York: Routledge.

Naser, Shereen C., Jorge Verlenden, Prerna G. Arora, Bonnie Nastasi, Lindsay Braun, and Rokeoshia Smith (2020), "Using Child Rights Education to Infuse a Social Justice Framework into Universal Programming," *School Psychology International*, 41 (1): 13–36.

Office of the Special Representative of the Secretary-General on Violence Against Children (2012), *Tackling Violence in Schools: A Global Perspective*, New York: United Nations.

Pais, Marta Santos (2020), "Placing Children's Freedom from Violence at the Heart of the Policy Agenda," in Jonathan Todres and Shani M. King (eds.), *The Oxford*

Handbook of Children's Rights Law, Oxford: Oxford University Press. https://doi.org/10.1093/oxfordhb/9780190097608.013.16.

Quennerstedt, Ann and Zoe Moody (2020), "Educational Children's Rights Research 1989–2019: Achievements, Gaps and Future Prospects," *International Journal of Children's Rights*, 28 (1): 183–208.

Shue, Henry (2020), *Basic Rights: Subsistence, Affluence, and U.S. Foreign Policy*, 40th anniversary edn., Princeton, NJ: Princeton University Press.

Sirota, Sandra (2017), "The Inconsistent Past and Future of Human Rights Education in the United States," *Prospects*, 47 (1–2): 101–17.

Spreen, Carol Anne and Chrissie Monaghan (2017), "Leveraging Diversity to Become a Global Citizen: Lessons for Human Rights Education," in Monisha Bajaj (ed.), *Human Rights Education: Theory, Research, Praxis*, 291–316, Philadelphia: University of Pennsylvania Press.

Tibbitts, Felisa (2005), "Transformational Learning and Human Rights Education: Taking a Closer Look," *Intercultural Education*, 16 (2): 107–13.

Tibbitts, Felisa (2017), "Evolution of Human Rights Education Models," in M. Bajaj (ed.), *Human Rights Education: Theory, Research, Praxis*, 69–95, Philadelphia: Pennsylvania University Press.

Tibbitts, Felisa and Peter G. Kirchschlaeger (2010), "Perspectives of Research on Human Rights Education," *Journal of Human Rights Education* 2 (1): 8–29.

Todres, Jonathan (2006), "Analyzing the Opposition to U.S. Ratification of the U.N. Convention on the Rights of the Child," in Jonathan Todres, Mark E. Wojcik, and Cris Revaz (eds.), *The United Nations Convention on the Rights of the Child: An Analysis of Treaty Provisions and Implications of U.S. Ratification*, 19–31, Leiden: Brill.

Todres, Jonathan (2018), "The Trump Effect, Children, and the Value of Human Rights Education," *Family Court Review*, 56 (2): 331–43.

UN Committee on the Rights of the Child (2001), *General Comments: No. 1: The Aims of Education*, UN/CRC/GC/2001/1, Geneva: United Nations.

UN Committee on the Rights of the Child (2009), *General Comments: No. 12: The Right of the Child to be Heard*, UN/CRC/GC/2009/12, Geneva: United Nations.

UN General Assembly, Human Rights Council (2011), *United Nations Declaration on Human Rights Education and Training*. Available online: https://documents-dds-ny.un.org/doc/RESOLUTION/GEN/G11/124/78/PDF/G1112478.pdf?OpenElement (accessed January 20, 2021).

United Nations Children's Fund (Unicef) (2019), "Primary Education," October. Available online: https://data.unicef.org/topic/education/primary-education/ (accessed January 20, 2021).

United Nations Educational, Scientific and Cultural Organization (UNESCO) (2006), *Plan of Action: UN World Programme for Human Rights Education*. Available online: https://unesdoc.unesco.org/ark:/48223/pf0000147853 (accessed January 20, 2021).

United Nations Educational, Scientific and Cultural Organization (UNESCO) (2017), *School Violence and Bullying: Global Status Report*, Paris: UNESCO.

Verhellen, Ellen (2001), "Facilitating Children's Rights in Education," in Stuart N. Hart, Cynthia Price Cohen, Martha Farrell Erickson, and Malfrid Grude Flekkoy (eds.), *Children's Rights in Education*, 179–90, London: Jessica Kingsley.

Verhellen, Ellen (2015), "Convention on the Rights of the Child," in Wouter Vandenhole, Ellen Desmet, Didier Reynaert, and Sara Lembrechts (eds.), *Routledge International Handbook of Children's Rights Studies*, 43–59, New York: Routledge.

Wallberg, Pamela and Maria Kahn (2011), "The Rights Project: How Rights Education Transformed a Classroom," *Canadian Children*, 36 (1): 31–5.

CHAPTER SIX

Teaching and Teacher Education

The Education, Certification, and Employment of Teachers

SUZANNE E. ECKES AND CHARLES J. RUSSO

In the American constitutional context, can teachers be dismissed for voicing their opinions about matters of public concern in their classrooms? What right, if any, do teachers have to make pedagogical decisions, including the selection of instructional materials and teaching methods? Can educators lose their teaching license if public school officials disapprove of their decisions? In this chapter, we review the legal landscape for the certification and employment of teachers in public schools in the United States. We then examine First Amendment issues associated with the regulation of teachers' conduct inside and outside the classroom.

TEACHER EDUCATION AND CERTIFICATION STANDARDS

Horace Mann (1796–1859) is credited not only with establishing public schooling throughout the United States but also with instituting *norms* for the education and certification of teachers. In his twelve annual reports as Secretary of the Massachusetts State Board of Education, Mann vigorously defended nonsectarian, publicly funded schools staffed by virtuous graduates of his normal schools (Cremin 2020). Most of these teacher training institutes have since been reorganized as schools of education in public and private universities and colleges.

Because eligibility for employment as a teacher in American public schools generally requires a teaching degree from an accredited school of education, teacher education programs typically offer specified courses in pedagogical methods and theory, along with supervised practice teaching opportunities. And because eligibility for employment as a teacher in American public schools requires a state-issued certificate or license, accredited teacher education programs typically select and prepare teacher candidates to meet state standards for certification (Blokhuis et al. 2021: 452). Institutional and program accreditation is undertaken by national organizations including the Council for the Accreditation of Educator Preparation (CAEP), formerly the National Council for Accreditation of Teacher Education (NCATE), and the Interstate New Teacher Assessment and Support Consortium (INTASC), using standards aligned with professional standards for teacher certification set by each state.

At Washington State University (WSU 2021), for example, these standards are explicitly framed in dispositional terms: "Professional dispositions are the principles or standards that underpin a teacher's success in the classroom. They are the values, commitments, and professional ethics that govern how a teacher acts with students, families, colleagues, and communities." WSU Standard 9 indicates that "Good teachers … are responsible colleagues." The indicia for meeting this standard include "arriving punctually and prepared for class and required activities." WSU aligns this dispositional standard with CAEP Standard R1.4 (Professional Responsibility), formerly NCATE Standard 1 (Professional Growth), which is in turn aligned with INTASC Standard 9 (Professional Learning and Ethical Practice) (CAEP 2021). At Niagara University (2021), a private, faith-based institution, professional standards are explicitly framed in dispositional terms. In other words, the indicia for meeting the same standard include "demonstrating compliance with laws, regulations, policies, and standards," and "being prepared for classes and appointments," and "being punctual."

John Dayton (2019: 411) cites rules for female teachers in Sacramento, California in 1915 prohibiting marriage, keeping company with men, leaving home after dark, traveling beyond city limits, smoking cigarettes, dressing in bright colors, and using hair dye. He notes that it would clearly be unconstitutional for public school districts and state certification agencies to apply such standards today. Nonetheless, affective or dispositional certification and employment standards continue to apply to public school teachers, both inside and outside the classroom. For example, at Washington State University, a teacher candidate who meets INTASC Standard 9 (Professional Learning and Ethical Practice) is one who, inter alia, "dresses appropriately" and "communicates professionally with others" (WSU 2021). At Niagara University

(2021), a teacher candidate who meets this standard is one who, inter alia, maintains a "professional appearance" and "demonstrates honesty."

In the American constitutional context, the Due Process Clause of the Fourteenth Amendment prohibits the state from depriving "any person of life, liberty, or property without due process of law." Because teaching certificates are a form of property, states may not deny certification arbitrarily to candidates who meet their requirements. Because teaching certificates are not contracts, however, states may change hiring and retention requirements without violating constitutional prohibitions against the impairment of contracts (Blokhuis et al. 2021: 453). Teachers may be dismissed for cause, including failure to comply with laws, policies, and professional standards on and off campus. But as we shall see, there must be a logical nexus between the off-campus speech or conduct of a teacher and their ability or fitness to teach (Dayton 2019: 412). Teachers may be dismissed by school boards for cause without necessarily losing their teaching certification, but if state officials revoke their certificates or licenses, they necessarily lose their jobs.

STATE LAWS AND LOCAL SCHOOL BOARD POLICIES

Education, as defined by their constitutions, governors, state boards, statutes, regulations, and courts, is one of the most highly regulated responsibilities of state governments. Importantly, because state legislatures have the power to make laws governing education, a significant portion of state budgets are devoted to public schooling. State legislatures thus play important roles in setting educational standards and certifying, hiring, and evaluating public school teachers and administrators. Statutes, which are enacted by state legislatures, and accompanying regulations promulgated by their state departments of education, establish the minimum qualifications educators need to work in public schools. All states set teacher certification and licensing standards while requiring teachers in public schools to maintain valid licenses. Further, state officials have the power to suspend or revoke these licenses, based on criteria in state law.

State laws also govern collective bargaining. For example, collective bargaining might allow teachers to advocate for smaller class sizes, recess, health benefits, higher salaries, and other important issues related to the terms and conditions of their employment. Although states have the legal authority to impose restrictions extending to many different areas in education, they often delegate considerable authority to local school boards. More specifically, if educational matters are not delineated in state law, they are ordinarily left to local school boards to regulate. Hiring and curricular decisions, then, are generally under the purview of local boards.

FEDERAL STATUTES

Although education matters have generally been reserved for the states, Congress has enacted laws with important implications for teachers' rights. For instance, in 1990 Congress enacted the Americans with Disabilities Act (ADA), 42 U.S.C.§ 12101, which protects teachers with disabilities who are otherwise qualified for the jobs they seek or occupy with reasonable accommodations. Likewise, under the Age Discrimination in Employment Act (ADEA), 29 U.S.C. § 621, teachers over age forty may claim age discrimination when the criteria used to make adverse employment decisions are linked to age. Additionally, Congress enacted Title VII of the Civil Rights Act of 1964 (Title VII), 42 U.S.C. § 2000e, an expansive federal law prohibiting employers with fifteen or more employees, including schools, from discriminating against individuals on the basis of sex, race, color, national origin, and religion.

Courts frequently interpret the meaning of federal and state laws. While decisions from the Supreme Court apply nationwide, the opinions of federal district courts (trial courts of the first instance for cases involving federal issues or questions) and the federal circuit courts of appeal (the twelve regional appellate courts with a thirteenth housed in Washington DC for federal agencies), as well as those of state courts, provide guidance to teachers that can vary by state or region. Until 2020, one unresolved question had been whether Title VII provides protections from discrimination based on sexual orientation or gender identity. That is, there had been uncertainty about whether the prohibition of discrimination "because of sex" included protections from discrimination based on sexual orientation and gender identity. Due to different interpretations of Title VII in the federal appellate courts, if a gay educator in Georgia, which is in the Eleventh Circuit, was fired because of his sexual orientation, there were no protections under Title VII, while a gay educator in Wisconsin, housed in the Seventh Circuit, would have been protected under the law.

In *Bostock v. Clayton County*, 140 S. Ct. 1731 (2020), the Supreme Court resolved the split between the circuit courts by ruling that employers who fire persons for being gay or transgender violate Title VII. "The statute's message for our cases is equally simple and momentous," wrote Justice Neil Gorsuch for the majority. "An individual's homosexuality or transgender status is not relevant to employment decisions. That's because it is impossible to discriminate against a person for being homosexual or transgender without discriminating against that individual based on sex."

US CONSTITUTION

Many issues related to teachers' rights involve federal constitutional protections, including the Equal Protection Clause of the Fourteenth Amendment. Under this provision, agents of the state are prohibited from denying to any person "the equal protection of the laws." In rough terms, to deny equal protection of the laws is to treat an individual or group differently from others without sufficient reason. In other words, the Equal Protection Clause requires that similarly situated persons be treated similarly.

Because the actions of public school boards and officials are "state action," teachers in private schools generally lack constitutional protections. However, some federal courts have agreed that private school teachers are protected by federal laws including the ADEA. In *DeMarco v. Holy Cross High School*, 4 F.3d 166 (2d Cir. 1993), for example, a math teacher whose contract was not renewed prior to his eligibility for tenure at age forty-nine successfully sued his employer under the ADEA.

If employees establish discrimination on the part of their employers, the latter must establish nondiscriminatory bases for their actions. In *DeMarco*, Catholic school officials claimed that they had not renewed the teacher's contract for cause, alleging that he had not begun his classes with prayer or attended Mass with his students. Officials also claimed a religious exemption from the ADEA. The Second Circuit disagreed, finding the federal prohibition against age discrimination could apply to faith-based schools. "Given that the religious duties that DeMarco allegedly failed to carry out are easily isolated and defined, we are confident that the able district judge will be able to focus the trial upon whether DeMarco was fired because of his age or because of failure to perform religious duties," wrote the court, "and that this can be done without putting into issue the validity or truthfulness of Catholic religious teaching."

The First Amendment protects both free speech and the freedom not to speak. In *Janus v. AFSCME*, 138 S. Ct. 2448 (2018), a public employee challenged the dues deducted from his paychecks to cover the cost of collective bargaining and other union activities. The Supreme Court ruled that collecting fees from non-consenting public sector employees violates the First Amendment as a form of compelled speech. As a result, public school teachers must now affirmatively opt into union membership. Teachers in faith-based and other nonpublic schools, on the other hand, have no right to engage in collective bargaining with their employers. In *National Labor Relations Board v. Catholic Bishop of Chicago*, 440 U.S. 490 (1979), the Court held that even though the National Labor Relations Board is charged with overseeing disputes in the private sector, it lacks jurisdiction over faith-based schools due to their religious affiliations.

THE FIRST AMENDMENT

The First Amendment provides that "Congress shall make no law respecting an establishment of religion, or prohibiting the free exercise thereof; or abridging the freedom of speech, or of the press; or the right of the people peaceably to assemble, and to petition the Government for a redress of grievances." The Establishment Clause, the Free Exercise Clause, and the Free Speech Clause have particularly important implications for teachers in American public schools.

In a nation comprised of people of every conceivable religious or political persuasion, questions undoubtedly arise about the First Amendment rights of teachers, both inside and outside of the classroom. We have already seen how private, faith-based schools have invoked the Free Exercise Clause and the Establishment Clause to limit the labor rights of teachers. This inapplicability of anti-discrimination laws to religious schools in their relationships with teachers categorized as "ministers" is referred to as an "ecclesiastical exception." The principle that religious schools have First Amendment rights to select their own "ministers" without government oversight or entanglement was established in *Hosanna-Tabor Evangelical Lutheran Church and School v. E.E.O.C.*, 565 U.S. 171 (2012).

To be certain, the First Amendment does not eradicate religious speech from public schools. Personal religious expression is not only allowed but also protected in public schools. Under the Free Exercise Clause, school officials generally need to have a compelling reason to place a substantial burden on a teacher's sincerely held religious beliefs and practices. Public school officials might violate the Free Exercise Clause if, for example, they prohibit teachers from reading religious texts such as the Koran or Bible in an empty classroom. Yet, such a restriction is likely permissible while teachers are supervising students in detention or students taking examinations. Further, because Title VII prohibits school boards and, by extension, their officials from discriminating against teachers based on religion, they may not impose unjustified burdens on their free exercise rights by denying time off for religious observances or holidays.

At the same time, the Supreme Court has outlined when the religious activities of school officials or teachers can cross the line into compulsion, in violation of the Establishment Clause. The Establishment Clause prevents government officials from preferring one faith over others, compelling belief in any religion or faith, or advancing or hindering religion. Courts use three primary tests when trying to determine whether a public school policy or teaching practice violates the Establishment Clause.

In *Lemon v. Kurtzman*, 403 U.S. 602 (1971), a case involving a state subsidy program for the salaries of teachers in parochial schools, the Court employed a framework for analyzing alleged violations of the Establishment Clause. Under the three-part "*Lemon* test," a government policy or practice violates the Establishment Clause if (a) its purpose is to endorse or disapprove of religion; (b) its primary effect is to aid or inhibit religion; or (c) it creates excessive entanglement between church and state (Blokhuis et al. 2021: 51).

An alternative to the three-pronged "*Lemon* test" is the "Endorsement test," as outlined in *Lynch v. Donnelly,* 465 U.S. 668 (1984), and applied in *Wallace v. Jaffree*, 472 U.S. 38 (1985). Employing this test, courts will strike down public school policies or teaching practices if a reasonable person would perceive them as endorsing or disapproving of religion. There is also the "Coercion test," as enunciated in *Lee v. Weisman*, 505 U.S. 577 (1992), which has largely fallen into disuse. Employing this test, courts find public school teachers or school officials violate the Establishment Clause if they proselytize or coerce students or audiences to participate in prayer. If a public school teacher were permitted to lead a prayer at a graduation ceremony, this would violate the *Lemon*, Endorsement, and Coercion tests. Of course, no such restrictions apply in parochial or other private schools.

"It can hardly be argued that either students or teachers shed their constitutional rights to freedom of speech or expression at the schoolhouse gate," wrote the Supreme Court in *Tinker v. Des Moines Independent Community School District*, 393 U.S. 503 (1969). There are limits, however, to the First Amendment rights of teachers on and off campus. In recent years, teachers have been dismissed for posting offensive comments on social media about immigration (Zavari 2019) and race (Schiferl 2020).

In *Pickering v. Board of Education*, 391 U.S. 563 (1968), a case involving a teacher who wrote a letter to a local newspaper voicing concerns about the funding policies of his school board, the Supreme Court recognized that public employees have First Amendment rights to speak about matters of public concern. When a teacher speaks about matters of public concern, the courts apply a balancing test, weighing the teacher's interests against the interests of the school board in providing efficient educational programs. In *Connick v. Myers*, 461 U.S. 138 (1983), a case involving an assistant district attorney who was dismissed for insubordination after circulating a questionnaire soliciting the support of coworkers for her criticisms of her superiors, the Supreme Court held that if a teacher's speech on matters of public concerns jeopardizes (a) classroom performance, (b) relationships with supervisors or colleagues, or (c) the efficiency and effectiveness of school operations, the school board will generally prevail.

Pickering has generally been applied to teachers' speech *outside* of their classrooms. In *Givhan v. Western Line Consolidated School District*, 439 U.S. 410 (1979), the Court decided that a teacher did not lose her free speech rights when she spoke about a matter of public concern with her principal rather than in public.

In *Garcetti v. Ceballos*, 547 U.S. 410 (2006), the Supreme Court distinguished between a public employee speaking "pursuant to his [or her] official duties" and a public employee speaking "as a citizen." The case concerned a disagreement between a deputy district attorney and his superiors over the handling of a criminal prosecution. Ceballos expressed concerns about irregularities in a case in a memo to his superiors and testified for the defense that a police affidavit contained inaccuracies. Ceballos was subsequently reassigned and denied a promotion. The Supreme Court held that expression directly related to the official job duties of a public employee is not protected under the First Amendment.

Later, in *Evans-Marshall v. Board of Education*, 624 F.3d 332 (6th Cir. 2010), a public high school teacher claimed a First Amendment right to select books for use in her classroom without interference from her employer. "Because the right to free speech protected by the First Amendment does not extend to the in-class curricular speech of teachers in primary and secondary schools made 'pursuant to' their official duties, we affirm the judgment rejecting this claim as a matter of law," wrote the Sixth Circuit. In *Demers v. Austin*, 746 F.3d 402 (9th Cir. 2014), the Ninth Circuit concluded that "*Garcetti* does not—indeed, consistent with the First Amendment, cannot—apply to teaching and academic writing that are performed 'pursuant to the official duties' of a teacher and professor."

Other Circuit Courts have relied on *Hazelwood v. Kuhlmeier*, 484 U.S. 260 (1988), a case involving a student newspaper published as part of a journalism course, to regulate the content of "school-sponsored expressive activities so long as their actions are reasonably related to legitimate pedagogical concerns"—to reject teacher claims of academic freedom. In *Boring v. Buncombe County Board of Education*, 136 F.3d 364 (4th Cir. 1998), a teacher was disciplined for allowing students to perform a play featuring a same-sex couple with an unplanned pregnancy.

The Fourth Circuit found for the board, citing *Hazelwood*. In *Kirby v. Yonkers School District*, 767 F.Supp.2d 452 (S.D.N.Y. 2011), a federal district court found no First Amendment violation after a health teacher was disciplined for asking middle school students to draw male reproductive organs on the blackboard, applying the "legitimate pedagogical concern" standard in *Hazelwood*. And in *Kramer v. New York City Board of Education*, 715 F. Supp. 2d 335 (E.D.N.Y. 2010), a federal district court upheld the discipline of a middle school teacher who had permitted her students to use "vulgar slang" in a sex education class, citing *Hazelwood* (Blokhuis et al. 2021: 420).

Some cases include both free speech and free exercise claims. In *Johnson v. Poway Unified School District*, 658 F.3d 9654 (9th Cir. 2011), the Ninth Circuit addressed whether a teacher in San Diego who hung religious banners in his classroom was allowed to do so. School officials permitted teachers to decorate their classroom with posters that included various messages. While some teachers displayed posters of the Beatles, others posted pictures of Mahatma Gandhi or the Dalai Lama.

The teacher in *Poway* displayed two large banners in his classroom. The first stated "In God We Trust," "One Nation Under God," "God Bless America," and "God Shed His Grace on Thee." The second included a quote from the Declaration of Independence that "All Men are Created Equal, They are Endowed By their Creator" and the word "Creator" in all capital letters. When school officials directed the teacher to remove the banners for fear of religious entanglement, he argued school officials were violating his free speech rights.

Applying *Pickering* in *Poway*, a unanimous Ninth Circuit ruled that because the teacher was speaking pursuant to his "official duties" as a public school employee, he had no First Amendment rights to display these banners. The court stressed that both because teachers occupy positions of trust and authority over impressionable high school students and this teacher was speaking for a public school board, officials could limit his expression. In addition, the court ordered the teacher to pay the school board's legal costs. Along with the government speech discussion, the Ninth Circuit addressed issues related to the Establishment Clause. Importantly, the court pointed out that not all speech referencing religion infringes on the Establishment Clause: "In essence, the Clause serves not as a closed door, but as a judicious chaperone; it permits a certain degree of impartial and friendly dialogue, but is swift to step in once that dialogue turns stigmatic or coercive."

Poway was consistent with other Ninth Circuit opinions related to teachers who posted materials in public schools. For example, in *Downs v. L.A. Unified School District*, 228 F.3d 1003 (9th Cir. 2000), the court held that educational officials could remove posters that a teacher displayed denouncing homosexuality in response to other posters in the school recognizing Gay and Lesbian Awareness Month. Although *Poway* only applies to states in the Ninth Circuit, other circuits have taken similar approaches to teacher expression in the classroom.

Similarly, the Fourth Circuit determined that school officials did not violate a teacher's First Amendment rights when they required him to remove religious material from his classroom bulletin board in *Lee v. York County School Division*, 484 F.3d 687 (4th Cir. 2007). The teacher displayed a poster of George Washington praying, an article highlighting the religious differences of presidential candidates, and another article discussing a student's missionary activities. The court observed that the teacher had no First Amendment rights because the displays constituted school-sponsored speech.

Other federal appellate courts have addressed political expression by public teachers in the classroom. In *Mayer v. Monroe County Community School Corporation*, 474 F.3d 477 (7th Cir. 2007), the contract of a probationary teacher was not renewed after she recalled honking her horn in support of demonstrators protesting the American-led war in Iraq in response to a student's question about political activism. Upholding the board's action, the court explained that the First Amendment does not allow teachers to advocate viewpoints to captive audiences or to depart from school-adopted curricula. Relying on *Garcetti*, the Seventh Circuit concluded that "the First Amendment does not entitle primary and secondary teachers, when conducting the education of captive audiences, to cover topics, or advocate viewpoints, that depart from the curriculum adopted by the school system." Interestingly, the Sixth Circuit seemed to deviate from this general trend when it entered a judgment in favor of a public school teacher who invited Woody Harrelson to meet with fifth-graders about the environmental benefits of growing industrial hemp in *Cockrel v. Shelby County School District*, 270 F.3d 1036 (6th Cir. 2001). The court ruled the teacher was speaking on a matter of public concern.

In the American constitutional context, public school officials may place restrictions on teachers who express their religious and political views in class. Courts have consistently agreed that K–12 classrooms contain captive audiences of impressionable students. As such, teachers cannot use their public positions to influence a captive classroom of students about religious or political issues.

Related to the First Amendment rights of public school teachers in the classroom is the amount of leeway they have regarding curricular materials and classroom activities. In *Ambach v. Norwick*, 441 U.S. 68 (1979), the Supreme Court observed that American public schools are charged with the important task of "inculcating fundamental values necessary to the maintenance of a democratic political system." Consequently, public school curricula are often at the center of legal controversies. Though the Supreme Court has recognized that parents have a constitutional right to direct the upbringing of their children, it has not permitted parents to make curricular decisions. Nonetheless, widely read books such as *To Kill a Mockingbird* and *The Great Gatsby* have been challenged by parents seeking to have them removed from lesson plans or library shelves (Fetter-Harrot, Irwin, and Eckes 2016). Parents have also challenged public school curricula in science, health, social studies, and even gym classes. In *Sedlock v. Baird*, 185 Cal. Rptr. 3d 739 (2015), parents argued that teaching yoga in a gym class promoted religion. Disagreements persist over health education pertaining to sexuality, birth control, AIDS, and other topics. In various disciplines, the debate over who controls what is taught in US public school classrooms continues to be lively.

In *Parker v. Hurley*, 514 F.3d 87 (1st Cir. 2008), the First Circuit declined to grant an exemption from curricular content designed to encourage respect for diversity and other civic values. In that case, two families contended that their rights under the Free Exercise Clause were violated when teachers discussed books depicting same-sex relationships with their children without notice or an opt out opportunity. The First Circuit observed the parents had an unquestioned right to determine whether to send their children to public school. However, this right did not authorize the parents to direct the school curriculum. Moreover, the parental rights granted under the Constitution do not require public school teachers to "shield individual students from ideas which potentially are religiously offensive." Other courts have agreed that parents' rights do not include the right to challenge curricular choices (Fetter-Harrott, Irwin, and Eckes 2016).

In *ACLU of Florida v. Miami-Dade County School Board*, 557 F.3d 1177 (11th Cir. 2009), the Eleventh Circuit addressed the issue of curricular control after a parent opposed the inclusion of a children's book about Cuba in his daughter's school library. The father, who claimed to have been a prisoner of conscience in Cuba, argued the book failed to depict life in Cuba accurately. The school board ultimately agreed with the father, citing inaccuracies in the text. Another group of parents then filed suit, arguing that removing the book was politically motivated and unconstitutionally suppressed ideas in contravention of the First Amendment (see Fetter-Harrot, Irwin, and Eckes 2016). The Eleventh Circuit held that while removal of the book might be unlawful if it was motivated by a desire to suppress an idea, the school board's decision was lawful because it was based on factual inaccuracies in the book.

In addition to what they teach in the classroom, public school teachers have been challenged on how they teach. In *Lee-Walker v. New York Department of Education*, 712 F. App'x 43 (2d Cir. 2017, *cert. denied*, 138 S. Ct. 1318 (2018)), a teacher ignored an assistant principal's directive to not teach a lesson to her ninth-grade class involving the Central Park Five attack in which five African American teenagers were wrongfully convicted of raping a white woman. The teacher attempted to use this event to show that there is sometimes a "societal tendency to rush to adverse legal conclusions against black males." Because the assistant principal disagreed with the teacher's approach, stating it would "unnecessarily 'rile up' black students," he told her to deliver a more impartial lesson. After the teacher's contract was not renewed, she alleged retaliation. The Second Circuit found in favor of the board. The court acknowledged that "the ultimate authority to determine what manner of speech in the classroom is inappropriate properly rests with the school board, rather than with the federal courts," adding that public school officials are best situated to ensure students are not exposed to material inappropriate to their developmental level.

In *Ali v. Woodbridge Township Schools*, 957 F.3d 174 (3d Cir. 2020), a school board in New Jersey fired a teacher for presenting inaccurate information about the Holocaust and the September 11, 2001 terrorist attacks. After he was dismissed, the teacher contended he had been discriminated against based on his Egyptian descent and perceived religion. The Third Circuit affirmed an order in favor of the board.

In another case involving controversial classroom discussions, the Seventh Circuit in *Brown v. Chicago Board of Education*, 824 F.3d 713 (7th Cir. 2016), upheld the suspension of a teacher for giving an "impromptu lesson on racial epithets" to his sixth-grade class. The principal overheard the teacher trying to instruct his students not to use an odious term from a song lyric in a note from a student. After he read the note, the teacher quickly stopped his grammar lesson to describe just how offensive the term is and why it should not be used. The principal suspended the teacher for violating a school policy against verbally abusive language. The teacher then sued, unsuccessfully arguing that the school board violated his First Amendment rights. The Seventh Circuit, although clearly sympathizing with the teacher, described the incident as "a well-intentioned but poorly executed discussion of why such words are hurtful and must not be used." Even so, based on *Garcetti* and Seventh Circuit precedent, the court agreed that the board did not violate the teacher's free speech rights. The court thus rejected the teacher's claim that he used the word in an educational manner to explain why it was hurtful.

The preceding cases demonstrate the constitutional limits to the First Amendment rights of teachers in public school classrooms in the United States. Indeed, school officials often find themselves at the center of complex controversies involving teachers and curricula. At the K–12 level, courts approach curricular challenges on case-by-case bases, often balancing teachers' interests in having the freedom to teach as they wish against the interests of their boards in ensuring efficient and appropriate instructional programs. To help avoid legal challenges, some boards have adopted policies limiting the academic freedom that public school teachers possess. As noted earlier, teachers in private schools lack First Amendment protections unless they are spelled out in their contracts.

TEACHER OUT-OF-SCHOOL CONDUCT

Can the speech or conduct of public school teachers outside of classrooms be regulated? In the past, it was not uncommon for public school teachers to be dismissed for their out-of-school conduct. In *Sullivan v. Meade*, 530 F.2d 799 (8th Cir. 1976), a teacher was dismissed for cohabiting with a boyfriend. In *Littlejohn v. Rose*, 768 F.2d 765 (6th Cir. 1985), the contract of an untenured teacher was not renewed after her divorce became public. Moreover, in *Gaylord v. Tacoma*, 559 P.2d 1340 (Wash. 1975), *Rowland v. Mad River Local School District*, 730 F.2d 444 (6th Cir., 1984), and *Glover v. Williamsburg*

Local School District, 20 F. Supp. 2d 1160 (S.D. Ohio 1998), teachers were dismissed for their sexual orientation.

Recent cases and media reports have raised questions about how far school officials may go in regulating teachers' out-of-school conduct. For example, the Associated Press (2013) reported that the parties reached a settlement when a teacher alleged that she was fired because she worked as a stripper before becoming a teacher. School officials claimed that they dismissed the teacher due to poor classroom management and attendance issues. In similar cases, boards have disciplined or fired teachers due to jobs or activities that they were involved in outside of school time. In Florida, a teacher lost her job after modeling swimsuits and appearing in some racier photographs (Joseph 2013). In *San Diego Unified School District v. Commission on Professional Competence*, 124 Cal.Rptr.3d 320 (Cal. Ct. App. 2011), the court ruled in favor of a school board that dismissed a teacher who posted graphic photographs of his genitals on an internet site, finding his immoral conduct rendered him unfit to teach.

Historically, American public school officials had a great deal of control over teachers' private lives. This control related to teachers being "exemplars" of their schools and role models to their students and communities. While public school teachers are held to a higher standard of conduct than the general population, they are still afforded some protections with regard to their out-of-school conduct. As a federal court noted in *Ponton v. Newport News School Board*, 632 F. Supp. 1056 (E.D. Va. 1986), the "teacher's interest in exercising her rights" must be "balanced against the state's interest in promoting the efficiency of the public services it performs." Specifically, citizens' rights to privacy are an implied right under the concept of personal liberty embodied in the Fourteenth Amendment.

In *Meyer v. Nebraska*, 262 U.S. 390 (1923), and in *Pierce v. Society of Sisters*, 268 U.S. 510 (1925), the Supreme Court held that states could not interfere with the rights of parents and teachers to contract for the educational services of their choosing. In *Pierce*, the Supreme Court declared that the substantive due process rights of parents under the Fourteenth Amendment included "the right of the individual to contract, to engage in any of the common occupations of life, to acquire useful knowledge, to marry, establish a home and bring up children, to worship God according to the dictates of his own conscience, and generally to enjoy those privileges long recognized at common law as essential to the orderly pursuit of happiness by free men." Since then, American courts have recognized equal protection, due process, freedom of speech, and privacy claims when public school teachers are disciplined for off-campus speech or conduct.

ESTABLISHING A NEXUS

Some courts have allowed public school officials to discipline teachers for off-campus speech or behaviors in cases linking the off-campus behavior with the ability of the teacher to fulfill her professional duties. The nexus theory requires that teachers' off-duty conduct have a negative impact on their teaching ability or effectiveness. For example, in *McCullough v. Illinois State Board of Education*, 562 N.E.2d 1233 (Ill. App. Ct. 1990), after a teacher was dismissed for failure to file income taxes, the appellate court affirmed that the teacher's conviction harmed his reputation and credibility as a teacher and role model. In *Board of Education of Cape Giradeau v. Thomas*, 926 S.W.2d 163 (1996), a teacher who fired gun shots at her husband's mistress was fired. The appellate court concluded the teacher was unfit to teach because her impressionable ninth-grade students would have received mixed messages about violence.

In contrast, in *Teacher Standards & Practices Commission v. Bergerson*, 153 P.3d 84 (Or. 2007), the Supreme Court of Oregon concluded that the Teacher Standards and Practices Commission (TSPC) had erred in suspending a teacher as a result of her off-duty conduct. The teacher consumed large quantities of prescription drugs and then ran her car into her estranged husband's truck at 80 miles per hour. The school board dismissed the teacher after articles appeared in the local newspapers about the incident. The high court could find no clear nexus between the teacher's actions and her professional duties at school.

SOCIAL MEDIA

Other teachers have been fired for criticizing school board programs or policies on their personal social media sites (McWilliams 2020) because they spoke out in their official capacities. From Facebook to Twitter to Instagram, in recent years, teachers have been involved in controversies involving their activities on social media. In *Land v. L'Anse Creuse Public School Board*, 2010 Mich. App. LEXIS 999, for example, a middle school teacher was fired after photographs of her simulating fellatio with a male mannequin at a bachelorette party appeared online.

An appellate court in Michigan overturned the dismissal absent a clear nexus between the teacher's behavior and her ability to teach. Concurring in the result, Justice Bandstra wrote:

> The record here could not support a determination that, as a result of the photographs being posted on the internet, petitioner's ability to teach effectively was adversely impacted enough to justify her discharge. That is not to say, however, that I agree with the commission or the majority

> opinion to the extent they conclude that, absent some misbehavior by a teacher involving students directly, a discharge decision can only be justified by a finding of professional misconduct. There may well be situations where misbehavior short of professional misconduct negatively impacts the teaching environment (either a teacher's ability to teach or the school community more generally) sufficiently to conclude that the misbehavior constitutes a "reasonable and just cause" for discharge under the statute.

A similar case arose in Pennsylvania after someone posted a picture of a teacher at a bachelorette party featuring a male stripper on Facebook. The board suspended the teacher for thirty days, but she ultimately won back pay and a clean disciplinary record (American Civil Liberties Union [ACLU] 2010). Without question, social media can, and does, blur the line between educators' private and public lives. Moreover, there is no doubt that teachers face increased scrutiny of their private lives as a result of social media. For example, a teacher in Utah who was a bikini model and body building competitor challenged school officials who requested that she remove photographs related to these activities from her Facebook and Instagram pages or be dismissed (Free 2015).

During the same year a board in Wisconsin placed a teacher on administrative leave over a picture on her Facebook page that featured her looking down the sight of her hunting rifle, which was aimed at the camera (Associated Press 2009). In *Munroe v. Central Bucks School District*, 805 F.3d 454 (3d Cir. 2015), a Pennsylvania high school teacher received national attention after being fired for unflattering descriptions of her students on her blog. She appeared on ABC, CBS, NBC, CNN, Fox News, and other television stations. The Third Circuit affirmed that the board did not violate the teacher's First Amendment rights because her unprotected speech would have disrupted the educational mission of the school.

Other internet postings have generated similar reactions from public school officials. In *Murmer v. Chesterfield County School Board*, 2007 WL 2914769 (E.D. Va. Oct. 4, 2007), an art teacher in Virginia appeared in a YouTube clip in which he painted pictures using his buttocks. The teacher wore a thong, a Groucho Marx disguise, and used a pseudonym. The video became public when someone posted it without the teacher's consent. After being dismissed, the teacher sued, arguing that there was no evidence that this video related to his teaching effectiveness. Conversely, school officials claimed that his conduct was unbecoming of a teacher and that he was not serving as a role model. The teacher and school board ultimately settled the case for $65,000 (ACLU 2008).

In another case, an art teacher from Texas was dismissed after her partner posted, and students learned about, a topless picture of her on Flickr.com. The *Houston Chronicle* apparently considered the pictures to be "no more erotic than the Statue of David" (Rothberg 2006: 1). The teacher was awarded a monetary settlement from the board of $14,850 and agreed to resign (May 2006). The State Board for Educator Certification took no adverse action against the teacher.

MARIJUANA

Some public school teachers might incorrectly assume they can smoke marijuana during nonschool hours in states where recreational marijuana has been legalized. After all, they can freely drink alcohol during off-duty hours. Teachers might be surprised to learn, though, that school officials may still be able to regulate this type of out-of-school conduct if employee handbooks prohibit this activity, even in states where recreational marijuana use is legal (see Eckes and Weiler 2017; Russo, Eckes, and Osborne 2017). Of course, in those states where marijuana is illegal, teachers can be disciplined, regardless of whether a prohibition is included in faculty handbooks if they come to work under the influence of marijuana, as in *Younge v. Board of Education*, 788 N.E.2d 1153 (Ill. App. Ct. 2003).

To date, because eleven states and the District of Columbia now permit the recreational use of marijuana, questions have arisen about whether employers can prohibit its use during nonschool hours (Murse 2020). In *Proposal for Decision, Texas Educational Agency v. Maryam Roland*, No. 701-16-47-EC, 2017 WL 238391 (Texas St. Off. Admin. Hgs. Jan. 10, 2017), an administrative law judge (ALJ) examined this issue after a teacher who worked in Texas ingested a marijuana product while on holiday in Colorado, where the recreational use of marijuana is legal. The Texas Education Agency sought to suspend the teacher's license for two years; she resigned from her job after testing positive for marijuana. The ALJ found that the teacher should not be disciplined, reasoning that if she had gambled in Nevada, she would not have been fired. Moreover, the ALJ continued, there was no evidence showing she was unfit to teach. Although there is not a great deal of litigation about teachers and the new recreational use laws, the media continues to report that teachers are disciplined in states where recreational is and is not legal under state law (Dura 2018; Joyce 2017).

Employees have also been fired for using marijuana for medicinal purposes even though it is legal in thirty states. In *Coats v. Dish Network*, 350 P.3d 849 (Colo. 2015), the Supreme Court of Colorado ruled that an employee was not subject to any protections for his off-duty use of medical marijuana because it was illegal under federal law. Public school teachers might not be aware that it may be impermissible to ingest marijuana even if they have been prescribed medical marijuana by a doctor in compliance with state law. It is also important to note that the Americans with Disabilities Act does not cover medical marijuana.

These cases highlight some of the issues relating to public school teachers' off-duty conduct and raise questions about how far boards and school officials may go. Although not every jurisdiction has adopted the nexus theory, it is a helpful framework for school leaders to follow. If school officials can clearly demonstrate that teachers' off-duty conduct has negatively impacted their teaching effectiveness, especially if the activities are illegal, then they are likely to be subject to discipline.

CONCLUSION

States, through their elected and appointed officials, have authority over public schools but federal laws and constitutional principles are important to consider. As discussed, the Constitution places constraints on the government and teachers are entitled to certain rights in public schools. Controversies related to teachers' rights in schools will continue to generate legal activity. It would therefore be wise to consider the limitations to teacher expression both inside and outside of schools. Likewise, in certain circumstances, teachers' out-of-school conduct may be regulated. In most cases, school board officials need to demonstrate that the conduct impairs the teachers' effectiveness in their classrooms.

REFERENCES

American Civil Liberties Union (ACLU) (2008), "Fired Art Teacher Wins $65,000 Settlement from Chesterfield County School Board," ACLU.org, March 7. Available online: https://www.aclu.org/press-releases/fired-art-teacher-wins-65000-settlement-chesterfield-county-school-board (accessed January 22, 2021).

American Civil Liberties Union (ACLU) (2010), "Settlement Reached with School District over Teacher Who Was Suspended over Photo with Stripper at Bachelorette Party," ACLU.org, August 17. Available online: https://www.aclu.org/press-releases/settlement-reached-school-district-over-teacher-who-was-suspended-over-photo-stripper (accessed January 21, 2021).

Associated Press (2009), "Schoolteacher Suspended for Facebook Gun Photo," *FoxNews.com*, February 5. Available online: https://www.foxnews.com/story/schoolteacher-suspended-for-facebook-gun-photo (accessed January 23, 2021).

Associated Press (2013), "Fired West Michigan Teacher Reaches Deal over Work as Stripper," *The Oakland Press*, May 30. Available online: https://www.theoaklandpress.com/news/fired-west-michigan-teacher-reaches-deal-over-work-as-stripper/article_7d370278-a995-5f5d-8318-c67c7df49196.html (accessed January 22, 2021).

Blokhuis, J.C., Jonathan Feldman, Michael Imber, and Tyll van Geel (2021), *Education Law*, 6th edn., New York: Routledge.

Council for the Accreditation of Educator Preparation (CAEP) (2021), "2022 Initial Level Standards," NCATE. Available online: http://www.ncate.org/~/media/Files/caep/standards/2022-initial-standards-1-pager-final.pdf?la=en (accessed January 27, 2021).

Cremin, Lawrence A. (2020), "Horace Mann," *Encyclopedia Britannica*, December 17. Available online: https://www.britannica.com/biography/Horace-Mann (accessed January 27, 2021).

Dayton, John (2019), *Education Law: Principles, Policies, and Practice*, 2nd edn., Athens, GA: Wisdom Builders.

Dura, Jack (2018), "Western N.D. Teacher Charged for Marijuana," *Grand Forks Herald*, February 9. Available online: https://www.grandforksherald.com/news/4401519-western-nd-teacher-charged-marijuana (accessed January 22, 2021).

Eckes, Suzanne and Spencer Weiler (2017), "Canned for Cannabis," *NASSP's Principal Leadership Magazine*, September: 58–60.

Fetter-Harrott, Allison, Cory Irwin, and Suzanne Eckes (2016), "Keep Voldemort Out of Our Schools," *Principal Leadership*, January: 58–60.

Free, Cathy (2015), "Utah Teacher Who Came under Fire for Posting Body Building Bikini Shots," *People*, October 23. Available online: https://people.com/celebrity/utah-teacher-who-came-under-fire-for-posting-body-building-bikini-shots/ (accessed January 21, 2021).

Joseph, Chris (2013), "Olivia Sprauer, Boca Raton English Teacher, Fired for Being 'Eye Candy Model'," *Broward Palm Beach New Times*, May 7. Available online: https://www.browardpalmbeach.com/news/olivia-sprauer-boca-raton-english-teacher-fired-for-being-eyecandy-model-6453491 (accessed January 21, 2021).

Joyce, Kathleen (2017), "Elementary School Teachers Smoked Marijuana in Office Every Day before School Began, Cops Say," *Fox News*, December 6. Available online: http://www.foxnews.com/us/2017/12/06/elementary-school-teachers-smoked-marijuana-in-office-everyday-before-school-began-cops-say.html (accessed January 21, 2021).

May, Michael (2006), "Hoover/AISD Settlement Leaves Naughtiness Undefined," *Austin Chronicle*, August 25. Available online: https://www.austinchronicle.com/news/2006-08-25/397740/ (accessed January 21, 2021).

McWilliams, Jennifer (2020), "Indiana Teacher Fired for FB Post Questioning Social-Emotional Learning," *Vanderburgh Independent Press*, February 24. Available online: http://www.theofficialvipnews.com/google2badecc5bb02684b.html/2020/02/24/indiana-teacher-fired-for-fb-post-questioning-social-emotional-learning/ (accessed January 21, 2021).

Murse, Tom (2020), "States Where Smoking Recreational Marijuana Is Legal," *ThoughtCo*, February 4. Available online: https://www.thoughtco.com/states-that-legalized-marijuana-3368391 (accessed January 21, 2021).

Niagara University (2021), "Dispositions." Available online: https://www.niagara.edu/dispositions/ (accessed January 27, 2021).

Rothberg, Steven (2006), "Texas Teacher Fired for Posting Topless Photos On-line," *College Recruiter*, June 19. Available online: https://www.collegerecruiter.com/blog/2006/06/19/texas-teacher-fired-for-posting-topless-photos-on-line/ (accessed January 21, 2021).

Russo, Charles J., Suzanne E. Eckes, and Allan G. Osborne (2017), "Schools and the Legalization of Marijuana: An Emerging Legal Issue," *Education Law Reporter*, 343 (2): 647–53.

Schiferl, Jenna (2020), "Summerville Teacher Accused of Posting Racist Comments Online No Longer Employed with DDS," *The Post and Courier*, June 10. Available online: https://www.postandcourier.com/news/summerville-teacher-accused-of-posting-racist-comments-online-no-longer-employed-with-dd2/article_1a6b7c9a-ab1c-11ea-9cc0-5f1c01d3228a.html (accessed January 21, 2021).

Washington State University (WSU) (2021), "Professional Dispositions." Available online: https://education.wsu.edu/undergradprograms/teachered/professionaldisposition/ (accessed January 27, 2021).

Zaveri, Mihir (2019), "Teacher Fired after Asking Trump to 'Remove' Immigrants Wins Her Appeal," *New York Times*, November 29. Available online: https://www.nytimes.com/2019/11/29/us/teacher-trump-tweets-reinstated.html (accessed January 21, 2021).

CHAPTER SEVEN

Assessment and Evaluation

Statutory Frameworks for the Assessment and Evaluation of Students, Teachers, and Schools

PATRICK J. MCGUINN

This chapter examines the growth of the federal role in American education law and policy over the past sixty years, with a focus on growing incentives and intensifying mandates around the assessment and evaluation of students, teachers, and schools. The seminal report, *A Nation at Risk* (Gardner et al. 1983) highlighted America's large and persistent racial and socioeconomic achievement gaps and the poor performance of American students compared to their international peers. While the original version of the largest federal education law—the Elementary and Secondary Education Act (ESEA)—contained little about assessment and evaluation, subsequent reauthorizations of the law—the Improving America's Schools Act of 1993, the No Child Left Behind of 2001, and the Every Student Succeeds Act of 2015—created, expanded, and sustained (respectively) federal legal mandates on student and teacher performance and school quality, as well as accountability for academic results, particularly for disadvantaged students.

NATIONAL GOALS FOR LOCAL SYSTEMS

The American approach to educational policy-making is unusual. In most countries, it is centralized. In the United States, it is divided between the federal and state levels and across separate legislative and executive branches. This decentralized system of policy-making is intended to prevent any one political actor from consolidating too much power. Americans also have a particularly strong historical attachment to local control in the area of education. The word "education" does not appear anywhere in the US Constitution, and there was very little federal (or even state) involvement in schools until the second half of the twentieth century. As a result, schools and education systems evolved over time through local competition and organic growth. Rather than a single national education system, in most other nations around the world, the United States has fifty distinct state education systems with widely divergent policies and outcomes. This has been particularly true when it comes to the assessment and evaluation of students, teachers, and schools.

Since the 1950s, however, US policy-makers have articulated three major goals for increased federal involvement in education: *integration* (fixing the legacy of racial injustice), *national security* (promoting defense research), and *economic* (alleviating poverty and enhancing global competitiveness). Each of these rationales mutated over time while continuing to provide a justification for federal expansion. The integration rationale shifted under George W. Bush from access to *achievement*. The national security rationale was redoubled with *A Nation at Risk*, when Americans got the sense that education was not merely a tool for national defense, but for a broader national *competitiveness* in the global marketplace. The economic rationale, meanwhile, seems to have shifted under the Clinton administration, moving from an anti-poverty issue to an *economic growth* imperative.

The federal government has had to rely on indirect levers of influence to encourage states to reform their schools and embrace national goals. The primary tool for federal policymakers has been the grants-in-aid system—or more simply, money. States are always eager to accept federal education funding—which has grown dramatically over time—and generally willing to accept the strings that come with it. A strong tradition of local control, however, has meant continued resistance to the expansion of federal authority. The result has been an increasingly contentious relationship between the growing ambitions of federal education policy, the willingness of state officials to accept it, and the ability of educators to implement it. This has led to a cyclical dynamic of federal education policy expansion and retrenchment.

During the 1950s and 1960s the country underwent a conceptual realignment as it started thinking about education in national terms for the first time. This was followed by a period of expansion and friction (1965–80) when federal involvement took root and expanded. Local control was curtailed and education bureaucratized, but the federal government did not have enough power to *control* reform efforts at the local level. A period of retrenchment (1980–8) followed, with a backlash against this expansion leading to a period of deregulation. In the background, a state-based "excellence agenda" started to form, which ultimately led to another conceptual realignment (1988–94) during which the federal government attempted to direct states toward standards-based reform. Another period of expansion and friction began (1994–2000) but few states embraced the federal call for new standards, tests, and accountability measures. With the passage of the No Child Left Behind Act of 2001 (NCLB), the dam constraining federal power was broken, and a new paradigm of test-based accountability was consolidated (McGuinn 2006).

CONCEPTUAL REALIGNMENT (1950–65)

The federal role began to grow in the 1950s in response to a series of perceived national crises. The first crisis centered on race and segregation. In *Brown v. Board of Education*, 347 U.S. 483 (1954), the Supreme Court declared segregated schools to be "inherently unequal" and ordered states to integrate. But states, particularly southern states, were angered and engaged in "massive resistance." All three branches of the federal government had to take concerted action to prompt states to integrate. States still made objections on the grounds of states' rights and local control, but these objections were viewed with increasing suspicion by the federal government and the civil rights community.

The second national crisis that precipitated an expanded federal role in education came in 1957 when the Soviet Union launched Sputnik, the world's first orbiting satellite, and heightened fears that the United States was losing the space race and the arms race in the Cold War. The National Defense Education Act of 1958 was enacted to help states expand their offerings in math, science, and foreign language. While the investment was small in absolute terms (less than $1 billion), the political precedent and psychological breakthrough was profound.

The third national crisis occurred in the 1960s when President Lyndon Johnson (LBJ) declared a "war on poverty" in his effort to create a "great society." LBJ believed that improved educational opportunity was the best path out of poverty. This economic rationale, joined with the other two, pushed Congress to enact the most expansive and expensive federal education law in American history, the Elementary and Secondary Education Act of 1965 (ESEA).

EARLY ESEA AND EXPANSION (1965–80)

Upon signing the ESEA, President Johnson (1966) declared that "I believe deeply no law I have signed or will ever sign means more to the future of America." The law put a powerful equity rationale at the heart of federal education policy and created a plan to provide supplemental resources and programs to increase opportunity for disadvantaged children. The centerpiece of this effort and of the legislation itself was the Title I program, which was designed to assist communities with a high concentration of low-income families by raising per-pupil expenditures. Together, the NDEA and the ESEA were to dramatically increase federal education funding.

But even as an active federal role in education became increasingly institutionalized over time, ESEA was not particularly well targeted, and did not have strong mechanisms to deliver on its original promise. The policy paradigm undergirding this equity regime was that the majority of schools were doing fine, that federal education reform efforts should target schools with high concentrations of poor and minority students, and the primary problem facing these schools was a lack of integration and/or adequate funding.

It quickly became clear that the implementation challenges would be especially difficult. The legislation incorporated multiple goals and methods and gave federal administrators few tools to force compliance. Even if such tools had been available, the agency charged with implementing the ESEA, the United States Office of Education (USOE), lacked the capacity and political will to rigorously administer it. The USOE—a small, passive organization that focused on collecting and disseminating statistical data—was ill-suited to a compliance role. As John and Anne Hughes (1972: 50) have noted, "The state agencies and the local districts, by and large, were used to going their own ways, which often meant disregarding federal requirements."

The politics and implementation of the ESEA were also greatly complicated by the addition of new purposes and programs and an increasingly contentious racial politics following 1965. The consequence of the ESEA's initial flexibility was that federal funds were used in a wide variety of ways for a wide variety of purposes, and local districts often diverted funds away from redistributive programs (Peterson, Rabe, and Wong 1986: 136–40). The large amount of discretion accorded to states and districts ensured that compliance with federal goals was spotty at best. Initially the USOE merely relied on the assurances of state officials. Over time, however, federal legislative enactments, bureaucratic regulations, and court mandates became increasingly numerous and prescriptive, and federal influence grew significantly.

The ESEA quickly developed formidable political constituencies that successfully pushed for incremental expansions in its size and scope. Continuing opposition to federal micromanagement in education and the lack of consensus on how to measure the effectiveness of school reform efforts, however, led federal administrators to focus on districts' spending patterns and administrative compliance. The result was that large numbers of bureaucratic regulations were created during the 1970s without any concomitant focus on student or school results—everything was judged by procedure and process. Between 1964 and 1976 the number of pages of federal legislation affecting education increased from 80 to 360, while the number of federal regulations increased from 92 in 1965 to nearly 1,000 in 1977 (Ravitch 1983).

Despite local frustration, expanding the ESEA remained a winning political proposition for Congress. As opponents of federal control had feared, the ESEA had given a crucial foothold to those who sought to further increase the federal role in education policy. It was expanded in 1968, 1974, and 1978. Over one hundred new programs were added, covering everything from migrant children to children with disabilities. Democratic President Jimmy Carter continued the institutionalization of the federal role in education when he created a cabinet-level Department of Education (ED) in 1979. The move was widely regarded as a political payback for the endorsement and support of the National Education Association (NEA) and the American Federation of Teachers (AFT) during the 1976 election. Legislation to create a new federal department for education had been introduced 130 times between 1908 and 1975, but the idea had always generated a great deal of political opposition from a variety of interests (Stallings 2002: 677). The new department quickly became a powerful symbol to both proponents and opponents of federal involvement.

By 1980 federal spending had expanded dramatically and the ESEA had facilitated the centralization, bureaucratization, and judicialization of American education and educational policy-making (Blokhuis and Curren 2021). The logic behind the ESEA—that the federal government needed to defend the most vulnerable children from local majorities—had led to increasing federal involvement but also increasingly inflexible and copious regulations and increasingly intrusive court intervention. By 1980 the Department of Education administered approximately five hundred different federal education programs (Paterson 1983). Ironically, however, the ESEA reduced the autonomy of schools and districts without really giving the federal government any *control*—it just fostered an increasingly stifling compliance culture. And most importantly, this period saw no federal attempt to push states to assess or evaluate the actual academic performance of students, teachers, and schools; such decisions were left completely to states, which in turn did little to nothing in this area.

RETRENCHMENT (1980–8)

The federal focus remained on access and equity rather than on assessing or evaluating students', teachers', or schools' academic performance; there was little effort to measure the educational progress of students who received federal funds. This fueled the growing perception in the 1970s that federal education policy—like many other Great Society policies—had become more about providing entitlements and protecting rights than about enhancing opportunity. This eventually led to growing discontent among Republicans, states' rights advocates, and even some Democrats about the nature and effectiveness of federal aid.

As part of his "New Federalism" program, President Ronald Reagan passed the Education Consolidation and Improvement Act of 1981 (ECIA), dramatically reforming many provisions of ESEA. The changes reduced the amount of federal funding for education by almost 20 percent and increased flexibility for states. One scholar estimated that the number of regulatory mandates was reduced by 85 percent during the Reagan administration (UC Santa Barbara [UCSB] 1991). Reagan hoped to either eliminate the federal role in schools or to redefine the nature of the federal policy by making privatization, choice, and competition—rather than equity—its guiding principles (Stallings 2002: 678).

Though Reagan's efforts to disband the U.S. Department of Education were unsuccessful, he substantially reduced its staffing, budget, and regulatory authority. However, Republican efforts to roll back federal influence also brought a flurry of media attention to the fact that American public schools were in very poor shape. *A Nation at Risk* painted a dire portrait of the country's public schools and highlighted how far American students lagged behind their foreign counterparts. The report's title also emphasized the authors' conclusion that although education had long been primarily a *state* issue, it had become a *national* problem. This point was also cast as a matter of national security in the Cold War struggle with the Soviet Union and in the competition in the global economy (Gardner et al. 1983): "If an unfriendly foreign power had attempted to impose on America the mediocre educational performance that exists today, we might well have viewed it as an act of war."

The federal rationale shifted—now it was not about the United States versus the USSR, but rather about the United States versus the world. The federal government, the report declared, has "the primary responsibility to identify the national interest in education. It should also help fund and support efforts to protect and promote that interest ... and provide the national leadership." The report's striking tone and conclusions ignited a frenzy of media attention. The Reagan administration highlighted the report's findings as evidence that the growth in federal involvement had been ineffective, and Education Secretary Terrell Bell began a very visible (and controversial) effort to urge state reform by providing public rankings of the states according to the quality of their public education systems.

Perhaps the most important consequence of *A Nation at Risk* was that states began to play a much more active role in education reform. In what became known as the "excellence movement," many states increased spending on schools and established new curricular and achievement standards in the 1980s to guide local school districts. Thomas Toch has written that "the national debate on public education produced scores of reforms ... Through 1984, 1985, 1986, and beyond, education was a dominant issue in state capitols nationwide ... In all, there were an estimated 3,000 separate school-reform measures enacted in the states during the mid-1980s" (1991: 36). The decade thus saw the building of a public and elite consensus around standards-based education reform (Manna 2002). The 1988 Reauthorization of the ESEA—which required school districts to assess the effectiveness of Chapter 1 programs and develop improvement plans for underperforming schools—represented the first step shifting federal education policy away from the equity approach and toward a focus on outcome accountability.

REALIGNMENT: GEORGE H.W. BUSH AND CLINTON (1988–94)

Reagan's Republican successor, George H.W. Bush, campaigned on a pledge to be an "education president." In office he convened a national education summit in Charlottesville, Virginia in 1989, bringing the nation's governors together to discuss school reform under presidential leadership for the first time. The meeting produced a series of national education goals that Bush attempted (but failed) to codify with his "America 2000" proposal to Congress in 1991. It called for the development of more detailed voluntary national standards in the core academic subjects and also called for the creation of "a system of voluntary examinations" called "American Achievement Tests" for all fourth, eighth, and twelfth graders, which would be made available to governors for adoption (UCSB 1991). It also proposed the creation of a "New American Schools Development Corporation" to design model schools, publish report cards (for schools, districts, and states), encourage merit pay and alternative certification for teachers and principals, and establish a number of private school choice demonstration projects.

As Governor of Arkansas, Bill Clinton had joined with Bush during the 1989 Charlottesville summit. During his 1992 presidential campaign, a centrist consensus had developed around these ideas. Clinton's Goals 2000 proposal (enacted in 1994) created a blueprint for the subsequent ESEA reauthorization and called for the creation of voluntary national standards and assessments based on the six national education goals outlined in America 2000. However, Goals 2000 greatly circumscribed the federal role in creating standards and assessments or in holding states accountable. The final legislation stated that national standards must be "sufficiently general" that they "will not restrict state and local control over curriculum and instruction methods … [and that states] can modify them to suit their own circumstances." It also emphasized that the standards were voluntary and that "states and communities can develop their own standards or modify and adopt those developed under national consensus." Federal funds were to flow to states and communities to "help them develop their own rigorous standards and implement their own programs of school reform." The law clearly indicates that "no state is required to have its standards or assessments certified or participate in Goals 2000 systemic improvement programs as a condition of participating in any federal education program" (Bodell 1994: 8).

Clinton's Education Secretary Richard Riley declared that education is "a local function, a state responsibility, and a national priority," and Goals 2000 reflected this complicated division of authority. Despite its flexibility and the lack of new mandates, however, Goals 2000 was widely recognized as a watershed moment. Riley noted that "for the first time in the nation's history, a statutory framework defines the federal role as one of supporting and facilitation to improve all schools for all children" (1995: 1). Previous federal programs had been categorical and addressed narrow purposes or populations, but Goals 2000 comprehensively addressed the nation's entire K–12 education system. Goals 2000 marked a fundamental break with the historical focus on promoting resource equity for disadvantaged groups and initiated a new era in emphasizing academic improvement for all students. Reformers hailed the focus on standards and school performance as an important step, but recognized that its voluntary nature and the restrictions on federal leadership limited its potential impact.

EXPANSION AND FRICTION: IMPROVING AMERICA'S SCHOOL ACT (1994–2000)

Goals 2000 signified an important new direction, but participation in the program was voluntary and the only incentive for states to take part was to claim a share of the small pot of money. The ESEA, on the other hand, was enormous in size and scope, housing the majority of federal education programs and allocating over $10 billion. The original ESEA created a large number of targeted, categorical federal education programs to provide assistance to specifically identified groups and purposes. Subsequent reauthorizations added additional groups and programs, which only exacerbated the disjointed nature of the original law. Federal programs continued to embody federal purposes, operating separately from state and local programs, and focusing on compliance rather than student achievement.

But by the 1990s there was a growing sentiment among Democrats and Republicans alike that the ESEA was in dire need of reform. The Clinton Administration's 1994 reauthorization proposal, entitled the Improving America's Schools Act (IASA), 108 Stat. 3518, called for tying federal aid for disadvantaged students (Title I), bilingual education, and many other programs to the standards developed under *Goals 2000*. Clinton's linking of education to economic growth established a strong rationale for broader federal involvement.

His emphasis on the need for increased reform, as opposed to merely increased spending, was also very important. However, continuing opposition to a more rigorous federal role in promoting school reform would limit the ability of the Clinton administration to implement even the weak enforcement provisions of the new laws.

Even so, the new federal concern about *every* child was remarkable given the historic focus on only *disadvantaged* children. In a major shift, Clinton argued that disadvantaged students in Title I schools should now be expected to make progress toward the challenging content and performance standards and assessments that were applied to all of the other children in the state. The changes to the ESEA required states to develop school improvement plans and challenging content standards in core academic subjects to receive federal funds. States were also required to develop assessments and set benchmarks for the "adequate yearly progress" that a district's Title I students would have to make. Schools would publish disaggregated test results and those that failed to meet state targets for two consecutive school years would be identified as needing improvement. States and districts were encouraged to take "corrective action" with failing schools, such as withholding funds, reconstituting staff, instituting new governance, or transferring students. The legislation also contained an important boost to public school choice by allowing school districts to use federal Title I funds to enable eligible students to transfer to another public school within that system and by providing a small amount ($15 million in the first year) of federal start-up funds for charter schools.

Much had been made during the Congressional debate over Goals 2000 about the voluntary nature of the national standards and federal programs, but this changed with the IASA. As Mike Smith, Clinton's Education Undersecretary, noted, the combination of "Goals 2000 and the 1994 ESEA changes imposed on the states a particular kind of reform—to play ball states had to go along with standards based reform" (interview with author, March 23, 2003). Many conservatives in Congress worried the new law would federalize education policy. This growing politicization of education in Washington occurred even as a consensus was building across the country among education reformers, governors, business leaders, and the public behind national standards and assessments. While the IASA forced states to "play ball" on standards-based reform, it allowed them to write their own rules for how the game would be played and states were given the freedom to design their own standards, assessments, and accountability systems.

Many ideas that would later form the core of the No Child Left Behind Act of 2001 (NCLB)—such as standards, assessments, adequate yearly progress, school report cards, and corrective action—were first expressed in the IASA. But in the early 1990s the lingering conservative opposition to a strong federal role in education and the continuing liberal reservations about testing and accountability meant that Goals 2000 and the ESEA reauthorization contained few truly mandatory reforms. In addition, the federal expansion came under determined attack by a Republican controlled and conservative-led Congress between 1995 and 1999. Republicans advanced proposals to eliminate the Department of Education, cut federal education spending, and to convert what funds remained into private school vouchers and block grants. These proposals made progress in the House but were defeated by a coalition of Democrats and Republican moderates in the Senate. The steadfast support of the business community and the National Governors Association for federal leadership around educational assessment and accountability was an important influence during this period.

Though unsuccessful in fundamentally redirecting federal education policy, conservatives were successful in significantly undermining federal influence over state reform efforts. The 1994 reforms gave states great flexibility and discretion in designing and implementing their school reform plans. By 2000, however, it was clear that this approach had failed to bring about major policy change at the state level or to improve student achievement. Whereas the ESEA had a limited scope of action yet achieved broad penetration in the form of bureaucratic compliance, the IASA had a broader ambition of policy alignment, but received shallow buy-in from the states.

BUSH, NO CHILD LEFT BEHIND, AND THE FEDERAL BREAKTHROUGH

Compliance with the IASA's requirements was poor. As of spring 2002, only sixteen states had fully met the requirements of the 1994 law. President George W. Bush made education reform and accountability a central theme of his 2000 election campaign and of his pledge to govern as a "compassionate conservative." Seizing the mantle of the civil rights movement, he called for a focus on exposing and closing racial achievement gaps and battling the "soft-bigotry of low expectations." By the beginning of the twentieth century then, each of the three original rationales for expanded federal involvement in education had shifted to take on a broader, more ambitious character.

Bush made a grand bargain with Congressional Democrats. In exchange for meeting new federal demands and greater federal accountability, NCLB provided a significant increase in federal spending on education and new flexibility in how states could spend it. In 2002, the year after NCLB was enacted, federal education appropriations increased by 34 percent, going from \$42.1 billion in 2001 to \$56.2 billion the following year. The increase in education funding from 2000 to 2010 was 64 percent, as the department saw an added $24.6 billion to its budget (Harrington 2011).

The most important requirements of NCLB were that states had to adopt academic standards to guide their curricula and adopt a testing and accountability system aligned with those standards. States had to test all students in grades 3 to 8 every year (as well as once in high school) in math and reading beginning in the 2005/6 school year. Beginning in 2002/3, states were required to annually test the English proficiency of students for whom English is not their first language, and by the 2007/8 school year, states also had to test all students in science at certain grade levels. States were free to develop and use their own standards and tests, but every school, school district, and state had to make student test results publicly available and disaggregated for certain groups of students including: major racial and ethnic groups; major income groups; students with a disability; students with limited English proficiency; and migrant students.

NCLB mandated that every state and school district issue report cards detailing student test scores and identifying schools failing to meet proficiency targets. NCLB explicitly required that states use this information to track their efforts to close the achievement gaps on reading and math between different racial, ethnic, and income groups and those with special needs. States were required to establish a timeline for making "adequate yearly progress" toward eliminating these gaps and moving all students to state proficiency levels within twelve years (by 2014). The law's accountability provisions required states to take a number of escalating actions with schools that did not reach their performance objectives. A school that failed to meet state performance targets for two consecutive years was to be given technical assistance from the district to help it improve, and students in that school had to be given the option to transfer to another public school in the district. If a school did not improve in the third year, students had to be given the option of using their share of Title I funds to pay for tutoring or other supplemental educational services. Schools that failed for four consecutive years were to implement corrective actions such as replacing staff or adopting a new curriculum, and in the fifth year the failing school had to be reconstituted with a new governance structure (such as by reopening as a charter school).

NCLB represented the most significant overhaul and expansion of the federal role in education since the ESEA was enacted in 1965. Like the IASA before it, NCLB was centered on standards, testing, and school accountability. But NCLB was much more prescriptive—a response to the perceived failure of the IASA to generate sufficient state reform and increasing pressure on national leaders to bring about better school results. While forty-eight states had standards and tests in place in 2000, for example, only thirteen states were testing students every year in reading and math between the third and eighth grades as NCLB required and even fewer had strong accountability systems of the sort mandated by the law.

Thus, prior to NCLB, even in states that had adopted standards and testing reforms, there were few consequences for schools that failed to perform well. NCLB's significance was in mandating that *all* states adopt a standards and testing regime, and that they conform to a federal timetable for achieving student proficiency. Under the new federal law, all states also had to collect and disseminate a tremendous amount of school performance data. In stark contrast to the implementation of previous federal education legislation, the Bush Department of Education also developed tough, detailed regulations in support of NCLB and threatened to withhold federal funds from states that did not comply with its mandates (Robelen 2003).

FROM NCLB TO THE ESSA

The election of Obama as president in 2008 gave the Democratic Party an opportunity to assert a new vision of education reform. The post-NCLB era witnessed a growing divide between civil rights groups and teachers unions (two crucial members of the Democratic coalition) over school reform, as they engaged in an increasingly charged fight over school testing, accountability, choice, and teacher evaluation reforms—all of which the teachers unions generally opposed (Rhodes 2011). Many civil rights leaders believed that NCLB's testing, disaggregated data, and accountability provisions offered an unprecedented and powerful tool in the fight for educational equity. A 2009 report by the Citizens Commission on Civil Rights observed that teachers unions "have battled against the principle that schools and education agencies should be held accountable for the academic progress of their students ... [And] they have attacked assessments designed to measure the progress of schools" (Taylor and Rosario 2009). Many in the education community, however, believed that the law unfairly held schools responsible for resolving educational problems that have their roots elsewhere, in broader social ills such as poverty (Taylor and Rosario 2009; Hartney and Flavin 2011; Moe 2011). How President Obama decided to navigate these intraparty disagreements would be of enormous import for his party and for education reform.

Many observers initially assumed that Barack Obama (who previously had one of the most liberal voting records in the Senate) would embrace the vocal criticisms of NCLB by many Democrats (particularly the influential teachers unions) and move away from school accountability and toward a reassertion of the traditional liberal focus on school resources, integration, and social welfare programs. But to the surprise of many, this was not to be, and observers went so far as to call Obama's education agenda "NCLB 2.0" (Ravitch 2009) or "NCLB on steroids" (Matthis 2011).

Early in his administration, President Obama called for the continuation of annual testing in ESEA, for expanded federal efforts to restructure the worst performing schools, for improved teacher evaluation and accountability, and for a new focus on innovation and charter schools (Stout 2009). During his two terms in office, the federal government would intervene more aggressively in education than perhaps any other domestic policy area other than health care. Faced with divided control and partisan gridlock in Congress—which was not able to reauthorize ESEA, the largest federal education program, until his last year in office—the Obama administration opted to make education policy unilaterally from the executive branch with a creative, expansive, and controversial use of executive power.

Through the use of competitive grant programs such as Race to the Top (RTTT), School Improvement Grants (SIGs), Investing in Innovation (I3), and the NCLB waiver process, the administration was able to push states to enact important policy changes, particularly around charter schools, common core standards and assessments, school turnarounds, and teacher evaluation.

RACE TO THE TOP

The "Great Recession" that helped usher Barack Obama into office in 2008 also led Congress to enact the American Recovery and Reinvestment Act (ARRA) of 2009, colloquially known as the "Stimulus." The $800 billion program directed $100 billion in spending to education, including $4.35 billion for "state incentive grants." The legislation provided little detail on the purposes of the grants or the process for distributing them and thus gave wide discretion to the U.S. Department of Education. Secretary Arne Duncan ultimately decided that the grants would be distributed through a competitive state application process, which he called Race to the Top (RTTT). RTTT, along with the related $3 billion School Improvement Grants (SIGs) and $650 million Investing in Innovation (I3) fund, was intended to provide a major federal investment to support promising educational reforms, and to reward states and districts at the "intersection of courage, capacity, and commitment," as Duncan put it in an interview with *Education Week* (2009). The ED announced that state applications would be graded on a 500 point scale according to the rigor of the reforms proposed and their compatibility with four administration priorities: improving teacher training, evaluation, and retention policies; the development of common standards and assessments; developing better data systems; and the adoption of certain school turnaround strategies.

The use of a competitive grant process to distribute such a large amount of federal education funds was innovative and unprecedented, as most federal funds have historically been distributed through categorical grant programs that allocated money to districts on the basis of need-based formulas (Mead 2010). States and districts in this traditional model received funding automatically based on their state educational needs (the number of ELLs or special education students, for example), regardless of the performance of their schools or the alignment of state education policies with federal priorities. Under RTTT (as well as I3 and SIG), however, states had to compete with one another and only received a grant if they adopted (or promised to adopt) reforms that were compatible with federal goals and approaches (McGuinn 2012a). The administration's guidelines for RTTT applications were "extraordinarily prescriptive" and incentivized states to enact policies that aligned with the Obama administration's education agenda (Smarick 2009).

Desperate for federal funds during a time of state budget crises, forty-six states applied during the first two rounds of the RTTT competition, with only Alaska, North Dakota, Texas, and Vermont declining to participate. The application guidelines also encouraged (and rewarded) states to engage a wide variety of education stakeholders in the crafting of their applications. This stimulated a lot of new conversations between education policymakers, reform advocacy groups, and practitioners and precipitated a great deal of media attention to the issue of school reform, helping to create new political coalitions to drive policy change.

RTTT's emphasis on expanding charter schools, adopting common academic standards and tests, and revamping teacher accountability helped open up a rift in the Democratic Party on school reform and change the political climate around these controversial issues, paving the way for states to adopt new policies. As Dana Goldstein observed in 2009, "the major fight on education policy isn't between Republicans and unions, or even between Republicans and Democrats, but rather within the Democratic coalition" (Smarick 2009).

RTTT succeeded in pushing states to enact a wide variety of education reform policies to make their grant applications more competitive or to fulfill the commitments they made in them. A 2011 Center on Education Policy survey of state education officials concluded that "Nearly all of the dozens of ARRA-related reform strategies included in our survey are being acted on by a majority—often a large majority of the responding states." State actions on teacher quality reforms are illustrative in this regard. Despite recognition of the importance of teacher quality to educational outcomes and considerable research that questioned the efficacy of existing state teacher evaluation, tenure, and dismissal policies, before RTTT very few states had taken action to address the issue (Gordon, Kain, and Staiger 2006; Glazerman et al. 2011).

Prior to the Obama era, the norm across the country was to give teachers tenure automatically after three years in the classroom, with no meaningful evaluation of their teaching effectiveness and little risk of their being fired during their career no matter how ineffective they were (McGuinn 2010). The opposition of teachers' unions to changes to evaluation and tenure had made the issue the "third rail" of education policy and stymied any effort at reform (Hartney and Flavin 2011; Moe 2011). President Obama and Secretary Duncan effectively used the bully pulpit to draw attention to problems in existing state teacher-evaluation and tenure systems and, combined with the incentives of RTTT and NCLB waivers, prompted an unprecedented wave of reforms (Council of Chief State School Officers [CCSSO] 2010; Sawchuk 2010). The National Council on Teacher Quality (NCTQ) reported that thirty-six states (and DC) changed their teacher evaluation policies between 2009 and 2012. There was a large increase in the number of states that required annual teacher evaluations (43 states), incorporated student achievement (32), differentiated levels of performance (26), conducted annual classroom observations (39) and multiple observations each year (22), and utilized performance-based tenure decisions (9) (Mead 2012; NCTQ 2012). The NCTQ (2012) found that "the landscape is quickly and dramatically changing when it comes to rethinking and rebuilding teacher evaluations in school systems in the United States."

In the most in-depth analysis of the impact of RTTT conducted to date, William Howell (2015: 62) found that in the wake of the competition (2009–14) states on average enacted 68 percent of the "reform policies" it encouraged while they averaged only a 10 percent adoption rate in the seven years before the competition (2001–8). "The surge of post-2009 policy activity constitutes a major accomplishment for the Obama administration," he concluded. "With a relatively small amount of money, little formal constitutional authority in education, and without the power to unilaterally impose his will on state governments, President Obama managed to jump-start policy processes that had languished for years in state governments across the country" (66).

However, building the capacity at both the district and state education agency level to implement the reforms pushed by RTTT (and the NCLB waiver program) proved to be a major challenge across the country (McGuinn 2012b, 2015). States and districts struggled to secure the financial, personnel, and technical resources to support schools with this work (Kober and Rentner 2012). In a survey of SEAs, Cynthia Brown and her colleagues (2011) noted that the wave of reforms had "put immense stress on agencies that were originally conceived as tiny departments primarily designed to funnel money to local school districts. Yet it is not at all clear that state education agencies are prepared for this demanding new role."

While policy enactment is significant, educational improvements are unlikely to occur in the absence of effective implementation of those policies, and it is clear that SEAs continue to face large capacity gaps as they undertake this work (Jochim and Murphy 2013). Some observers have argued that the Obama administration made a major strategic miscalculation with RTTT and NCLB waivers by pushing states to adopt multiple major education reforms simultaneously and to implement them concurrently on a short timetable, thus increasing the odds of implementation problems and political pushback (Hess 2015).

NCLB WAIVERS

NCLB had originally been scheduled for reauthorization in 2007, but disagreements between Congress and President Obama—and between Congressional Democrats and Republicans—about the future of federal education policy delayed reauthorization until 2015. In the interim, states struggled with the costs and consequences of implementing the law as more and more schools failed to meet their NCLB-mandated goals of increased student proficiency (and 100 percent proficiency by 2014) and as education leaders clamored for relief. As Kenneth Wong has observed, "the Obama administration saw a policy window in the absence of ESEA reauthorization to advance some of its reform priorities" (2015: 409). It decided to act unilaterally, announcing an ESEA flexibility plan in 2011 that would enable states to apply to the U.S. Department of Education for a waiver from NCLB's accountability provisions.

The administration made the granting of NCLB waivers *conditional*, which was much more controversial and appears to be unprecedented in education. Secretary Duncan created a list of eighteen sets of policy commitments across four reform areas that states had to make to be eligible to receive a waiver: develop a plan for SEA systems and processes to monitor and assist district school improvement efforts; adopt college and career ready standards (such as the Common Core); develop a plan to identify and improve the bottom 15 percent of schools; and create teacher and principal evaluation systems "based on multiple valid measures, including student progress over time" (Wrabell et al. 2016). Members of Congress from both parties criticized the administration for attempting to legislate education policy from the executive branch, and called the conditional waiver program a violation of the separation of powers.

Despite these reservations, most states were desperate to get out from under the NCLB accountability system and the majority of states applied for a waiver and as of November 2014, forty-three states had received them (Klein 2015b). Significantly, the U.S. Department of Education threatened to revoke a state's waiver if it did not meet the commitments in its application and it issued regular state-by-state monitoring reports on their progress. The department placed several states on warning status for losing their waivers and did in fact revoke the waivers of Washington (for failing to reform its teacher evaluation system) and Oklahoma (for rejecting Common Core). As with RTTT, the application process for NCLB waivers succeeded in driving a significant—if widely varying—amount of education reform in states. An analysis of state waiver applications by the Center for American Progress concluded: "States have proposed interesting and promising ideas in each principle area. Some states are pushing new ideas, many of which are promising or innovative, by ensuring all students graduate college and career ready, developing differentiated accountability systems, and improving teacher and leader effectiveness" (Ayers and Owen 2012). Kenneth Wong, meanwhile, found that while "states made greater progress in meeting some of the federal expectations than others," overall the "administration has enjoyed substantial success in using the waiver process to leverage states to adopt policy changes" (2015: 411, 406).

COMMON CORE

Perhaps the most significant policy change spurred by RTTT and NCLB waivers was widespread state adoption of Common Core academic standards and its aligned assessments. The United States' decentralized and fragmented education system had previously proved an insurmountable barrier to the creation of the kind of national academic standards and tests that are the norm in much of the rest of the world (Manna and McGuinn 2013). The Common Core State Standards (CCSS) in mathematics and English language arts were developed at the behest of the National Governors Association (NGA) and the Council of Chief State School Officers (CCSSO). The CCSS set forth what students should know and be able to do in mathematics and English language arts at each grade level from Kindergarten to twelfth grade. Advocates argued that high, uniform academic standards would improve the academic performance of American students and better prepare them for college and careers.

Standards advocates also believed that states needed incentives and support to build the systems necessary, but that a direct federal mandate (grant-in-aid condition) to adopt the Core would infuriate people across the political spectrum and likely doom the effort. The strategy that emerged was to cast the standards as "national but not federal" and have the federal government incentivize (but not require) states to adopt them. As noted above, the carrots that the federal government used to encourage states to adopt the Core were the RTTT grant competition and the NCLB waiver application process. By 2010, forty-six states and the District of Columbia had adopted the Core standards (McDonnell and Weatherford 2013). Forty-four also initially signed on to use one of the aligned assessments that was developed by the Partnership for Assessment of Readiness for College and Careers (PARCC) and the Smarter Balanced Assessment Consortium (SBAC) and funded by the federal government (Forgione 2012).

However, as states moved toward full implementation of the new standards and aligned assessments during the 2014/15 school year, an anti-Common Core coalition gained strength. Some objections to the Common Core were shared across ideologies: a perception that the standards took a one-size-fits-all approach, created a de facto national curriculum, put too much emphasis on standardized tests, might threaten student privacy, and undermined teacher autonomy. Moreover, the Common Core was quickly linked to the emerging anti-testing backlash. While the Core standards were separate from the new assessments—states could and did adopt the standards but not the tests—they became conflated in the public mind.

These problems were exacerbated by the Republican electoral landslide in the November 2014 elections, during the first full year of implementation and testing. Many of the invested public officials who had made the original decision to adopt the new standards and tests were now gone. The Obama administration's use of RTTT and NCLB waivers to encourage states to adopt the standards, and its funding of the two consortia that developed the aligned assessments, fed concerns that Uncle Sam was becoming the national schoolmaster. This involvement, along with the Obama administration's vocal and oft-repeated support for the Core, made it easy for opponents to cast it as a federal initiative.

As state implementation of the CCSS proceeded, many teachers became concerned that states were tying evaluation systems to the new standards and assessments before the kinks had been ironed out and feared this would result in arbitrary or unfair personnel decisions. A 2014 Gallup poll found that 76 percent of teachers continued to support the goals of the Common Core, but only 27 percent supported using computerized tests to measure student performance, and only 9 percent supported using those test scores to evaluate teachers (Lyons 2014). At its 2015 convention, the NEA formally adopted resolutions in support of the testing opt-out movement and in opposition to the use of Common Core aligned tests to evaluate teachers or rate schools (Sawchuk 2015). Finally, many left activists have argued that the Common Core movement misses the mark because it does not address the core underlying social inequities that are at the root of educational performance gaps. Thus, the debate over the Common Core became entangled with long-standing liberal concerns that governments are not doing enough to address poverty, safety, health, and other out-of-school factors affecting student achievement, and that teachers lack sufficient training and resources to meet the needs of disadvantaged students.

While many were quick to declare that ESSA (see below) amounted to a death knell for Common Core, it is important to note that the law itself does not automatically repeal the Core in the states. It merely prohibits the federal government from mandating or incentivizing states to adopt/maintain the standards in the future. This means that whether or not individual states that have already adopted the Common Core (which is the majority) end up dropping the Core will ultimately come down to state level political dynamics. But the more time that states are aligned with the Common Core standards, the less likely they will drop them. State governments, school administrators, and teachers have already invested a tremendous amount of time, effort, and money in implementing the Core and realigning their education systems around the new standards and assessments (Thompson 2012). These represent "sunk costs" that cannot be recouped if a state changes direction, and the replacement of the Core with something truly new would require significant new investment to develop. As a result, states are likely to become increasingly "path dependent" with regard to the Core as time goes on (Pierson 2004; Soss, Hacker, and Mettler 2010). These dynamics mean that large numbers of states are unlikely to repeal the Core and that even in those states that do, many (such as Indiana and Pennsylvania) are likely to simply rename their standards or adopt a slightly modified version.

As we have already seen, however, it is more likely that states will pull out of the two major assessment consortium (PARCC and SBAC), which may ultimately constrain the impact that the new standards can have on American education. Of the forty-six states that originally joined one of the two testing consortia, only sixteen remained as of 2019. Opposition to high-stakes standardized testing mobilized opposition among parents—and particularly influential suburban parents—in a way that concern about standards did not. Nonetheless, while the Common Core "brand" has been damaged, support for the idea of national standards remains strong among teachers and the general public. Thus, the brand of the Common Core may fade, even while the concept of standards-based reform persists.

ESSA

Congress finally reauthorized NCLB in 2015, with bipartisan passage of the Every Student Succeeds Act (ESSA). Many observers saw the new law as a reaction against the Obama administration's activism in education, with Rick Hess and Max Eden (2015) saying it "treat[ed] the U.S. Department of Education like a national school board." ESSA went into effect, officially replacing NCLB and its associated waivers, during the 2017/18 academic year (Klein 2016). Upon its passage, when asked about the future of the federal role in education, Senator Lamar Alexander remarked: "I think it will be very different. Everybody was really fed up with Washington telling 100,000 public schools so much about what to do and it was really creating a backlash on efforts to set higher standards, namely Common Core and teacher evaluation" (Klein 2015a).

While media coverage emphasized that the new law "ends" NCLB and dramatically reduces the federal role in education, these are overstatements. The law maintains the annual testing and reporting provisions at the heart of NCLB. States will continue to be required to test all students in math and language arts in grades 3 to 8 and once in high school, and to test them in science at three different points in time. The ESSA also maintains the requirement that states publicly report student test score data for schools and disaggregate it for different subgroups of students (special education, English language learners, racial minorities, and students in poverty). The NCLB requirement that at least 95 percent of students participate in the tests remains as well. States are, however, given greater flexibility in selecting the tests they want to use, including the option of having the SAT or ACT substitute for a state assessment in high school. States must also continue to have academic standards that are aligned to those tests; the standards are set by each state itself, but they must be "challenging" and connected to college readiness. There is strong language in the law prohibiting the US Secretary of Education from forcing or encouraging states from adopting any *particular* set of standards such as the Common Core.

The ESSA's most significant change from NCLB involves accountability, both in terms of how states identify struggling schools and what states have to do if and when that process reveals that students in a school are performing poorly. This was the area where NCLB was most prescriptive and most controversial, establishing an "adequate yearly progress" system and a specific menu of remedies that states had to choose from to intervene in schools that failed to make "AYP" toward 100 percent student proficiency, and were therefore labeled "in need of improvement." Under the ESSA, states still have to submit accountability plans to the US Department of Education, but states are given much more latitude in picking their own academic goals for schools, though there must be an expectation of progress and schools must be rated somehow on their performance in relation to these goals.

States have to include at least four indicators in these school ratings. Three of these are supposed to be academic indicators: proficiency on state tests in math and language arts, English-language proficiency, and one other such as student growth in test scores. States must also choose an additional nonacademic indicator of school quality such as a measure of student or teacher engagement, or school climate. Additionally, high school ratings must incorporate graduation rates. States also get to decide how to weight the individual indicators in their accountability systems though the law stipulates that academic factors have to count "much" more collectively than the others. Under the ESSA, states are also required to intervene in a smaller percentage of underperforming schools, with more flexibility in deciding how they want to intervene.

The big shift from NCLB is that federal compliance monitoring of state accountability and school improvement efforts is considerably reduced. The ESSA explicitly prohibits the attaching of conditions to federal education waivers, thus denying future education secretaries the tool that Duncan used to such effect. A federal focus on compliance auditing for civil rights violations, waste, fraud, and abuse will continue, but beyond this, the federal government will have to rely on guidance more than enforcement to steer state accountability and school improvement policies, and states are not required to intervene in 95 percent of their schools. Predictably, the reduced role of the federal government outlined in the ESSA met with both praise and alarm, with some hopeful that increased state flexibility will return schools to local control and unleash innovation, while others warn that states are likely to respond by devoting less effort and fewer resources toward improving schools, and particularly those that serve disadvantaged students (Aldeman 2015). Thus while many of NCLB's key components remain in place and a significant role for the national government in K–12 education policy will continue, it is possible that Americans may well have witnessed the apogee of federal power in education.

The passage of the ESSA in 2015 was greeted with two very divergent expectations about how states would respond to their newfound flexibility from NCLB era mandates around school accountability and turnarounds. The optimistic view was that states would use their increased authority to enact innovative policies that would experiment with different approaches to school improvement that were better matched with local conditions and needs. The pessimistic view was that states were likely to use their discretion to retreat from the pursuit of greater educational equity and struggle to muster the political will or administrative capacity necessary to address persistent racial and socioeconomic achievement gaps (Robinson 2018).

An analysis of the US Department of Education's implementation of ESSA over its first two years, however, indicates that the reality of educational federalism today remains complicated (McGuinn 2019). Many observers were surprised when the department released its first feedback on state plans (for Delaware, Nevada, and New Mexico) in June of 2017. The feedback and guidance on the plans was very extensive and in a number of cases requested clarifications and/or revisions to be made before they would be granted approval. As Erica Green

(2017) of the *New York Times* noted, "[Education Secretary Betsy] DeVos, who made a career of promoting local control of education, has signaled a surprisingly hardline approach to carrying out an expansive new federal education law, issuing critical feedback that has rattled state school chiefs and conservative education experts alike."

ESSA contains statutory language requiring that state plans be "ambitious," but it does not define what that means, thus, leaving it up to the department to define. Ultimately USED staff (along with a panel of peer reviewers) apparently decided that key elements of many state plans did not meet that standard. Despite the fact that the ESSA gave states flexibility to design new accountability systems, for example, an independent review found that most state plans were not very innovative or ambitious. A 2017 Bellwether report concluded that "states were not taking full advantage of the opportunities ESSA presented. Instead, with few exceptions ... [they] found state ESSA plans to be mostly uncreative, unambitious, unclear, or unfinished" (Aldeman et al. 2017).

USED continued to scrutinize subsequent state plans as they were submitted and to request modifications. In a March 2018 speech to the CCSSO, DeVos criticized states for the many ways in which their ESSA plans had fallen short. She told them that state accountability systems were too complex; that state ideas for school improvement were uncreative; that states were not focusing enough on supporting students directly; that state testing systems were outdated and weak; and that states were not doing enough to ensure that education funds were spent wisely and equitably (Hyslop 2018). She noted that "ESSA was enacted ... to give you the flexibility and opportunity to address your state's unique challenges. This law gives you that chance. The trouble, I don't see much evidence that you've yet seized it ... Whatever the reasons, I see too many plans that only meet the bare minimum required by the law" (Green 2018a).

Interestingly, at least nine governors agreed with DeVos's criticisms of their own state plans, including seven Republicans. Nathan Deal (R-GA) remarked that his state plan "does not take full advantage of the opportunities for flexibility and innovation, nor does it set adequately high expectations for Georgia's students." Wisconsin Governor Scott Walker criticized his state's plan as just "bureaucratic paperwork" that "does little to challenge the status quo." And Maryland Governor Larry Hogan called his state plan a "farce," in part because it failed to specify what steps the state would take if significant numbers of schools failed to improve. The state plan answered only "N/A" in this section (Green 2018b). These governors' criticisms were echoed by several civil rights organizations and think tanks who did their own independent analyses of state ESSA plans. The left-leaning Center for American Progress concluded that DeVos "put students at risk" by deregulating education and in particular by “attempting to de-emphasize the federal government’s role in oversight of education funding; eliminating key student protections; and weakening accountability for school and college performance” (Jimenez and Flores 2019). The Alliance for Excellent Education (2018) similarly warned that “too many states minimize student subgroup performance in their ESSA accountability systems,” while a November 2018 review by the Collaborative for Student Success found that equity was not prioritized in half of the seventeen states they analyzed and that many states were not taking their new oversight responsibilities seriously (Cowen 2018).

What are the major policy changes that states have made using the ESSA’s new flexibility? States are broadening their accountability systems beyond NCLB’s focus on test scores in reading and math. Many states have added science and a more accurate measure of student attendance, as well as indicators of college and career readiness, progress toward high school completion, and school climate (Klein 2019). In addition, the majority of state plans included measures of student academic growth year-to-year rather than the single year-end summative assessments used under NCLB.

CONCLUSION

Eventually—and controversially—all fifty states’ ESSA plans were ultimately approved by the Department of Education even though many were criticized for being inadequately ambitious or innovative (or both). The implementation of ESSA has really only just begun, however, and it is far too early to predict how state plans will evolve or what the law’s ultimate impact on state education systems will be over the long term. Not surprisingly given their different philosophical views on the appropriate federal role in education, Congressional Republicans criticized the ED for being too heavy-handed in their review of state plans while Democrats criticized the department for being a rubber stamp that fails to hold states accountable.

The intergovernmental negotiations between the ED and SEAs have been complicated under ESSA and will continue as states work to implement their plans, as the ED engages in compliance monitoring, and as states submit their inevitable requests to modify their plans and receive federal waivers from the law’s mandates. Margaret Spellings, the Secretary of Education under George W. Bush, recently remarked that she found the implementation of ESSA “depressing.” “The pressure is too great at the local level not to have that ballast of the federal government saying, ‘We mean it. We’re serious about accountability.’” She also predicted that the political pendulum around the federal role is likely to shift again, with calls for a return to greater federal activism, observing "that's our history isn't it?" (Educators for Excellence 2018).

Ever since the passage of the original Elementary and Secondary Education Act in 1965, periods of federal activism in education have been followed by periods of retrenchment (McGuinn 2016). The Bush and Obama administrations embraced an expansive view of the federal role in education and one built on a test-based accountability framework. Their aggressive push on school reform, however, eventually led to a political backlash against federal involvement in education, which resulted in an ESEA reauthorization (the Every Student Succeeds Act) that rolls back the federal role in K–12 schooling in some important ways. However, there is some debate about the extent to which the ESSA undoes important elements of the Obama education agenda (Weiss 2015). The legacy of the Bush and Obama administrations in education is thus bifurcated: On the one hand, federal activism effectively advanced the standards-based accountability movement in states. On the other hand, it mobilized opposition against "federal overreach," which helped to enact a law that constrains the power of the national government in K–12 schooling in the future (Ujifusa 2015).

While the legacy of the Trump administration in education remains unclear (and complicated by the COVID-19 pandemic), it does seem that the ESSA is *not* likely to result in a return of education policy-making authority to the local level, but rather to the state level. A 2015 report from the Council of Chief State School Officers, for example, proclaimed that "Regardless of this uncertainty at the federal level, state education leaders remain firmly committed to state accountability systems that support educators, parents, and students by providing useful information that leads to improved outcomes for all students" (Weiss and McGuinn 2017).

While states have historically been relatively minor players in school reform, one of the enduring legacies of the George W. Bush, Obama, and Trump administrations may well be the invigoration and expansion of the state role in education (Anagnostopoulos, Rutledge, and Bali 2013). Going forward, states now have considerably more latitude to determine their own education agendas, though also less political cover from federal mandates. What remains to be seen is if states have developed (or can develop) sufficient political will and administrative capacity to maintain the momentum that has built up behind education reform over the past two decades (Camera 2015). Precisely how states will utilize this newfound authority is unknown, but one thing is certain: flexibility from federal mandates will result in widely divergent state levels of commitment to school reform, a wide range of policy approaches, and widely varying levels of effectiveness in improving student, teacher, and school outcomes across the fifty states (Weiss and McGuinn 2016). This is American federalism at work in the assessment and evaluation of schools, for better or worse.

REFERENCES

Aldeman, Chad (2015), "New K-12 Education Law Leaves Schools Behind," *Washington Post*, December 11. Available online: https://www.washingtonpost.com/opinions/new-k-12-education-law-leaves-schools-behind/2015/12/11/e0ffb894-9f73-11e5-a3c5-c77f2cc5a43c_story.html (accessed February 11, 2021).

Aldeman, Chad, Anne Hyslop, Max Marchitello, Jennifer O'Neal Schiess, and Kaitlin Pennington (2017), "An Independent Review of ESSA State Plans," Bellwether Education Partners. Available online: https://bellwethereducation.org/sites/default/files/Bellwether_ESSAReview_ExecSumm_1217_Final.pdf (accessed February 11, 2021).

Alliance for Excellent Education (2018), "Too Many States Minimize Student Subgroup Performance in ESSA Accountability Systems," All4Ed.org, December 14. Available online: https://all4ed.org/reports-factsheets/too-many-states-minimize-student-subgroup-performance-in-essa-accountability-systems/ (accessed February 10, 2021).

Anagnostopoulos, Dorothea, Stacey Rutledge, and Valentina Bali (2013), "State Education Agencies, Information Systems, and the Expansion of State Power in the Era of Test-Based Accountability," *Educational Policy*, 27 (2): 217–47.

Ayers, Jeremy and Isabel Owen (2012), "No Child Left Behind Waivers: Promising Ideas from Second Round Applications," Center for American Progress, July 1. Available online: https://www.americanprogress.org/article/no-child-left-behind-waivers/ (accessed February 11, 2021).

Blokhuis, J.C. and Randall Curren (2021), "The Judicialization of American Education," in Kathy Hytten (ed.), *Oxford Encyclopedia of Philosophy of Education*, New York: Oxford University Press. https://doi.org/10.1093/acrefore/9780190264093.013.1602.

Bodell, Heather (1994), *Goals 2000: A National Framework For America's Schools*, Arlington: Education Funding Research Council.

Brown, Cynthia G., Frederick M. Hess, Daniel K. Lautzenheiser, and Isabel Owen (2011), "State Education Agencies as Agents of Change," Center for American Progress, July 27. Available online: https://www.americanprogress.org/issues/education-k-12/reports/2011/07/27/9901/state-education-agencies-as-agents-of-change/ (accessed February 11, 2021).

Camera, Lauren (2015), "States Eager to Shirk Obama Era Education Policies," *U.S. News and World Report*, December 18. Available online: https://www.usnews.com/news/articles/2015-12-18/states-eager-for-flexibility-in-new-education-law (accessed February 12, 2021).

Council of Chief State School Officers (CCSSO) (2010), *Charter and Innovative Schools: Emerging Trends Reflected in Phase I Race to the Top Applications*, American Institutes for Research, May. Available online: https://www.air.org/sites/default/files/downloads/report/Charter_and_innovative_schools_0.pdf (accessed February 12, 2021).

Cowen, Jim (2018), "ESSA and School Improvement: Promise to Practice," Collaborative for Student Success, November 15. Available online: https://forstudentsuccess.org/promise-to-practice-announcement/ (accessed February 10, 2021).

Education Week (2009), "An Interview with Arne Duncan," *Education Week*, December 2. Available online: https://www.edweek.org/leadership/an-interview-with-arne-duncan/2009/12 (accessed February 11, 2021).

Educators for Excellence (2018), “Does DeVos Want to Gut Impact Aid to Fund School Choice?” *Politico*, April 20. Available online: https://www.politico.com/newsletters/morning-education/2018/04/20/does-devos-want-to-gut-impact-aid-for-school-choice-177946 (accessed February 10, 2021).

Forgione, Pascal D. (2012), *Coming Together to Raise Achievement: New Assessments for the Common Core State Standards*, Princeton, NJ: Center for K–12 Assessment & Performance Management.

Gardner, David P. et al. (1983), *A Nation at Risk: The Imperative for Educational Reform*, Washington, DC: National Commission on Excellence in Education.

Glazerman, Steven, Dan Goldhaber, Susanna Loeb, Stephen Raudenbush, Douglas Staiger, Grover J. Whitehurst, and Michelle Croft (2011), *Passing Muster: Evaluating Teacher Evaluation Systems*, Washington, DC: Brookings Institution.

Gordon, Robert, Thomas J. Kane, and Douglas O. Staiger (2006), *Identifying Effective Teachers Using Performance on the Job*, Washington, DC: Brookings Institution.

Green, Erica L. (2017), “DeVos’s Hard Line on New Education Law Surprises States,” *New York Times*, July 7. Available online: https://www.nytimes.com/2017/07/07/us/politics/devos-federal-education-law-states.html (accessed February 10, 2021).

Green, Erica L. (2018a), “After Demanding Local Control, DeVos Finds That it Limits Her Influence,” *New York Times*, March 9. Available online: https://www.nytimes.com/2018/03/09/us/politics/betsy-devos-education-reform-states.html (accessed February 10, 2021).

Green, Erica L. (2018b), “As DeVos Approves Education Plans, She Finds Skeptics in G.O.P. Governors,” *New York Times*, February 11. Available online: https://www.nytimes.com/2018/02/11/us/politics/betsy-devos-education-reform-governors-essa.html (accessed February 10, 2021).

Harrington, Elizabeth (2011), “Education Spending Up 64% under Non Child Left Behind But Test Scores Improve Little,” *U.S. News and World Report*, September 26. Available online: http://www.cnsnews.com/news/article/education-spending-64-under-no-child-left-behind-test-scores-improve-little (accessed February 10, 2021).

Hartney, Michael and Patrick Flavin (2011), “From the Schoolhouse to the Statehouse: Teacher Union Political Activism and U.S. State Education Reform Policy,” *State Politics & Policy Quarterly*, 11 (3): 251–68.

Hess, Frederick (2015), “Lofty Promises but Little Change for America’s Schools,” *Education Next*, 15 (4). Available online: http://educationnext.org/lofty-promises-little-change-americas-schools (accessed February 11, 2021).

Hess, Frederick M. and Max Eden (2015), “A New Bipartisan Education Bill Curbs Obama-Era Overreach,” *National Review*, November 18. Available online: https://www.manhattan-institute.org/html/new-bipartisan-education-bill-curbs-obama-era-overreach-8758.html (accessed February 11, 2021).

Howell, William G. (2015), “Results of President Obama’s Race to the Top,” *Education Next*, 15 (4): 58–67.

Hughes, John and Anne Hughes (1972), *Equal Education: A New National Strategy*, Bloomington: Indiana University Press.

Hyslop, Anne (2018), “ESSA Analysis: Betsy DeVos Set the Rules for States’ New Education Plans, So Why Is She Blaming Local Leaders for Following Them?” *The 74*, April 18. Available online: https://www.the74million.org/article/essa-analysis-betsy-devos-set-the-rules-for-states-new-education-plans-so-why-is-she-blaming-local-leaders-for-following-them/ (accessed February 10, 2021).

Jimenez, Laura and Antoinette Flores (2019), "3 Ways DeVos Has Put Students at Risk by Deregulating Education," Center for American Progress, May 30. Available online: https://www.americanprogress.org/issues/education-k-12/reports/2019/05/30/470509/3-ways-devos-put-students-risk-deregulating-education/ (accessed February 10, 2021).

Jochim, Ashley and Patrick J. Murphy (2013), "The Capacity Challenge: What it Takes for State Education Agencies to Support School Improvement," Center on Reinventing Public Education, December 1. Available online: https://www.crpe.org/publications/capacity-challenge-what-it-takes-state-education-agencies-support-school-improvement (accessed February 11, 2021).

Johnson, Lyndon B. (1966), "Remarks in Johnson City, Texas, Upon Signing the Elementary and Secondary Education Bill, April 11, 1965," in *Public Papers of the Presidents of the United States: Lyndon B. Johnson, 1965*, Vol. 1, entry 181, 412–14, Washington, DC: Government Printing Office.

Klein, Alyson (2015a), "Alexander: Federal Role on K-12 Will Be 'Very Different' Under ESSA," *Education Week*, December 17. Available online: https://www.edweek.org/policy-politics/alexander-federal-role-on-k-12-will-be-very-different-under-essa/2015/12 (accessed February 11, 2021).

Klein, Alyson (2015b), "States Pitch Changes as They Seek NCLB Waiver Renewals," *Education Week*, April 15. Available online: http://www.edweek.org/ew/articles/2015/04/15/states-pitch-changes-as-they-seek-nclb.html?qs=NCLB+waivers (accessed February 11, 2021).

Klein, Alyson (2016), "The Every Student Succeeds Act: An ESSA Overview," *Education Week*, March 31. Available online: http://www.edweek.org/ew/issues/every-student-succeeds-act/index.html?cmp=eml-enl-eu-news1 (accessed February 11, 2021).

Klein, Alyson (2019), "States, Districts Tackle the Tough Work of Making ESSA a Reality," *Education Week*, April 2. Available online: https://www.edweek.org/ew/articles/2019/04/03/states-districts-tackle-the-tough-work-of.html (accessed February 10, 2021).

Kober, Nancy and Diane Stark Rentner (2012), "State Education Agency Funding and Staffing in the Education Reform Era," Center on Education Policy, February. Available online: https://files.eric.ed.gov/fulltext/ED529269.pdf (accessed February 11, 2021).

Lyons, Linda (2014), "Teachers Favor Common Core Standards, Not Testing," Gallop.com, October 29. Available online: https://www.gallup.com/poll/178997/teachers-favor-common-core-standards-not-testing.aspx (accessed February 12, 2021).

Manna, Paul (2002), "Federalism, Agenda Setting, and the Dynamics of Federal Education Policy," Paper presented at the Annual Meeting of the American Political Science Association, Boston, MA, August 29–September 1, 2002.

Manna, Paul and Patrick McGuinn, eds. (2013), *Education Governance for the Twenty-First Century: Overcoming the Structural Barriers to School Reform*, Washington, DC: Brookings Institution.

Matthis, William J. (2011), "No Child Left Behind on Steroids," *Washington Post*, August 25. Available online: https://www.washingtonpost.com/blogs/answer-sheet/post/no-child-left-behind-on-steroids/2011/08/25/gIQA92bzdJ_blog.html (accessed February 11, 2021).

McDonnell, Lorraine M. and M. Stephen Weatherford (2013), "Organized Interests and the Common Core," *Educational Researcher*, 42 (9): 488–97.
McGuinn, Patrick (2006), *No Child Left Behind and the Transformation of Federal Education Policy 1965–2005*, Lawrence: University of Kansas Press.
McGuinn, Patrick (2010), "Ringing the Bell for K–12 Teacher Tenure Reform," February, Washington, DC: Center for American Progress. Available online: www.americanprogress.org/issues/2010/02/teacher_tenure_reform.html (accessed February 11, 2021).
McGuinn, Patrick (2012a), "The State of Evaluation Reform: State Education Agency Capacity and the Implementation of New Teacher Evaluation Systems," Center for American Progress, November 13. Available online: https://www.americanprogress.org/wp-content/uploads/2012/11/McGuinn_TheStateofEvaluation-1.pdf (accessed February 11, 2021).
McGuinn, Patrick (2012b), "Stimulating Reform: Race to the Top, Competitive Grants and the Obama Education Agenda," *Educational Policy*, 26 (1): 136–59.
McGuinn, Patrick (2015), "Evaluating Progress: State Education Agencies and the Implementation of New Teacher Evaluation Systems," Consortium for Policy Research in Education, September 1. Available online: https://files.eric.ed.gov/fulltext/ED564263.pdf (accessed February 11, 2021).
McGuinn, Patrick (2016), "From *No Child Left Behind* to the *Every Student Succeeds Act*: Federalism and the Education Legacy of the Obama Administration," *Publius: The Journal of Federalism*, 46 (3): 392–415.
McGuinn, Patrick (2019), "Assessing State ESSA Plans: Innovation or Retreat?" *Phi Delta Kappan*, 101 (2): 8–13.
Mead, Sara (2010), "Competitive Grants Are Nothing New," *Education Week*, August 3. Available online: https://www.edweek.org/education/blogs-of-the-week/2010/08 (accessed February 11, 2021).
Mead, Sara (2012), "Recent State Action on Teacher Evaluation," Bellwether Education Partners, August 22. Available online: https://bellwethereducation.org/publication/recent-state-action-teacher-effectiveness (accessed February 11, 2021).
Moe, Terry M. (2011), *Special Interest: Teachers Unions and America's Public Schools*, Washington, DC: Brookings Institution.
National Council on Teacher Quality (NCTQ) (2012), *State of the States 2012: Teacher Effectiveness Policies*. Available online: https://www.nctq.org/dmsView/State_of_the_States_2012_Teacher_Effectiveness_Policies_NCTQ_Report (accessed February 11, 2021).
Paterson, Paul E. (1983), *Making the Grade: Report of the Twentieth Century Fund Task Force on Federal Elementary and Secondary Education Policy*, New York: Twentieth Century Fund.
Peterson, Paul E., Barry G. Rabe, and Kenneth K. Wong (1986), *When Federalism Works*, Washington, DC: Brookings Institution.
Pierson, Paul (2004), *Politics in Time: History, Institutions, and Social Analysis*, Princeton, NJ: Princeton University Press.
Ravitch, Diane (1983), *Schools in Cities: Consensus and Conflict in American Educational History*, New York: Holmes & Meier.
Ravitch, Diane (2009), "Obama and Duncan Launch NCLB 2.0," *Education Week*, December 8. Available online: http://blogs.edweek.org/edweek/Bridging-Differences/2009/12/obama_and_duncan_launch_nclb_2.html (accessed February 11, 2021).

Rhodes, Jesse Hessler (2011), "Progressive Policymaking in a Conservative Age? Civil Rights and the Politics of Federal Education Standards, Testing, and Accountability," *Perspectives on Politics*, 9 (3): 519.

Riley, Richard W. (1995), "Reflections on Goals 2000," *Teachers College Record*, 96 (3): 1.

Robelen, Erik W. (2003), "Department Levies $783,000 Title I Penalty on GA," *Education Week*, May 28. Available online: https://www.edweek.org/policy-politics/department-levies-783-000-title-i-penalty-on-ga/2003/05 (accessed February 10, 2021).

Robinson, Kimberly Jenkins (2018), "Restructuring the Elementary and Secondary Education Act's Approach to Equity," *Minnesota Law Review*, 103 (2): 915–98.

Sawchuk, Stephen (2010), "States Strive to Overhaul Teacher Tenure," *Education Week*, April 5. Available online: http://www.edweek.org/ew/articles/2010/04/07/28tenure_ep.h29.html (accessed February 12, 2021).

Sawchuk, Stephen (2015), "NEA To Support Opt-Out, Oppose Common-Core Testing," *Education Week*, July 7. Available online: http://blogs.edweek.org/edweek/teacherbeat/2015/07/nea_to_support_opt-out_oppose_.html (accessed February 11, 2021).

Smarick, Andy (2009), "Stimulus Watch, Special Report 2," American Enterprise Institute, September 4. Available online: https://www.aei.org/research-products/working-paper/education-stimulus-watch-special-report-2/ (accessed February 11, 2021).

Soss, Joe, Jacob S. Hacker, and Suzanne Mettler (2010), *Remaking America: Democracy and Public Policy in an Age of Inequality*, New York: Sage.

Stallings, D.T. (2002), "A Brief History of the U.S. Department of Education, 1979–2002," *Phi Delta Kappan*, 83 (9): 677.

Stout, David (2009), "Obama Outlines Plan for Education Overhaul," *New York Times*, March 10. Available online: http://www.nytimes.com/2009/03/11/us/politics/11web-educ.html?_r=0 (accessed February 11, 2021).

Taylor, William L. and Crystal Rosario (2009), "National Teachers' Unions and the Struggle over School Reform," Citizens' Commission on Civil Rights, July. Available online: http://www.mikemcmahon.info/CCRTeacherUnionSchoolReform09.pdf (accessed February 11, 2021).

Thompson, Frank J. (2012), *Medicaid Politics: Federalism, Policy Durability, and Health Reform*, Washington, DC: Georgetown University Press.

Toch, Thomas (1991), *In the Name of Excellence*, Oxford: Oxford University Press.

UC Santa Barbara (UCSB) (1991), "White House Fact Sheet on the President's Education Strategy, April 18, 1991." Available online: https://www.presidency.ucsb.edu/documents/white-house-fact-sheet-the-presidents-education-strategy (accessed February 10, 2021).

Ujifusa, Andrew (2015), "Duncan's Legacy Undercut as ESEA Rewrite Advances," *Education Week*, December 3. Available online: https://www.edweek.org/policy-politics/duncans-legacy-undercut-as-esea-rewrite-advances/2015/12 (accessed February 12, 2021).

Weiss, Joanne (2015), "ESSA Cements the K-12 Obama-Duncan Legacy," *Education Week*, December 10. Available online: https://www.edweek.org/policy-politics/opinion-essa-cements-the-k-12-obama-duncan-legacy/2015/12 (accessed February 11, 2021).

Weiss, Joanne and Patrick McGuinn (2016), “States as Change Agents under ESSA,” *Phi Delta Kappan*, 97 (8): 28–33.

Weiss, Joanne and Patrick McGuinn (2017), “The Evolving Role of the State Education Agency in the Era of ESSA and Trump: Past, Present, and Uncertain Future,” CPRE Working Paper #WP 2017–1, Philadelphia: Consortium for Policy Research in Education.

Wong, Kenneth K. (2015), “Federal ESEA Waivers as Reform Leverage: Politics and Variation in State Implementation,” *Publius: The Journal of Federalism*, 45 (3): 405–26.

Wrabell, Stephani L., Andrew Saultz, Morgan S. Polikoff, Andrew McEachin, and Matthew Duque (2016), “The Politics of Elementary and Secondary Education Act Waivers,” *Educational Policy*, 32 (1): 117–40.

CONTRIBUTORS

Maryam Ahranjani holds an LLM from the University of Pennsylvania Law School, USA, a JD from American University Washington College of Law, USA, and a BS Ed. from Northwestern University, USA. She is Professor of Law and recipient of the Ron & Susan Friedman Faculty Excellence Award at the University of New Mexico School of Law (UNMSOL), USA. Professor Ahranjani has won numerous awards for teaching, scholarship, and service, including the University of New Mexico's New Teacher of the Year Award, the American Bar Association's Raeder-Taslitz Award for Criminal Law, and the Education Law Association's Steven S. Goldberg Award for Distinguished Scholarship. An active member of the District of Columbia Bar Association, she is a former Teaching Fellow in the Marshall-Brennan Constitutional Literacy Project in Washington, DC and later served as the national director of the Project. She has published widely, is a sought-after commentator and speaker, and is co-author (with Andrew G. Ferguson and Jamin B. Raskin) of *Youth Justice in America, 2nd edition* (2014).

J.C. Blokhuis holds a Ph.D. in Educational Thought and Policy from the University of Rochester, USA, a JD from the University of Ottawa Faculty of Law, Canada, and a MS Ed. from Niagara University, USA. He is Professor of Social Development Studies at Renison University College, University of Waterloo, Canada and a former Kluge Fellow at the Library of Congress in Washington, DC, USA. He is a senior member of the Education Law Association and Associate Editor for *Theory and Research in Education*. Professor Blokhuis has published in academic journals including *Public Affairs Quarterly*, the *Harvard Education Review*, the *Journal of Philosophy of Education*, the *American Educational Research Journal*, and the *Oxford Research Encyclopedia* *of Education*. He is co-author (with Katherine Covell and R. Brian Howe) of *The Challenge of Children's Rights for Canada, 2nd edition* (2018) and lead author of *Education Law, 6th edition* (2021).

Katherine Covell holds a Ph.D. in Developmental Psychology from the University of Toronto, Canada and an MA in Psychology from Simon Fraser University, Canada. She is Professor Emerita in Psychology and former Executive Director of the Children's Rights Center at Cape Breton University, Canada. Professor Covell has served as a member of the Official Canadian Delegation to the United Nations Committee on the Rights of the Child, and represented North America on the International NGO Advisory Council on Violence Against Children from 2007 to 2013. She is co-author (with R. Brian Howe and J.C. Blokhuis) of *The Challenge of Children's Rights for Canada, 2nd edition* (2018); and co-author (with R. Brian Howe) of *Education in the Best Interests of the Child: A Children's Rights Perspective on Closing the Achievement Gap* (2013), *Children, Families, and Violence: Challenges for Children's Rights* (2009), and *Empowering Children: Children's Rights Education as a Pathway to Citizenship* (2005).

Suzanne E. Eckes holds a Ph.D. in Education from the University of Wisconsin, USA, a JD from the University of Wisconsin Law School, USA, and an EdM in Educational Administration, Planning, and Social Policy from Harvard University, USA. She is the Susan S. Engeleiter Professor in Educational Leadership and Policy Analysis at the University of Wisconsin-Madison, USA. A National Education Policy Center Fellow, Professor Eckes is a longtime member of the Education Law Association (ELA), serving as its President in 2017–18. She is a frequent contributor to the *Education Law Reporter* and has published in leading academic journals including *Education Law into Practice*, *Educational Policy Review*, the *American Educational Research Journal*, and the *Education and Law Journal*. Professor Eckes is co-author (with Martha M. McCarthy and Janet Decker) of *Legal Rights of School Leaders, Teachers and Students, 8th edition* (2019) and co-author (with David M. Schimmel and Matthew C. Militello) of *Principals Avoiding Lawsuits* (2017).

Jonathan Feldman holds a JD from the New York University School of Law, USA. He is Legal Director at the Empire Justice Center in Rochester, New York, USA, where he has served as lead or co-counsel in a number of high-profile civil rights and school funding cases, including class action suits under Section 1983 of the Civil Rights Act, the Individuals with Disabilities Education Act (IDEA), and the Americans with Disabilities Act (ADA). Professor Feldman is a member of the bar in New York, New Jersey, and Pennsylvania. He has served as a Lecturer of Law at Cornell University Law School, USA and has also served as a Teaching Fellow at the Cornell Legal Research Clinic, USA. He is a frequent contributor to the *Legal Services Journal* and has published work in the *California Law Review*, the *Rutgers Law Journal*, and the *American University Journal of Gender, Social Policy, and the Law*. Professor Feldman is co-author, most recently, of *Education Law, 6th edition* (2021).

R. Brian Howe holds a Ph.D. in Political Science from the University of Toronto, Canada and an MA in Political Science from Simon Fraser University, Canada. He is Professor Emeritus in Political Science and former Director of the Children's Rights Center at Cape Breton University, Canada. An award-winning researcher, teacher, and advocate, Professor Howe has an extensive publication record. He is co-author (with Katherine Covell) of *Education in the Best Interests of the Child: A Children's Rights Perspective on Closing the Achievement Gap* (2013), and of *Empowering Children: Children's Rights Education as a Pathway to Citizenship* (2005) and a frequent contributor to the *Education and Law Journal*, the *Cambridge Journal of Education*, *Human Rights Quarterly*, the *International Journal of Children's Rights*, and the *Journal of Educational Thought*.

Patrick J. McGuinn holds a Ph.D. in Government, an MA in Government, and an M.Ed. in Education Policy from the University of Virginia, USA. He is Professor of Political Science and Education at Drew University and a Senior Research Specialist at the Consortium for Policy Research in Education at the University of Pennsylvania. Professor McGuinn has held fellowships at the Institute for Advanced Study in Princeton, New Jersey; the Rockefeller Institute of Government in Albany, New York; the A. Alfred Taubman Center for Public Policy and American Institutions at Brown University, and the Miller Center of Public Affairs at the University of Virginia. He is co-editor (with Christopher P. Loss) of *The Convergence of K–12 and Higher Education: Policies and Programs in a Changing Era* (2016); and co-editor (with Paul Manna) of *Education Governance for the 21st Century: Overcoming the Structural Barriers to School Reform* (2013).

David Hòa Khoa Nguyễn holds a Ph.D. in Educational Policy Studies from Indiana University, USA, an LLM from Faculty of Law at Leiden University, the Netherlands, a JD from the Robert H. McKinney School of Law at Indiana University-Purdue University, Indianapolis (IUPUI), USA, and an MBA from the Kelley School of Business at Indiana University, USA. He is Assistant Professor of Urban Education Leadership and Policy Studies at the School of Education and Adjunct Professor of Law at the Robert H. McKinney School of Law at

IUPUI, USA. Professor Nguyễn is a member of the Education Law Association, a Fellow of the American Bar Association Law Practice Division, and a member of the bar in Indiana, North Dakota, and Texas. He is a frequent contributor to the *Education Law Reporter* and has published in the *Belmont Law Review*, the *North Dakota Law Review*, the *Cleveland State Law Review*, and the *BYU Education and Law Journal*.

Charles J. Russo holds an Ed.D. in Educational Administration and Supervision from St. John's University, USA, a JD from St. John's University School of Law, USA, and an MDiv. from the Seminary of the Immaculate Conception, USA. He is the Joseph Panzer Chair in Education at the School of Education and Health Sciences at the University of Dayton, USA and Research Professor of Law in the University of Dayton School of Law, USA. Professor Russo is a longtime member of the Education Law Association, serving as its President in 1998–9. He received the McGhehey Achievement Award from the Education Law Association in 2002, a Distinguished Scholar Award from the American Educational Research Association's Special Interest Group on Religion and Education in 2021, and a Lifetime Achievement Award from the South African Education Law Association in 2021. Professor Russo has authored, co-authored, edited, or co-edited seventy-seven books. Most recently, he is editor of *Law, Education, and the Place of Religion in Public Schools: International Perspectives* (2022); co-author (with Allan G. Osborne Jr.) of *Special Education and the Law: A Guide for Practitioners, 4th edition* (2021); co-author (with Kevin P. Brady, Cynthia A. Dieterich, and Allan G. Osborne Jr.) of *Legal Issues in Special Education: Principles, Policies, and Practices* (2020); and co-editor (with Steve Permuth) of *Legal Issues in Faith-Based Schools, 7th edition* (2018).

INDEX